The Future of Work in Asia and Beyond

The Future of Work in Asia and Beyond presents the findings and associated implications arising from a collaborative research study conducted on the potential impact of the Fourth Industrial Revolution (4IR – or Industry 4.0) on the labour markets, occupations and associated future workforce competencies and skills across ten countries.

The 4IR concerns the digital transformation in society and business – an interface between technologies in the physical, digital and biological disciplines. The book explores many related issues: the nature of the 4IR, as well as demographic, generational and socio-cultural issues, economic and political perspectives, public and private sector similarities and differences, business strategy and managerial implications, human resource management/planning strategies, policies and practices, industry innovations, 'best practice' cases and comparative country studies. Chapters are based on a framework which combines labour market and multiple stakeholder theories. Issues are explored through the perceptions of organisational managers based in Australia, China, India, Indonesia, Malaysia, Mauritius, Nepal, Singapore, Taiwan and Thailand to provide an analysis of organisational, industry and government preparedness for the 4IR.

This book is recommended reading for anyone wanting to gain an understanding of the 4IR and a range of related challenges and issues, as well as suggested strategies for governments, education and industry that are necessary to address them.

Alan R. Nankervis is an adjunct professor of human resource management at Curtin and RMIT universities, Australia. He has more than thirty years' teaching and research experience at universities in Australia, Canada, China, Singapore, Thailand and the UK, and is the author or co-author of more than 150 publications.

Julia Connell is Assistant Dean, Research Training, Faculty of Business and Law, University of Newcastle, Australia. Her research interests include: employment related topics, vulnerable workers/precarious jobs, change/people development, organisational effectiveness and issues related to higher education.

John Burgess is Professor of Human Resource Management at RMIT University, Melbourne, Australia. His research interests include the HRM practices of multinational enterprises; the gig economy and labour regulation; and transitional labour markets.

Routledge Studies in Innovation, Organizations and Technology

Strategic Renewal
Core Concepts, Antecedents, and Micro Foundations
Edited by Aybars Tuncdogan, Adam Lindgreen, Henk Volberda, and Frans van den Bosch

Service Innovation
Esam Mustafa

Innovation Finance and Technology Transfer
Funding Proof of Concept
Andrea Alunni

Finance, Innovation and Geography
Harnessing Knowledge Dynamics in German Biotechnology
Felix C. Müller

Business and Development Studies
Issues and Perspectives
Edited by Peter Lund-Thomsen, Michael Wendelboe Hansen and Adam Lindgreen

Frugal Innovation
A Global Research Companion
Edited by Adela J. McMurray and Gerrit A. de Waal

Digital Work and the Platform Economy
Understanding Tasks, Skills and Capabilities in the New Era
Edited by Seppo Poutanen, Anne Kovalainen, and Petri Rouvinen

The Future of Work in Asia and Beyond
A Technological Revolution or Evolution?
Edited by Alan R. Nankervis, Julia Connell and John Burgess

For more information about the series, please visit www.routledge.com/ Routledge-Studies-in-Innovation-Organizations-and-Technology/book-series/RIOT

The Future of Work in Asia and Beyond

A Technological Revolution or Evolution?

Edited by Alan R. Nankervis, Julia Connell and John Burgess

Routledge
Taylor & Francis Group

LONDON AND NEW YORK

First published 2020 by Routledge

2 Park Square, Milton Park, Abingdon, Oxon OX14 4RN

605 Third Avenue, New York, NY 10017

Routledge is an imprint of the Taylor & Francis Group, an informa business

First issued in paperback 2021

British Library Cataloguing-in-Publication Data
A catalogue record for this book is available from the British Library

Library of Congress Cataloging-in-Publication Data
Names: Nankervis, Alan R, editor. | Connell, Julia, 1956- editor.
Title: The future of work in Asia and beyond : a technological revolution or
   evolution? / edited by Alan R Nankervis, Julia Connell and John Burgess.
Description: First Edition. | New York : Routledge, 2020. | Series: Routledge
   studies in innovation, organizations and technology | Includes bibliographical
   references and index.
Identifiers: LCCN 2019051032 (print) | LCCN 2019051033 (ebook)
Subjects: LCSH: Labor market—Pacific Area. | Personnel management—Pacific Area. |
   Industrial policy—Pacific Area. | Technological innovations—Government policy.
Classification: LCC HD5850.43.A6 F88 2020 (print) | LCC HD5850.43.A6
   (ebook) | DDC 331.12095—dc23
LC record available at https://lccn.loc.gov/2019051032
LC ebook record available at https://lccn.loc.gov/2019051033

ISBN: 978-1-138-39001-0 (hbk)
ISBN: 978-1-03-217323-8 (pbk)
DOI: 10.4324/9780429423567

Typeset in Bembo
by Apex CoVantage, LLC

Contents

List of contributors   vii
Foreword by Ashley Braganza   xii

PART 1
The context of the Fourth Industrial Revolution   1

1   **Meeting the workforce challenges of the Fourth Industrial Revolution**   3
ALAN R. NANKERVIS, JULIA CONNELL, JOHN BURGESS AND ALAN MONTAGUE

2   **Conceptual research framework**   20
VERMA PRIKSHAT AND NUTTAWUTH MUENJOHN

PART 2
Country chapters   31

3   **Australia**   33
ROSLYN CAMERON, ALAN MONTAGUE, PAULINE STANTON, NUTTAWUTH MUENJOHN AND ROSLYN LARKIN

4   **Singapore**   52
AZAD SINGH BALI, CHRISTOPHER VAS AND PETER WARING

5   **Taiwan**   71
MIN-WEN SOPHIE CHANG

6   **China**   84
YI LIU, ZENGKE AN AND HAIYUE XIU

7 **India**   100
SANJEEV KUMAR, VERMA PRIKSHAT AND J. IRUDHAYA RAJESH

8 **Indonesia**   114
SASKIA P. TJOKRO, MATHEUS S. N. SIAGIAN AND SOEGENG PRIYONO

9 **Malaysia**   131
NOORZIAH MOHD SALLEH AND BADARIAH AB RAHMAN

10 **Mauritius**   149
VIKASH ROWTHO, KARLO JOUAN, SARITA HARDIN-RAMANAN,
SHAFIIQ GOPEE, ODYLLE CHAROUX

11 **Nepal**   167
SUBAS P. DHAKAL, DEVI P. DAHAL AND SIMON DAHAL

12 **Thailand**   184
MONTHON SORAKRAIKITIKUL

PART 3
Fourth Industrial Revolution – The Asia Pacific
and beyond   199

13 **Comparisons and conclusions**   201
ALAN R. NANKERVIS, JULIA CONNELL AND JOHN BURGESS

Appendix   212
Index   216

Contributors

Australia

Roslyn Cameron (PhD) is Director of the Centre for Organisational Change and Agility (COCA) at Torrens University Australia, Adelaide, South Australia. She is a fellow of the Australian Human Resources Institute (FAHRI), the Australian Institute for Training and Development (FAITD) and a member of the AHRI Advisory Panel for Research.

Roslyn Larkin is a human resource management/employment relations lecturer at the University of Newcastle, Australia. Current research interests include ethical leadership, knowledge management and ethical AI.

Alan Montague is the Program Director for the Masters of HRM at the Royal Melbourne Institute of Technology (RMIT), Australia. His research interests include skill/vocational shortages, employment/education program policy development, corporate ethics, and management and workforce planning.

Nuttawuth Muenjohn is a researcher and educator in the School of Management, RMIT University, Melbourne, Australia. His research focuses on leadership studies, international HRM and workplace innovation, and has been achieved through various international research collaborations.

Pauline Stanton is Head of the School of Management at RMIT and Deputy Pro Vice Chancellor Business (International). Her research interests include managing people in healthcare and human resource management in MNEs.

China

Zengke An is an associate professor of human resources management in the School of Business and Administration, Zhongnan University of Economics and Law. Dr. An has published articles on human resource management, employ-ment relations management and labour relations management.

Yi Liu is an associate professor in the International School of Innovation and Entrepreneurship, Shandong University, Qingdao, China. Her research interests include knowledge management, talent management and emerging country multinationals.

Haiyue Xiu is a master's degree candidate from the School of Business Admin-istration, Zhongnan University of Economics and Law, based in Wuhan, China. She majors in human resource management and has a strong research interest in HRM-related topics.

India

Sanjeev Kumar is an assistant professor in the Faculty of Business, Sohar Uni-versity, Sohar, India. His major areas of research include service quality, work-readiness challenges, retailing and marketing analytics.

Verma Prikshat is currently a senior lecturer at Cardiff Metropolitan Uni-versity. Verma's research interests include 4IR-readiness, transformational leadership and follower outcomes and graduate work-readiness challenges in the Asia Pacific region.

J. Irudhaya Rajesh is currently a lecturer at Flinders University, Australia. Previously, he was a faculty member at the University of South Australia and Australian Institute of Business.

Indonesia

Soegeng Priyono (DevOne Advisory) has completed successful consultancy assignments with clients in the public and private sectors. Prior to this, he worked for IBM, Lotus Consulting, EDS and Arthur Andersen. He holds a bachelor of science degree (electrical engineering) and postgraduate qualifications.

Matheus S. N. Siagian is the owner of the first hotel chain (Tree Group) that uses IoT for the rooms in Eco Tree O'tel. He holds a bachelor's degree from the Hospitality Management School in BHMS Luzern, Switzerland, together with an MBA degree from GSBA Zurich at Hörgen.

Saskia P. Tjokro is the Head of ANGIN Impact (angin.id), the largest Angel Investment Network in Indonesia. She has conducted market research for several Indonesian tourism sectoral policies and holds an MBA degree from the University of Gadjah Mada with a focus on entrepreneurship.

Malaysia

Badariah Ab Rahman is a lecturer in the industrial relations programme and a Research Fellow at the Borneo Institute of Indigenous Studies, Universiti Malaysia Sabah. Her research interest includes labour studies, employment relations and democracy at workplaces. She holds a doctorate in industrial relations from Universiti Malaysia Sabah.

Noorziah Mohd Salleh is a senior lecturer at the Faculty Business and Management, Universiti Teknologi MARA, Sabah, Malaysia. Noorziah's research interests focus on management, with specific interest in strategic management and human resource management.

Mauritius

Odylle Charoux is currently the Director of Innovation and Change Management at Curtin Mauritius (Charles Telfair Campus) and a member of the 'Charles Telfair Company' Board of Directors. She holds BSc (biology andand psychology), BEd and MSc qualifications, and an honorary doctorate from Curtin University.

Shafiiq Gopee has more than 16 years of teaching experience at tertiary level and currently heads the Office of Learning and Teaching at Curtin Mauritius. He holds a BSc in information systems, an MSc in information systems and human resources management and a doctorate from Curtin University.

Sarita Hardin-Ramanan is the Head of IT, Design and Communication at Curtin Mauritius. She holds a BEng, a master's in computer science and a PhD from Curtin University. Her research interests include graduate employability and the impact of 4IR technologies on the future of work.

Karlo Jouan is the Head of Faculty, Accounting Finance and Law at Curtin Mauritius. Karlo holds a diploma in mechanical and electrical engineering, a BA Hons in economics and a PhD in financial economics. His research interests include changes in the labour market and NGO sector.

Vikash Rowtho is the Head of Research at Curtin Mauritius. He completed his bachelor and master degrees in computer science, is qualified as a programming engineer, and a holds a PhD in education. His research interests include technology and the future of work, especially how 4IR technologies will shape the future of work.

Nepal

Devi P. Dahal is a team leader of the Nepal Vocational Qualifications System (NVQS) Project. An electrical engineer with a master's degree in technical and vocational education from the UK, Devi's current research interest revolves around the nexus between 4IR and education systems.

Simon Dahal is an academic coordinator at Pathik Gyan Niketan and has been involved in education for over a decade. He has a master's degree in physics (materials science and quantum mechanics). His research interest revolves around the socio-economic implications of the 4IR in the education sector.

Subas P. Dhakal is a senior lecturer in the Business School at the University of New England, Australia. Subas has research interests in community capitals framework, Fourth Industrial Revolution, work and work-readiness, and socially responsible businesses in the Asia Pacific.

Singapore

Azad Singh Bali is a lecturer in public policy at the University of Melbourne, and his research interests lie in comparative social policy in Asia. His academic training is from the National University of Singapore and the University of Madras.

Christopher Vas is Associate Professor and MBA Director at the University of Canterbury. In 2017, Dr Vas co-founded Futuresafe Technologies in Singapore. He holds a PhD in public policy from the ANU.

Peter Waring is Professor and Pro Vice Chancellor Transnational Education at Murdoch University in Singapore. He holds qualifications in commerce, law and management and has published extensively in the fields of employment relations, corporate governance and management.

Taiwan

Min-Wen Sophie Chang is an adjunct assistant professor at International College, Providence University in Taiwan. Her research interests include 4IR, human resource management, employability, e-learning, teamwork, creativity and innovation, amongst many others.

Thailand

Monthon Sorakraikitikul is a lecturer at Thammasat Business School, Thammasat University, Thailand. He teaches human resource management, organisational development and knowledge management. He has a bachelor's degree in marketing, an MBA, and a PhD from the Asian Institute of Technology.

Foreword

The basis of competitive advantage of nations, industries and organisations is being fundamentally transformed by technology. Whereas, conventional economic factors of production provide an indication of strategic strengths, there are other phenomenon that are emerging as critically vital to future prosperity. One such phenomenon is data. It is deemed to be the 'oil of the 21st century'. Yet, this analogy is limited. Oil is to be found in limited physical locations, it's difficult to extract, messy to process and environmentally unfriendly in its use. Data, on the other hand, is available to every nation, industry and organisation. Data are unconstrained by physical geography and do not respect nor recognise national boundaries – data can travel around the globe in seconds. They can be processed in elegant, yet complex algorithms and mathematical formulae. Another phenomenon is the skills systems and people needed to be able to analyse and exploit this data. The capabilities needed to develop emergent technologies such as: artificial intelligence, blockchain, the internet of things, augmented and virtual reality, smart algorithms and machine learning provide the bedrock of gaining sustainable advantage. These skills and capabilities are spread unevenly across nations. Many are simply unprepared and show little sign of preparing citizens for the future.

This book is significant and timely. The Fourth Industrial Revolution (the 4IR) is here right now and this book sets out clearly its ramifications, implications and actions to be taken. Its significance stems from the breadth of coverage – examining 4IR in countries and organisations located in Asia Pac and beyond. The countries examined include: Australia, China, India, Indonesia, Malaysia, Mauritius, Singapore, Thailand, Nepal and Taiwan.

The book is rigorous in the methods used to develop a strong evidence base, drawing on empirical data to address the question 'how prepared are you and your organisation to face the impact of 4IR?' The authors examine the changes taking place in organisations that are being driven by 4IR technologies. They report on enablers and impediments to developments and applications in practice. They assess the impact of 4IR on people, in terms of the work they will do, or the jobs that will be lost, anticipated workplace changes and employment attributes. The authors delve into preparations that organisations are making in different countries to both absorb and exploit 4IR. This work at a policy level is important to enable policy makers to set clear directions and help their industries gain from the 4IR.

As a result, this book makes essential reading for policy makers, researchers and students who want to lead companies, industries and countries towards success in the 4IR world.

Professor Ashley Braganza MBA PhD ACIB
Deputy Dean, College of Business, Arts and Social Sciences
Professor of Organisational Transformation, Brunel Business School

Part 1

The context of the Fourth Industrial Revolution

1 Meeting the workforce challenges of the Fourth Industrial Revolution

Alan R. Nankervis, Julia Connell, John Burgess and Alan Montague

Introduction

'History tells us that anxiety tends to accompany rapid technological change, especially when technology takes the form of capital which threatens people's jobs' (Citigroup, 2019). Much has been made of questions such as: will a robot steal your job (Waldrop, 2018) or will a robot be your boss (Kruse, 2018). Others have indicated that artificial and machine intelligence still do not match the full range of human abilities, and to date few companies have reportedly deployed these technologies at scale outside of the technology sector, as they are uncertain about the return on investment (McKinsey Global Institute, 2017). This chapter introduces the broad workforce issues and challenges associated with current and future developments and applications in artificial intelligence (AI), robotics and machine learning technologies. It also provides an introduction and overview of the book. Subsequent chapters will further explore these challenges and their impacts on the workforces of a wide range of countries in the Asia Pacific region and beyond. Many writers have envisaged a radically changing business landscape with consequent transformations in people management strategies. Thus far there has been considerable debate about the nature of what has been referred to as the Fourth Industrial Revolution (4IR) or Industry 4.0. The term '4IR' will be used throughout this book for consistency.

The 4IR is broadly characterised 'by a range of new technologies that are fusing the physical, digital and biological worlds, impacting all disciplines, economies and industries, and even challenging ideas about what it means to be human' (Schwab, 2016, webpage). Some authors have suggested that it is a natural 'fourth' stage in the evolution of new technologies and their effects on workplaces, jobs and associated skills and capacities; whilst others (for example, Williams, in O'Neill, 2017b; Chalmers, in Adams, 2017) argue that that it represents an all-encompassing revolutionary change which is totally dissimilar to all previous industrial revolutions. Chalmers (in Adams, 2017) argued that we are witnessing an industrial revolution phase that will have the 'biggest and most profound' impact ever on the work of humans, suggesting that every single occupation will be altered in one way or another, and although not every job will be totally supplanted, all workers and their managers will need to adapt. Even though the rise of the 4IR has the potential to become a driving force for social and economic growth, it will also simultaneously transform the patterns of production, consumption and employment, resulting in broader geopolitical and socio-economic changes in both developed and emerging economies (Ayentimi & Burgess, 2018).

Chalmers (in Adams, 2017, webpage) suggested that the jobs that will change most radically 'include accounting, some legal work, insurance, insurance underwriters, bank tellers, taxi drivers, truck drivers, retail and some medical' positions. Further enhancements in artificial intelligence will mean that various forms of robots replace more human job roles, with profound advances evident in automation, computers, research, medicine and legal services (Chalmers, in Adams, 2017; Williams, in O'Neill, 2017a). Other observers have highlighted the potential job losses and income polarisation associated with digitalisation. For example, Brynjolfsson and McAfee (2014) maintain that the 'computer revolution' has huge potential for disrupting labour markets and reducing labour costs. In addition to replacing and/or augmenting labour, the 4IR is already beginning to mimic human thinking. Romero et al. (2016: 1) propose that, in smart factories, 'operators 4.0' will be able to create trusting and interaction-based relationships between themselves and machines'. Given the ever-increasing scope and pace of such new technologies, changes will be significant and relatively unpredictable. Peters (2017: 2) proposes that if 'the Industrial Revolution was the First Machine Age, and Electricity the Second, then Electronics was the Third, and the Internet is the platform for the Fourth'. Therefore, is the 4IR destined to leave its forerunners in the shade (WEF, 2016a) with never-ending or 'perpetual' and revolutionary change taking place?

Given the turbulence that the 4IR is inducing in a rapidly evolving labour market (WEF, 2016b), the capacity to forecast and plan to meet future skill needs and formulate associated job requirements is a huge challenge. The short, and longer-term impacts of these new technologies and mindsets on employment is progressively becoming a critical issue for governments, businesses, educational institutions and individual workers (Scarpetta, 2017). The World Bank Report (2019) stresses the need for human capital investment as those people with higher levels of human capital adapt faster to technological change – a critical issue for the future of work – indicating that humans and machines will need to work in harmony together. It has been claimed that one in ten jobs have the potential to be automated (Arnold et al., 2018). A Cedefop (2019: 9) briefing report maintains that these technologies may transform rather than destroy jobs, especially those that demand worker autonomy, planning, teamwork, communication and customer-service skills which are expected to be more resistant to full automatisation. As a result, a key question concerns the impact of the 4IR, namely whether it will lead to mainly positive workplace, jobs and skills outcomes (WEF, 2016b).

The challenges of 4IR technologies

4IR technologies employ software that enables various devices, services and machines, robots, driverless vehicles, virtual personal assistants and more to learn and acquire knowledge like humans (O'Neill, 2017a, 2017b). 'The rate of learning is going to be exponential' and swift, which contrasts with human learning which is slow and painstaking at times (Walsh, in O'Neill, 2017b). They differ from other information technical systems (ITS) as they can be intuitive and perform complex tasks without any coding undertaken by human or manual input to boost their performance. The Price Waterhouse Coopers Workforce of the Future Report (2018: 8) suggests that there are three levels of AI:

i   *Assisted intelligence*, widely available today, improves what people and organisations are already doing (for example, global navigation systems)
ii *Augmented intelligence*, which helps people and organisations to do things they could not otherwise do (for example, ride-sharing services technologies)
iii *Autonomous intelligence*, which is currently being developed for the future (for example, autonomous vehicles).

The future of work

Digital disruption, machine learning, artificial intelligence and robotics are all part of the terminology surrounding the 4IR. In the realm of work, workplaces, jobs, careers and learning and development, the existing evidence and projections suggest profound change. The WEF (2016b) and the World Bank (2019) have both provided reports and predictions on how the 4IR will impact particular nations, industries and workplaces. Some of these predictions include:

1 Some jobs will be displaced creating problems of unemployment and structural adjustment, especially with respect to low-skilled and repetitive jobs in the services and manufacturing sectors
2 Work will be transformed through the way production is organised with respect to the interface between jobs and technology
3 The nature of workplaces will be transformed through external work, increased contracting, casual and multiple 'gigs' as well as remote work
4 Education and skill needs for new and future jobs will also change, involving changes in professions and occupations, together with the emergence of new sectors and professions
5 Many (if not most) jobs will be augmented by technology, in various forms
6 Skills and incomes will be polarised, leading to the intensification of emerging inequalities
7 There is likely to be a large productivity dividend for employers from job displacement and job augmentation
8 New jobs and professions will emerge, most likely in health services, energy generation and storage and logistics
9 Careers will become less predictable, non-linear and potentially disruptive
10 Work will become increasingly globalised through mechanisms such as increased offshoring and online work; and the mobility of high skilled workers will also increase, especially across the relatively newly incorporated ASEAN Economic Community.

What is likely to be the impact of the 4IR on global jobs? The World Bank (2019) identified both the fundamental changes, and features of the labour market that are not anticipated to change. First, the technology blurs the boundaries of organisations, and new global organisations can be created in a short time using web-based platforms that network service provision. Second, technology is shifting the demand for skills towards highly skilled technologically linked jobs. Third, industrial jobs have not disappeared through robotics; the major change is in the shift in manufacturing towards low cost labour economies from advanced economies. Finally, in emerging economies many jobs are informal, low paid and result in low productivity, and this is unlikely to change as a consequence of the 4IR.

The World Bank (2019) also identified the policy challenges for governments as investing in education and human capital; improving social protection and supporting fiscal sustainability, through effective taxation regimes that provide the support for investment in education and infrastructure. The scope of all of these challenges and the public policy issues is beyond the scope of this book. However, as the next section of the chapter explains, its focus is on managerial perceptions of these challenges and whether it is considered that governments are well-prepared to meet the challenges across the Asia Pacific region and beyond.

The purpose and scope of the book

Discussion concerning the 4IR to date has tended to be generalised and Western-centric (Cedefop, 2019; McKinsey Report, 2012; Quigley & Chalmers, 2016). Many of the cited studies comprise consultants' reports that outline the changes that are taking place with respect to technology; discuss the implications of the applications across a multitude of criteria (jobs, work, skills, income, wealth distribution or training); or examine issues linked to readiness, adjustment and transition, or organisational, industry and public policy (McKinsey Global Institute, 2017; Price Waterhouse Coopers, 2018). The purpose of this book is to examine a number of key issues associated with the 4IR through the lens of managers at country and organisational levels.

In relation to the selected countries included in the book, each chapter addresses the following questions:

a   What changes are occurring within the organisation that are linked to technological developments associated with the 4IR?
b   What are the drivers and impediments to such developments and applications?
c   What is the impact on work, workplaces and employment?
d   What preparations are organisations making for the 4IR?
e   To what extent are national strategies or policies guiding and leading organisational developments with respect to the 4IR, and how effective are they?

As Chapter 2 points out, in all but two countries the data was collected by a standard survey questionnaire. Each country chapter reports and analyses the local research findings, which are then presented comparatively in the final chapter, with considerations of their similarities and differences. One key issue is whether different stages of economic development impact on the application of 4IR technologies. Some questions concern whether: the application and implementation of these technologies differ according to developed, intermediary or developing country status, and how the 4IR is likely to affect the nature of workplaces, jobs, skills and the entire future of work. These are the key macro and micro issues explored in this book.

For these purposes, the countries in this book have been divided into three economic and social categories – developed, intermediary and developing countries. There is some debate about the determinants of 'developed' or 'developing' country status, based on criteria such as gross domestic product (GDP) or per capita income. For example, the World Bank (2019) classifies developed countries as those with incomes of US\$12,275 per year. Human development indicators are also considered, such as literacy and poverty levels, the availability of tap water, mobile telephone density and the proportion of wealthy individuals (China Power, 2016; Sharma, 2019). Here, we argue that, unlike some of the developing countries in the study, both China and India have made sufficient progress in reducing poverty levels, increasing literacy standards and gross domestic product growth, to enable them to be considered (at least) at 'intermediary' country status. China, for example, has the highest GDP number in the world, above the US, Japan and most of Europe (China Power, 2016).

Theoretical foundations of the study

This study was broadly built upon the theoretical foundations derived from the confluence of two seminal management theories and models, namely, socio-technical theory (Applebaum, 1997; Baxter & Sommerville, 2011; Emery & Trist, 1965; Mumford, 2006; Scacchi, 2004; Trist, 1980) as well as the Job Characteristics Model (Hackman & Oldham, 1980). The conceptual framework presented in Chapter 2, which underpins the subsequent country research study, illustrates the amalgam of the components of these theories into an integrative framework.

Firstly, and perhaps most importantly, socio-technical theory represents the broad canvas of the interface between technology and humans towards productive engagement at the workplace. Developed by the Tavistock Institute for Human Relations in London in the 1940s, socio-technical systems (STS) theory initially focused on the manufacturing sector during the first and second industrial revolutions. STS considers organisations as 'social and technical systems' (Trist, 1980: 9) comprising three key levels (primary work systems, whole organisational systems and macro-social systems). According to this theory, employees are regarded as complementary to technology rather than an extension of it (Trist, 1980: 9), where the goal of management is to increase rather than decrease the task and job variety of employees in order to maximise productivity, profitability and competitiveness. As Baxter and Sommerville (2011) explain, socio-technical systems represent 'an approach to (organisational) design that considers human, social and organisation factors, as well as technical (technological) factors in the design of organisational systems, that is …"*human-centred design*"' (p. 1). The concept of 'human-centred design' has been promoted more recently as a means of 'humanising the potential emphasis on technology in a world of work where consistent organisational and economic change are the now' (Mumford, 2006: 340). The Third and Fourth Industrial Revolutions – or the 'human-technology interface' – emphasises 'how people accomplish their work in the organisational system using the information technology, people, resources and circumstances at hand' (Scacchi, 2004: 8).

At the institutional level, the Job Characteristics Model (JCM) (Hackman & Oldham, 1980) provides guidance on managing the impact of the implementation of new technologies on jobs, skills and workplaces, especially those with which this book is most concerned that are associated with the 4IR. First, the JCM suggests that there are five important 'job characteristics' which enhance employees' satisfaction and retention that are inherently linked to job outcomes such as employee retention, organisational performance, productivity and competitiveness. The five characteristics are skill variety, task variety, task significance, autonomy and feedback (Hackman & Oldham, 1980), all of which are likely to be significantly impacted (positively or adversely) by the new 4IR technologies. At the strategic management level, these theories suggest that the inputs, outputs and outcomes of employees need to be carefully managed and measured in order to ensure that their activities contribute in financial terms to organisation success. Thus, when considering whether or not to implement the new 4IR technologies, or which technologies to choose and in which organisational functions, managers need to consider the costs and consequences of these important high-level decisions. They especially need to calculate the human, financial and reputational costs associated with their choices, which are the focus of this study.

In order to provide a global context to the study, the comparative country-based Automation Readiness Index (ARI) designed by the Economist Intelligence Unit (EIU, 2018) was also used to locate countries on a scale measuring their capacity to effectively deal with the challenges posed by the 4IR. Only six of the countries discussed in this book are included in the ARI – Australia, China, India, Indonesia, Malaysia and Singapore. Table 1.1 provides a summary of criteria that supported the construction of the ARI – for a full list of categories see the ARI reference.

The principal components are the innovation environment; education policies; and labour market policies. The ARI indicates the relative ability of a selection of twenty-five countries to develop and apply automated solutions, together with their ability to support the innovation process (through education), and translate it into programs that support workplace adjustment and upskilling, ranking the selected countries against these criteria.

Table 1.1 Automation Readiness Index Categories

Innovation environment	Education policies	Labour market policies
Sub-categories		
Research and innovation	Basic education	
Infrastructure	Post compulsory education	Knowledge on automation
Ethics and safety	Continuous education	Workforce transition programs
	Learning environments	

Source: Economist Intelligence Unit Ltd (2018), The Automation Readiness Index, pp. 8–10

Table 1.2 Overall Index: Ranks and Scores

Rank	Country	Country status	Rank	Country	Country status
1	South Korea	Mature	14	**Malaysia**	Developed
2	Germany	Mature	15	Turkey	Developed
3	**Singapore**	Mature	16	Russia	Developed
4	Japan	Mature	17	Argentina	Developed
5	Canada	Mature	18	**India**	Emerging
6	Estonia	Mature	19	Brazil	Emerging
7	France	Mature	20	Colombia	Emerging
8	UK	Mature	21	Saudi Arabia	Emerging
9	US	Mature	22	South Africa	Emerging
10	**Australia**	Mature	23	Mexico	Emerging
11	Italy	Developed	24	Vietnam	Emerging
12	**China**	Developed	25	**Indonesia**	Emerging
13	UAE	Developed			

Source: Economist Intelligence Unit Ltd (2018), The Automation Readiness Index, pp. 8–10

Table 1.2 ranks the 25 countries included in the index – the countries featuring in this book are highlighted in bold. The country sample includes G20 countries as well as five additional nations that represent diverse regions of the world (EIU, 2018). South Korea is ranked first as it scored highly across all the three categories listed in Table 1.2 with Germany, Singapore and Japan ranked next – all countries that have demonstrated strong leadership in relation to industry digitisation. It should be noted that the ARI classifies countries as 'mature', 'developed' and 'emerging'; rather than 'developed', 'intermediary' and 'developing' as in the classification chosen for this book.

The 4IR and the Asia Pacific

The 4IR will impact almost every industry in every country (Schwab, 2016). On the positive side it presents countries in the Asia Pacific region and beyond with opportunities to 'leap-frog' from earlier stages of development and industrialisation into later stages. At a community level the 4IR has the potential to provide upgraded infrastructure across all locations, regardless of remoteness.

Satellite technology, community technology and AI offer opportunities for remote service delivery, especially in the key services of health and education. Satellite, battery and solar/wind technology supports improvements in the provision of information, market access, water quality, communications and energy. The potential to transform service provision, quality of life and overall human development is enormous (Ayentimi & Burgess, 2018). On the negative side, however, there will most likely be job displacement through mechanisation, robotics and digitalisation, although many jobs will remain in some Asia Pacific countries since labour costs (wages) are low, particularly in agriculture and in the informal sector.

As the country chapters illustrate, different countries in the Asia Pacific region may adopt diverse 4IR applications at different stages and in different ways, depending on their unique labour markets, government imperatives and socio-economic circumstances. Applications of the 4IR in engineering, health, construction and the design and entertainment sectors will be the most affected, with banking, clerical services, stevedoring and retail jobs already being transformed through technology (such as data storage and library services; security services; teaching; medical services) (Peters, 2017; WEF, 2017a, 2017b, 2017c).

The Asia Pacific region is one of the most dynamic regions in the world in terms of growth, comprising the intermediary global powers of China and India as well as a diverse range of countries by size, ethnicity, religion, economic structure and political systems (Dhakal et al., 2018). The WEF Report (2016a) on the future of work incorporated a survey of senior HR and Chief Strategy Officers across the globe with the intention of providing understanding about the future of jobs, work and skills provoke a global debate on these issues. The survey generated a report that was categorised by broad industry sectors, regions and selected countries which covered the following sectors: Financial Services and Investors; Information and Communication Technology; Energy; Basic and Infrastructure; Mobility; Consumer; Healthcare; Media, Entertainment and Information and Professional Services. The report included thirteen developed, intermediary and developing economies: Australia, Brazil, China, France, Germany, India, Italy, Japan, Mexico, South Africa, Turkey, United Kingdom and United States. It also embraced two broader regional groupings: ASEAN (combining findings from Indonesia, Malaysia, Singapore and Thailand), and the GCC (Kuwait, Qatar, Saudi Arabia and the United Arab Emirates). Regional groupings of country results were presented, including the Asia Pacific – China, India, Japan, Australia and ASEAN. The report assessed skill requirements, employment changes and the challenges and threats from the 4IR.

For the Asia Pacific the following trends (2015–2020) around industry and the workforce emerged (WEF, 2016b): growing industries/occupations (transport and logistics, sales, management, business services), and declining industries/occupation (manufacturing, education, computers and science, architecture and engineering); key technologies are cloud technology, big data, new energy and flexible work.

The regional findings are interesting in that (a) the industry changes include high skill areas such as education, science and engineering; (b) shareholder demands are seen as a major constraint on long term human resource development strategies; and (c) the drivers of change are linked to technological developments. The report also suggested that the most significant workforce management strategies to address these challenges include job rotation, employing migrant labour and upskilling employees.

Previous research on labour markets, particularly focusing on youth and job-readiness (Cameron et al., 2018; Dhakal et al., 2018) has highlighted the diversity of the region's labour markets in terms of industry distribution and supply characteristics, including skills, education, demography, wages and employment conditions. To differentiate these by stages of development and human capital capabilities, the Human Development Index and the Human Capital Index provide background information that highlights the diversity of the region. The Human Development Index (HDI) (UNDP, 2016) integrates three basic dimensions of human development (life expectancy, schooling and income), while the Human Capital Index (HCI) primarily incorporates four indicators: *capacity* – the stock of education across generations; *deployment* – the active participation in the workforce across generations; *development* – current efforts to educate, skill and upskill the student body and the working age population; and *know-how* – growth or depreciation of the skillsets of those of working age through opportunities for higher value-add work (WEF, 2017a: 5). The HDI reports where countries are located in terms of development, whilst the HCI indicates their human capital potential. The WEF (2016b) commentary on the HCI performance for the region stated that:

> Asia and the Pacific, the world's most populous region, score towards the middle of the range of the Human Capital Index results, with an overall average score of 67.83. The gap between the best and worst performers in the Asia and the Pacific region is the second largest of any region, reflecting in part the different stages of development of the 22 countries from the region covered in the Index, but also the varying degrees of human capital outcomes even between countries with similar income.
>
> (p. 9)

Previous research by Dhakal et al. (2018) highlighted the differences in the range of the HDI in the region from higher performing countries such as Australia and Singapore, to relatively impoverished countries such as Indonesia and Vietnam. Not surprisingly, there was a strong association between HCI and HDI. Countries with high HDI scores also had high HCI scores, and the same association applied for low scores. Consequently, it may be difficult for some countries to 'robot-proof' learning by 'blending an array of key competences (entrepreneurship, digital, STEM, languages, learning to learn) into curricula and learning methods, within comprehensive VET programmes and policy actions', as proposed by Cedefop (2019: 4).

Country coverage

This book explores nine Asia Pacific countries (Australia, China, India, Indonesia, Malaysia, Nepal, Singapore, Taiwan and Thailand) together with one Indian Ocean nation (Mauritius). As discussed in each country chapter, the challenges and impacts of the 4IR, as perceived by managers in a range of local industry sectors are likely to be mediated by the diversity of their political, economic, social and demographic characteristics. From table 1.2 and the ARI scale above it can be seen from the list of countries included that there are several in the top 10 in terms of automation readiness (Singapore and Australia); several that are located in the 11–20 range (China, Malaysia and India); with Indonesia ranked last at 25th among the listed countries. Unfortunately, not all countries included in this book feature in the ARI report; however, it does provide a comparative evaluation of countries located at different stages of readiness in terms of the ARI, providing a starting point for evaluating their experiences with the 4IR across the selected countries. *The Economist* (2018) report on the automation readiness index commented that South East Asia contains both countries that are protected from and countries that are vulnerable to 4IR developments. Those protected have large shares of informal and agricultural employment and are not susceptible to labour displacement due to these technologies since there is surplus labour; those vulnerable are emerging, middle–income economies that have skill shortages and infrastructure limitations in such areas as education, transport and communications.

The contribution of the book

This book is one of the first to consider the perceived impact of the 4IR on the future of organisations and their workforces in the Asia Pacific region through the lens of regional managers and HRM professionals. The perceptions of managers across ten different countries are presented in the specific country chapters, together with an analysis of the cross-regional similarities and differences which are examined later in the book.

These perspectives are useful in aiding our understanding of the extent to which the 4IR and its applications and impacts are linked to the unique contexts and state of development of each country represented. Finally, the book considers some broader global issues. For example, will the 4IR intensify existing national and global inequalities, and further concentrate economic power and wealth in the hands of a few multinational enterprises that have propriety rights over the technological platforms and applications that are transforming global business? Such scenarios have led those such as Peters (2017) to refer to 'technological unemployment' and Frey and Osborne (2017) to argue that job stagnation in the digital age can only be avoided by a shift towards inclusive growth.

Whatever the future holds, it is certain that change will continue in a future where humans and robots will interact ever more closely (Cedefop, 2019: 4).

The implications of this and other challenges outlined throughout the book are discussed in more detail in the concluding chapter. Specifically, the aims here are to identify the key impacts of the 4IR across the ten countries included in the book, as well as to explore innovative strategies that may help to address inequality and encourage inclusive growth.

Organisation of the book

As discussed earlier, this book features 10 countries which are categorised as developed, intermediary and developing, and, following the first two chapters, the country chapters are presented in these categories in alphabetical order.

Chapter 2, by Prikshat and Muenjohn, presents the conceptual research framework for the book. This chapter outlines the survey instrument that underpins the reporting of the research findings guiding all but two of the country studies (Nepal and Taiwan). The purpose of the survey was to scope the preparations, potential impact and policy challenges associated with 4IR-related forces (as outlined in this chapter). The unit of analysis for the survey was the organisation, and the informants for data collection were primarily senior managers. Through the survey instrument, senior managers were asked to reflect on the stages of the 4IR which their organisations have reached; how prepared their organisations and their workforces are for the 4IR; the likely consequences of the 4IR for their organisations; and their perceptions of the preparation and comprehensiveness of government policy towards the 4IR.

Developed countries

Chapter 3 (Australia) is the first of the country chapters in the developed countries section by Cameron, Montague, Stanton, Muenjohn & Larkin. The findings/analysis reported in this chapter focus on three large sectors in the Australian economy (health, ICT, and tourism and hospitality). The sample group represented was drawn from the Australian Human Resource Institute (AHRI) database, comprising senior human resource managers and professionals from a range of industry sectors – including the key sectors mentioned earlier. Findings indicate that there is a variety of pressures and trends impacting each sector and their respective growth and productivity. Ageing populations and workforces, national ICT infrastructures, skill shortages in key professions, and prohibitive costs for 4IR technologies for SMEs in particular, are contributing to Australia's ability to embrace the 4IR in order to meet demand and build and maintain global competitiveness. The authors contend that the Australian government, in partnership with industry labour market planners, needs to strategise and plan for policy infrastructure that is integrated, moving the economy and human capital towards greater readiness for the 4IR, and the rapid onslaught of digital disruption and associated technologies.

The next chapter (Chapter 4) by Bali, Vas and Waring focuses on Singapore. Here, the authors maintain that the 4IR poses both tremendous risks and opportunities for Singapore – a country which prides itself on being a 'Smart Nation'. Their chapter identifies the challenges associated with the 4IR, as well as the strategic choices of government, trade unions and industry. The results of their survey confirm that few jobs in Singapore's labour market will be untouched by the impact of 4IR with the impact of AI and automation already being felt within a number of key Singaporean industries.

Taiwan, third in the developed countries section and Chapter 5 in the book is authored by Min-Wen Sophie Chang. This chapter is one of two in this book that did not use the survey. Instead, key issues related to 4IR readiness are explored through a selection of case studies across the manufacturing, retail and healthcare sectors. Chang concludes that, after considering cases of 4IR technology upgrades across these three sectors, some large Taiwanese firms seem capable and ready to install robots, smart hardware and equipment, particularly in manufacturing. However, when comparing the service sector with the manufacturing sector, she maintains that, concerns over customers' responses or profitability may deter firms from effecting change, and that this may be one of the reasons why these sectors have been less successful in transitioning to the 4IR. Chang concludes that, it may be that some Taiwanese firms are not suitable for 4IR technological implementation because they do not have the right business models to support the required digitalisation, as per Cheng (2017) cited in this chapter.

Intermediary countries

As explained earlier China and India are classified as intermediary countries for the purposes of this book. In Chapter 6, by Liu, An and Xiu the authors examine the potential effects of the 4IR on the workforce in the Chinese context. China has its own 4IR plans referred to as "Made in China 2025" which were released in May 2015. However, due to the economic structure and its relatively low independent innovation capability, Liu et al. conclude that China is currently unable to take a leading position in the wave of the new industrial revolution. Overall, they report that, based on the survey findings, China's economy and society have achieved a great deal since the 1970s, and although China can adapt to the 4IR as required, there are still problems requiring attention. For example, the regional imbalance of economic and talent structures remain unresolved and are holding back economic sustainability and social development. There has also been a lack of investment and output in basic research, leading to a lack of innovation. Finally, the 4IR is likely to mean that a large number of traditional jobs will disappear, but employees are largely unaware of the relationship between job loss and the implementation of new technologies. Meanwhile, the existing labour market is unable to meet the labour demand brought by the emerging industries.

Chapter 7 focuses on India and was authored by Kumar, Prikshat and Irudhaya. The chapter considers the potential impacts of 4IR adoption and application in India. The findings indicate high levels of perceived impact on all the four dimensions (i.e. task productivity, task innovation, customer satisfaction and management control). As a result, the authors maintain that, given that the service sector is a mainstay of the Indian economy, the results of their study are particularly important for managers in the Indian service industry to assist their understanding of the importance of the adoption and application of 4IR technologies in business service processes. It is also proposed that, as some respondents from the Indian service organisations expressed concerns about losing their jobs due to the integration of new technologies, it is important that managers create a positive environment and prepare for their adoption. Another key issue was the reported lack of organisational preparedness with regard to the adoption of AI technologies, as findings showed that a significant percentage of employees reported very low to low levels of preparation for the anticipated technology changes. These concerns required urgent attention as the consequences of being unprepared for the 4IR may be detrimental in the longer term for organisations in terms of reduced productivity, profit, loss and sustained competitiveness.

Developing countries

Chapter 8 features Indonesia, the first of the developing countries in this section of the book. Tjokro, Siagian and Priyono explain that the Indonesian government has committed to developing *Smart Cities*, where 1000 new IT companies will be introduced as a strategic intervention by 2020 across the country. In addition, Indonesia is trying to rapidly integrate into the fast-moving ecosystem of the 4IR, although only one in seven businesses has implemented artificial intelligence in their business to date, and the manufacturing and consumer goods sectors are still mainly in the 3IR or 2IR automation phase. Overall, the authors state that the Indonesian government and the private sector have made significant steps towards building an economy and the infrastructure necessary for the country to become one of the most successful adopters of 4IR technologies in the Asia Pacific region, leveraging technology for future economic and social benefits. Further, the government has made allocations for training funding for youth through vocational training centres, where subjects include programming training, graphic design and general administration and computing skills – placing some areas of Indonesia in a unique state of 4IR preparedness.

Next, Chapter 9, authored by Noorziah Mohd Salleh & Badariah Ab Rahman focuses on Malaysia. The authors propose that, although implementing the 4IR has high potential in Malaysia, it is crucial that the necessary infrastructure is ready to meet the requirements for the inevitable transition. For example, infrastructure such as internet services currently requires further development and improved nationwide access in terms of coverage, speed and usefulness in order to fully capitalise on the Internet of Things (IoT) and big data. As such, the government, organisations and workforces have to work together to realise the national aspiration to fully embrace the 4IR. The research survey results establish that the desire to move forward into the 4IR era is apparent amongst respondents, although there was some uncertainty in relation to 'how' and 'why' it will benefit them. It was also clear that the implementation of 4IR technologies will require the Malaysian government and industry to develop strategies for affected workforces, thus ensuring that employees are being trained/retrained to enable them to be relevant in the digitalisation era.

Chapter 10 features Mauritius, written by Rowtho, Jouan, Hardin-Ramanan, Gopee and Charoux. The authors point out that it is essential to urgently address the current shortage of skills in AI, robotics and blockchain and to promote the emergence of a class of techno entrepreneurs. Survey respondents predicted that in future there will be a greater use of the platform economy, with easier access to a diverse pool of labour outsourced both locally and globally. Findings also indicate that pursuing progress with third industrial revolution technologies and hoping to be ready for disruptions brought about by the 4IR, are not sufficiently substantial strategies to support the country to move to the next level. Instead, the authors maintain that the government will need to put in place appropriate legislative frameworks to facilitate the deployment of new technologies and the necessary reskilling and upskilling of employees. Some initiatives in some sectors have been introduced to develop strategies for accelerating the implementation of big data analytics, cloud-based business, the internet of things, artificial intelligence, robotics and blockchain. However, unlike previous models of industrial revolution, the 4IR also implies the need to embark on a cultural transformational journey where the Mauritian government and businesses cooperate with employees, educational systems and communities to engage in a new model of development, eventually leading to the creation of a smart island with a circular and inclusive economy.

Chapter 11 by Dhakal, Dahal and Dahal features Nepal, the second country chapter in the book which does not include a survey, as interviews were used instead. The authors propose that the quest for an inclusive 4IR in the developing world requires that significant attention be paid to the UN's Sustainable Development Goals. As trends in 4IR-related opportunities and challenges have not been well-documented in Nepal, the chapter reviews existing policy landscapes in the education, employment and innovation sectors, alongside the perspectives of various stakeholders. The authors conclude that if transformative technologies associated with the 4IR are to contribute to SDG aspirations, the current Nepalese policy landscape is ill-equipped, requiring substantial investment in education, employment and innovation to be strategically prepared to exploit its potential. It is argued that, as Nepal ranks so poorly in many of the global indicators, there is an urgent need to integrate employment and education strategies driven by an emphasis on investment in ICT-related hard and soft infrastructure.

The last of the country chapters (12) features Thailand and was written by Sorakraikitikul who explains that, Thailand's Ministry of Information & Communication Technology introduced 'Thailand 4.0' – an economic model that aims to unlock the country from several economic challenges resulting from past economic development models. It specifically targets four industry sectors

(bio–economy, electronic and robotic parts, aviation–related and medical industries) as well as revitalising some of the more traditional sectors. The findings
indicate that most respondents are aware of the 4IR, and of the associated government strategies, plans and policies. That said, the author contends that the
research findings indicate the need for support in skill development that will
be necessary for the future – such as technical skills related to data security/
communication, data analytics, collaboration software, IT infrastructure and
automation technology, so as to equip Thai workers for the adoption of 4IR
technologies in their organisations. Moreover, it is proposed that organisations
will need to provide additional (and more sophisticated) learning and development opportunities, which will require collaboration between all relevant
stakeholders. as well as innovative strategies, plans, policies and programs that
are implemented in a proactive and ongoing manner.

The final chapter (13) is written by the editors, Nankervis, Connell and Burgess. The chapter summarises the key comparative findings of the study across
the 10 countries included in the book, and discusses the overall implications
for industry managers, their organisations and associations, government policy,
education strategies and nations more generally. In the process some insights
are offered towards addressing the research questions outlined in this chapter
that focus on how prepared managers and organisations are in relation to the
impact of the 4IR.

References

Applebaum, S. H. (1997). Socio-technical systems theory: An intervention strategy for organisation development. *Management Decision*, 35 (6), 452–463.

Arnold, D., Arntz, M., Gregory, T., Steffes, S., & Zierahn, U. (2018). No need for automation
angst but automation policies. In Neufeind, M., O'Reilly, J., & Ranft, F. (eds.), *Work in the
Digital Age, Challenges of the Fourth Industrial Revolution*. London: Rowman & Littlefield
International.

Australia urged to embrace AI revolution, as report says automation will affect all jobs: A new
revolution is upon us that will dramatically change the Australian workforce. *Lateline*
(ABC1); Time: 22:30; Broadcast Date: Tuesday, 8th August 2017; Duration: 6 min., 34 sec.
see mp4. Available at: http://searh.informit.com.au.ezproxy.lib.rmit.edu.au/documentSu
mmary;dn=TSM201708080182;res=TVNEWS, accessed 8 November 2017.

Ayentimi, D.T., & Burgess, J. (2018). Is the fourth industrial revolution relevant to Sub-Sahara
Africa? *Technology Analysis & Strategic Management*. doi:10.1080/09537325.2018.1542129

Baxter, G., & Sommerville, I. (2011). Socio-technical systems: From design methods to systems engineering. *Interacting with Computers*, 23, 4–17.

Brynjolfsson, E., & McAfee, A. (2014). *The Second Machine Age: Work, Progress, and Prosperity in
a Time of Brilliant Technologies*. New York: W.W. Norton & Company.

Cameron, R., Burgess, J., Dhakal, S., & Mumme, B. (2018). The future for work-readiness
and graduate employability in the Asia Pacific. In Cameron, R., Dhakal, S., & Burgess, J.
(eds.), *Transitions from Education to Work, Workforce Ready Challenges in the Asia Pacific*. Oxon:
Routledge, pp. 236–243.

Cedefop, K. (2019). *Artificial or Human Intelligence? Digitalisation and the Future of Jobs and Skills: Opportunities and Risks*. Briefing Note, June. ISSN 1831-2411. Available at: www.cedefop.europa.eu/files/9140_en.pdf, accessed 1 July 2019.

Chalmers, in Adams, P. {broadcaster} (2017). When robots come for your job. *Late Night Live*. Radio National Australian Broadcasting Commission Sydney, 27 September. Available at: www.abc.net.au/radionational/programs/latenightlive/when-the-robots-come/8992662

Cheng, T-Z. (2017). Management advice for entrepreneurs: turnaround struggling firms. *Business Weekly* (In Mandarin), Taipei.

China Power (2016). Is China a developed country? *China Power*, 9 March. Available at: https://chinapower.csis.org/is-china-a-developed-country/, accessed 2 August 2019.

Citigroup (2019). *Technology at Work v4.0, Navigating the Future of Work*. Citi GPS: Global Perspectives & Solutions. Available at: www.oxfordmartin.ox.ac.uk/publications/technology-at-work-4/, accessed 1 July 2019.

Dhakal, S., Prikshat, V., Nankervis, A., & Burgess, J. (2018). *The Transition from Graduation to Work: Challenges and Strategies in the Twenty-First Century Asia Pacific and Beyond*. Berlin: Springer.

Economist Intelligence Unit (EIU) Ltd (2018). *The Automation Readiness Index: Who Is Ready for the Coming Wave of Automation?* Commissioned by the ABB (ASEA Brown Boveri). Available at: www.automationreadiness.eiu.com/, accessed 1 July 2019.

Emery, F., & Trist, E. (1965). The causal texture of organizational environments. *Human Relations*, 18, 21–32.

Frey, C. B., & Osborne, M. A. (2017). The future of employment: How susceptible are jobs to computerisation? *Technological Forecasting & Social Change*, 114 (C), 254–280.

Hackman, J. R., & Oldham, G. R. (1980). *Work Redesign*. Reading, MA: Addison-Wesley.

Kruse, K. (2018). *In 2023 Your Boss Will Be a Robot (and You Will Love Her)*. Available at: www.forbes.com/sites/kevinkruse/2018/11/28/your-boss-will-be-a-robot-and-you-will-love-her/, accessed 1 July 2019.

McKinsey Global Institute (2017). *Artificial Intelligence the Next Digital Frontier?* Discussion Paper, McKinsey and Company. Available at: www.mckinsey.com/~/media/McKinsey/Industries/Advanced%20Electronics/Our%20Insights/How%20artificial%20intelligence%20can%20deliver%20real%20value%20to%20companies/MGI-Artificial-Intelligence-Discussion-paper.ashx

McKinsey Report (2012). *Education to Employment: Designing a System That Works*. Available at: www.mckinsey.com/industries/social-sector/our-insights/education-to-employment-designing-a-system-that-works

Mumford, E. (2006). The story of socio-technical design: Reflections on its successes, failures and potential. *Information Systems Journal*, 16 (4), 317–342.

O'Neill, M. (2017a). Explainer: What is artificial intelligence? *Lateline,* 7 August. Australian Broadcasting Commission Sydney. Available at: www.abc.net.au/news/2017-08-07/explainer-what-is-artificial-intelligence/8771632, accessed 16 August 2019.

O'Neill, M. (2017b). The AI race. *Lateline*, 8 August. Australian Broadcasting Commission Sydney. Available at: http://iview.abc.net.au/programs/ai-race/NS1732H001S00#playing (now removed from access)

Peters, M. A. (2017). Technological unemployment: Educating for the fourth industrial revolution. *Educational Philosophy and Theory*, 49 (1), 1–6. doi:10.1080/00131857.2016.1177412

Price Waterhouse Coopers (2018). *Workforce of the Future: The Competing Forces Shaping 2030*. Available at: www.pwc.com/gx/en/services/people-organisation/workforce-of-the-future/workforce-of-the-future-the-competing-forces-shaping-2030-pwc.pdf, accessed 13 January 2019.

Quigley, M., & Chalmers, J. (2016). *Changing Jobs, the Fair Go in the New Machine Age.* Melbourne: Redback Quarterly.

Romero, D., Stahre, J., Wuest, T., Noran, O., Bernus, P., Fast-Berglund & Gorecky, D. (2016). *Towards an Operator 4.0 Typology: A Human-Centric Perspective on the Fourth Industrial Revolution Technologies.* CIE46 Proceedings, 29–31 October, Tianjin, China, ISSN 2164-8670 CD-ROM, ISSN 2164-8689 ON-LINE

Scacchi, W. (2004). Socio-technical design. In Bainbridge, W. S. (ed.), *The Encyclopedia of Human Computer Interaction.* Great Barrington: Berkshire Publishing Group.

Scarpetta, S. (2017). *What Future for Work?* http://oecdobserver.org/news/fullstory.php/aid/5433/What_future_for_work_.html

Schwab, K. (2016). *The Fourth Industrial Revolution.* Geneva: World Economic Forum.

Sharma, M. (2019). Is India a developing country? America doesn't think so. *Business Today*, 15 April. Available at: www.businesstoday.in/current/world/india-developing-country-us-doesn-think-so-donald-trump-narendra-modi/story/337348.html, accessed 16 August 2019.

Trist, E. (1980). *The Evolution of Socio-Technical Systems: A Conceptual Framework and an Action Research Program.* Conference on Organisation Design and Performance, April, Wharton School, University of Pennsylvania.

UNDP (2016). *Human Development Report 2016: Human Development for Everyone.* New York: UNDP.

Waldrop, M. M. (2018). *The Future of Work: Will Robots Take My Job?* Available at: www.knowablemagazine.org/article/technology/2018/future-work-will-robots-take-my-job, accessed 1 July 2019.

World Bank (2019). *World Development Report 2019: The Future of Work.* Washington, DC: World bank.

World Economic Forum (WEF) (2016a). *Top Ten Skills in 2020 in 2015.* Future of Jobs Report. Available at: www.bing.com/images/search?view=detailV2&ccid=Ijh%2fsOXl&id=C41497B94D22DAE9C4E3164A9B3E2B4297EF1A04&thid=OIP.Ijh_sOXlZU_6l HdJPeskkAEsES&q=top+ten+skills+for+4th+industrial+revolution&simid=607988816 161869356&selectedIndex=0&ajaxhist=0

World Economic Forum (WEF) (2016b). *The Future of Jobs: Employment, Skills and Workforce Strategy for the Fourth Industrial Revolution.* Available at: http://www3.weforum.org/docs/WEF_Future_of_Jobs.pdf

World Economic Forum (WEF) (2017a). *This Is When a Robot Is Going to Take Your Job, According to Oxford University.* Available at: www.weforum.org/agenda/2017/07/how-long-before-a-robot-takes-your-job-here-s-when-ai-experts-think-it-will-happen/

World Economic Forum (WEF) (2017b). *Artificial Intelligence Will Transform Universities: Here's How.* Available at: www.weforum.org/agenda/2017/08/artificial-intelligence-will-transform-universities-here-s-how/

World Economic Forum (WEF) (2017c). *Accelerating Workforce Reskilling for the Fourth Industrial Revolution: An Agenda for Leaders to Shape the Future of Education, Gender and Work.* Geneva: WEF.

2 Conceptual research framework

Verma Prikshat and Nuttawuth Muenjohn

Introduction

The purpose of this chapter is to outline the survey instrument that underpins the reporting of the information contained in all but two of the country studies. The objective of the survey was to scope the preparations, likely impact and policy challenges associated with those forces associated with the 4IR that were outlined in chapter one. The unit of analysis for the survey is the organisation, and the informants for the data collection are senior managers. Through the survey instrument the book asks senior managers to reflect on: what stages of the 4IR their organisations have reached; how prepared their organisations and their workforces are for the 4IR; the likely consequences of the 4IR for their organisations; and their perceptions of the preparation and comprehensiveness of government policy towards the 4IR.

Senior managers are likely to be forward looking in terms of identifying potential opportunities and challenges in relation to the sustainability and future of the organisations and the workforces with which they are associated. To this extent, the presumption is that it is senior managers who are in a position and have a vested interest in reflecting on the positioning of their organisation for the 4IR. In turn, their responses provide a basis for examining the preparation and impact of the 4IR across the organisations, industries and countries included in the study. Not all chapters used the survey instrument. Nepal and Taiwan used interviews with managers and/or case studies for the research. In these cases, there were logistical and institutional factors that limited the application of a survey – in Nepal it was the large number of small enterprises that were difficult to access; in the case of Taiwan it was the difficulty in accessing a sufficient sample of managers who would agree to participate in the study.

The components of the survey

The linkages between the Fourth Industrial Revolution and the Future of Work (FoW) in this study are categorised against three main factors: namely, 'strategic factors', 'individual factors' and 'organisational factors'. The strategic factors are those that influence organisations to make conscious decisions about the adoption of particular 4IR technologies. Individual factors are associated with the effects of these choices on employees, workplaces, jobs and skills. Finally, organisational factors include the impacts on the organisation as a whole due to the adoption of 4IR technologies. In addition, the proposed conceptual framework includes the individual and organisational factors moderating the relationships between these factors.

Three main components were identified for the 4IR model based on extant research literature. The strategic factors comprised three variables: strategic orientation, top management support and innovative leadership. Individual factors comprised five variables: perceived usefulness and ease of use of new technologies, task innovation, task productivity, attitude, job satisfaction and job insecurity. Organisational factors comprised three variables: organisational innovation, organisational change readiness, and organisational performance/IT business value. The following section justifies and explains the identified variables.

Strategic factors

Strategic Orientation (SO)

In the context of the 4IR, strategic orientation can inform us about the intentions of organisations to recruit technical personnel, commit funds to new technology development and maintain a reputation of being at the forefront of a technological area in a particular industry (Salavou et al., 2004). Strategic orientation (SO) refers to an organisation's processes, practices and decision-making activities that lead to its growth (Lumpkin & Dess, 1996). It focuses on building competitive advantage and exploring new business opportunities through innovation, experimentation and risk-taking decisions (Morgan & Strong, 2003; Venkatraman, 1989). Strategic orientation, as an internal organisational factor (amongst others), with regard to the adoption of the latest technologies, rests on the premise that previous research observes SO as an innovation determinant (Wilson et al., 1999), whilst simultaneously reflecting the innovative attitude of an organisation and its commitment to innovation (Ettlie, 1983).

Top Management Support (TMS)

Previous research has observed that top management support (TMS) significantly affects the adoption of new information technologies (Lian et al., 2014; Teo et al., 2009; Wang et al., 2016). The TMS provided by an organisation can create a positive environment (or otherwise) to facilitate the adoption of new technologies. The level of TMS can influence perceptions of how adoption will benefit the organisation, support the procurement of sufficient resources and help overcome employees' resistance to the change (Premkumar & Roberts, 1999).

Innovative leadership

Although possession of the requisite technological or research and development capabilities and complementary assets are key enablers for technology adoption, leadership is of paramount importance to efficiently and effectively drive the innovation process (Oke et al., 2009). Leaders play an important role in determining which innovations to introduce (Victorino et al., 2006), and innovative leaders have the capacity to serve as behavioural role models for enhancing innovative behaviours and modifying the attitudes of their followers. As innovative leadership is also likely to influence organisational decision-making (Cyert & March, 1963), it could be considered to be one of the requisite variables of an organisation's foray into linking the 4IR with the FoW.

Individual factors

Perceived usefulness and ease of use of new technologies

The extant literature demonstrates strong empirical support (Doll et al., 1998; Karahanna & Straub, 1999) for the Technology Acceptance Model (TAM) (Davis, 1989; Venkatesh & Davis, 2000) as an analytical framework for examining the links between the 4IR and the FoW. From a conceptual perspective, it is proposed that the TAM needs to be extended to incorporate the attitudes of an organisation's employees towards the acceptance of new technologies related to the 4IR. The TAM posits that usage of information technology is determined by the beliefs a user holds about its perceived usefulness (PU) and its perceived ease-of-use (PEU). While PU is defined as the degree to which a person believes that use of a system would improve their performance, PEU refers to the degree to which a person believes that using a particular system would be effortless. Thus, this conceptualisation proposes that employees' acceptance of new technologies, based on their specific beliefs concerning PU and PEU, are the two key people-related factors that can influence the acceptance of the latest technologies, and thus can influence the degree to which jobs, workplace and skill changes occur in organisations.

Task innovation

Task innovation refers to the extent to which individual employees tend to try and create new ideas in their work. In the context of 4IR technologies and the FoW, workers will rely heavily on information processing which is likely to be increasingly abstract and mediated by sensing mechanisms (Torkzadeh & Doll, 1999). Thus, the overall impact of technology on the innovation of different tasks performed by employees becomes one of the important criteria for studying the 4IR and the FoW (Deng et al., 2008; Saeed et al., 2010).

Task productivity

The linking model of the 4IR and the FoW is characterised by a strong reliance on the latest technologies and software. Extant literature has observed the positive impact of information technology on task productivity (Danziger & Kraemer, 1985; Davis, 1989). Technologically advanced software has the capacity to improve employees' time management skills and to enhance the resultant productivity (Doll & Torkzadeh, 1998). Previous research on the adoption of IT-intensive systems has highlighted enhanced business process performance as a consequence of the successful adoption and implementation of new technologies in the workplace (Arnold, 2006).

Attitude and job satisfaction

Morris and Venkatesh (2010) highlighted the importance of analysing the influences of technological characteristics on job characteristics and/or job outcomes (cited in Maier et al., 2010). Based on Maier et al. (2010), we propose that there is a relationship between attitudes related to the usage of the latest technologies (due to FoW considerations) and the work-related outcomes of job satisfaction. However, it should be noted that employee attitudes rely heavily on the PU and PEU of new technologies, and attitudes are an outcome of these perceptions. The increased complexity of technological implementation for the FoW may impact on the job satisfaction of employees. For example, ineffective communication regarding the technological changes may give employees the impression that new technologies are being implemented to reduce costs rather than to facilitate work outcomes (Stone & Lukaszewski, 2009). Moreover, new 4IR technological implementation may require employees to change their work habits and adjust to new workflows, thus potentially creating more stress and resistance towards using the new technology (Ngai et al., 2007). Such behaviours may also result in lower job satisfaction levels among employees (Konradt et al., 2003). Consequently, attitudes towards new technologies and resultant job satisfaction are important work-related factors that assume greater importance in the context of the 4IR and the FoW.

Job insecurity

Technological investment has been central to theories of employment reduction (Autor et al., 2003; Goos & Manning, 2007) and job insecurity (Gallie et al., 2017) for some time. Due to changes in the world of work there is a greater need to study insecurity about particular job features (Lee et al., 2018). For example, as jobs in an organisation become more automated and employees' routine tasks are taken over by technology, less freedom and creativity tend to be required from humans (Lee et al., 2018). Consequently, perceptions about reductions in freedom and an absence of control over jobs raise important concerns about human replacement by machines (Nica, 2016; Peters, 2017) and associated perceptions of job insecurity.

Organisational factors

Organisational innovation

While task innovation refers to the extent that individual employees tend to create and implement new ideas in their work, organisational innovation on the other hand refers to an organisation's proclivity towards the initiation and/or implementation of different types of innovations, such as technological, administrative, products and processes (Salavou et al., 2004). The concept of organisational innovation is mainly captured in this framework around the technology-related notion rather than behaviour-related or product-related domains. The adoption of the latest technologies has the potential to assist individual employees in creating new ideas, and also potentially provides them with a platform to try out innovative ideas (Doll & Torkzadeh, 1998). Similarly, adoption of the latest technologies has the potential to influence organisational innovation, as these technologies improve rapid access to new knowledge within and across organisations, significantly impacting potential innovations.

Organisational change-readiness

Triggered by the 4IR, the FoW is characterised by digital innovation. Innovation can occur only when the organisation is ready to change its approaches to production, adoption, assimilation, exploitation, renewal, enlargement and development (Crossan & Apaydin, 2010). Organisational readiness for change in the context of the 4IR may reflect a state of being both psychologically and behaviourally prepared to take action and be receptive to innovations (Weiner, 2009). An organisation's members need to be committed to the change and have the change efficacy to implement digital organisational change (Weiner, 2008). Thus, organisational readiness for change provides the overarching theoretical scaffold to develop an assessment of organisational readiness for digital innovation concerning the FoW (Lokuge et al., 2019).

Organisational performance/IT business value

The term information technology (IT) business value is commonly used to refer to the organisational performance impacts of IT, as previous research has shown that information technology contributes to the improvement of IT business value (Brynjolfsson & Hitt, 1996; Kohli & Devaraj, 2003; Mukhopadhyay et al., 1995). Thus, in the context of the 4IR and the FoW, the term organisational or IT business value can be used to measure the impact of the associated technologies on the performance of an organisation. This impact needs to be measured at both the intermediate process level and the organisation-wide level and comprises both efficiency and competitive impacts (Melville et al., 2004). In general, it is suggested that organisations need to invest in quality IT assets that help IT business value generation and further enhance organisational performance (Trieu, 2017).

The survey instrument

Given that the target population of this study was industry managers, the survey instrument was designed as a self-evaluative report which comprised three sections covering different questions relating to the theoretical framework. All the measures for different variables were developed on validated scales derived from a review of the information systems and management literature.

The first two sections of the survey instrument requested organisation details (e.g. industry types and locations) and respondent demographics (e.g. gender, age, education). The third section examined the current IT infrastructure and capabilities of the organisations being surveyed, while the fourth investigated strategic orientation (this concerned the matching of IT strategies with business strategies); top management support (related to the adoption of AI/software/applications); perceived usefulness (PU) and the perceived ease of use (PEU) of technology, as discussed earlier. The fifth section investigated the links between 4IR technologies and task productivity-task innovation, organisation innovation, IT business value and organisation performance in the organisations studied. The sixth section was designed to assess respondents' views on their employees' attitudes, job satisfaction and job insecurity regarding the adoption of these new technologies. Finally, the last two sections comprised items in relation to innovative leadership behaviours and organisation change readiness levels.

The survey also comprised questions designed to provide an understanding of the current technological stage of the organisations being surveyed, the current skill levels of employees, and the different types of technologies being used in organisations. A further section comprised questions regarding the role of government policies. This section also asked respondents for their opinions on the percentage of jobs likely to be replaced in the next decade, due to the impact of the 4IR in their organisation. The survey used self-reporting, meaning that the respondents were asked to indicate the degree of their agreement or disagreement with each statement on a five-point Likert scale (1 = strongly disagree, 2 = disagree, 3 = undecided, 4 = agree, 5 = strongly agree).

Pre-testing and adjustments to the survey

To strengthen the content validity of the survey instruments, a pre-test was conducted prior to the pilot study. This was conducted by observing the degree of relevance of each variable item. The questionnaire was reviewed and examined by research experts from different partnering countries to check the veracity of the questionnaire and to ensure that it measured what it was designed to measure. The second stage of data collection comprised the pilot study which was conducted in Australia and involved organisations from different industry sectors. Piloting the survey can provide the researcher(s) with a better understanding and ensure that the final survey will achieve the research aims. In this case some small changes were made to the survey questionnaire, mainly to simplify questions to assist understanding and ensure that they were understood by respondents.

The initial instrument was developed in Australia and written in English. Within the other countries where the survey was utilised it was translated into the local language, pre-tested and modified. While the structure of the survey was similar across the countries, the details are not identical, due to local contextual factors.

Sampling and data collection

The sampling and data collection processes differed across the countries. In Indonesia the survey was directly administered in hard copy, while in Thailand and Mauritius it was distributed online. The Indonesian study was confined to three provinces, while the Thai and Mauritian cases were national. The number of surveys distributed and returned, and the industry coverage of the respondents, also differed across the countries as explained in each chapter.

Data cleaning and processing

In all cases the data was cleaned, coded and entered into a database to support subsequent analysis. For this book the purpose is to scope the state of preparation of organisations, employees and managers; and to track where they are located in terms of positioning and preparation for the 4IR.

Reporting the results

Analysis for this study was divided into the following four parts:

a) **Participant Analysis** covered the initial demographic section, i.e. organisational and respondent details
b) **Variables Analysis** was covered in the aforementioned sections
c) **Comparative Analysis** investigated respondent comparisons between gender, age, education and positioning in relation to different sections of the survey instrument
d) **Impact Analysis** examined the effect of strategic orientation, top management support and innovative leadership on the adoption of technology concerning the 4IR and the FoW (i.e. AI/Robotics, machine learning and associated software applications).

In this book only the descriptive statistics derived from the study are presented. As mentioned earlier in this chapter, two of the ten countries (Nepal and Taiwan) used interviews and/or case studies rather than a survey instrument due to the prevalence of small to medium size enterprises in those countries, or due to the difficulty of attracting survey respondents. However, these two chapters still followed the same conceptual and empirical frameworks as the other eight countries.

Directions for future research

This book reports on the descriptive findings arising from the survey reinforced by reference to secondary data, public reports and public policy on the 4IR from each of the respective countries.

The research can be extended through conducting statistical tests on the data set in order to establish linkages between the variables. To this end, a schematic model is proposed to guide future research (see figure 2.1). This model, linking the 4IR with the FoW, provides a conceptual framework that was designed based on the limited prior research conducted in this field of study. The model is based on a review of the extensive management information system literature, using socio-technical theory as its foundation, as discussed in Chapter 1. The framework and the propositions emerging from it provide a rich agenda for future research. The three components of the model identify a number of avenues for future research, that it is proposed, may help to track the movement of organisations towards the FoW. First, although this study mentions only three factors (i.e. innovative leadership, top management support and strategic orientation) as responsible for an organisation's trajectory, further exploration into more strategic factors has the potential to improve this framework considerably. Moreover, it will be important to assess the interplay among the three strategic variables to determine how they may influence and impact an organisation's move towards the FoW in the 4IR context.

A second avenue that should receive more attention relates to identifying the organisational change-readiness factors that are instrumental in facilitating the transition of an organisation towards the 4IR. Although recent research (Weiner et al., 2008; Weiner, 2009) has begun theorising about the development of measures and empirical assessment of organisational readiness for change, to our knowledge, it has not yet been associated with the 4IR and the FoW.

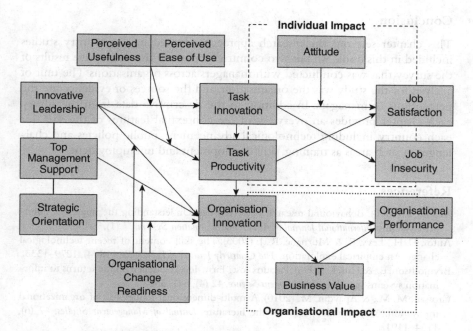

Figure 2.1 Conceptual Model for the 4IR and FoW

A more detailed exploration of 'organisational facilitators' (Schillewaert et al., 2005) has the potential to inform organisations with regard to how they can become ready for the FoW. Similarly, the role of 'organisational learning capabilities' (Nwankpa & Roumani, 2014) can inform researchers in relation to how various learning capabilities can boost organisational change readiness to meet the challenges of the 4IR and the FoW.

A third avenue for basic research concerning the FoW, may be to extend the proposed conceptual framework to include work-related outcomes for individual employees, such as technostress, employee knowledge-sharing and the relational quality of interactions due to the use of these new technologies. Last but not least, the construct of IT business value assumes importance in the context of the 4IR, and its further exploration regarding how this value can be enhanced; or can play an important role between organisational innovation and organisational performance, which can then better inform organisations when moving towards the FoW in a more deliberate manner.

Fourth, there is scope for different research approaches with, for example, detailed industry or organisational case studies that track the impact, preparations and responses to the 4IR through time.

Finally, the focus and scope of the research can be extended beyond the organisation to the sector or to the profession. The perceptions can be extended to different stakeholders, including training and education institutions, trade unions and employees.

Conclusion

This chapter sets out the research approach adopted in the country studies included in this book. All but two countries report on the descriptive results of the survey that was conducted with managers across organisations. The unit of analysis for the study was the organisation, and the sources of evidence are the perceptions of managers. In addition to the descriptive data from the survey, each chapter provides an overview of the contextual features of the 4IR for each country, including technological advancement, public policies and challenges in such areas as training, skill development and unemployment.

References

Arnold, V. (2006). Behavioural research opportunities: Understanding the impact of enterprise systems. *International Journal of Accounting Information Systems*, 7 (1), 7–17.

Autor, D. H., Levy, F., & Murnane, R. J. (2003). The skill content of recent technological change: An empirical exploration. *The Quarterly Journal of Economics*, 118 (4), 1279–1333.

Brynjolfsson, E., & Hitt, L. (1996). Paradox lost? Firm-level evidence on the returns to information systems spending. *Management Science*, 42 (4), 541–558.

Crossan, M. M., & Apaydin, M. (2010). A multi-dimensional framework of organizational innovation: A systematic review of the literature. *Journal of Management Studies*, 47 (6), 1154–1191.

Cyert, R. M., & March, J. G. (1963). *A Behavioural Theory of the Firm*. Englewood Cliffs, NJ: Prentice Hall.

Danziger, J. N., & Kraemer, K. L. (1985). Computerized data-based systems and productivity among professional workers: The case of detectives. *Public Administration Review*, 45 (1), 196–209.

Davis, F. D. (1989). Perceived usefulness, perceived ease of use, and user acceptance of information technology. *MIS Quarterly*, 319–340.

Deng, X., Doll, W. J., & Cao, M. (2008). Exploring the absorptive capacity to innovation/ productivity link for individual engineers engaged in IT enabled work. *Information & Management*, 45 (2), 75–87.

Doll, W. J., Hendrickson, A., & Deng, X. (1998). Using Davis's perceived usefulness and ease-of-use instruments for decision making: A confirmatory and multigroup invariance analysis. *Decision Sciences*, 29 (4), 839–869.

Doll, W. J., & Torkzadeh, G. (1998). Developing a multidimensional measure of system-use in an organizational context. *Information & Management*, 33 (4), 171–185.

Ettlie, J. E. (1983). Organizational policy and innovation among suppliers to the food processing sector. *Academy of Management Journal*, 26 (1), 27–44.

Gallie, D., Felstead, A., Green, F., & Inanc, H. (2017). The hidden face of job insecurity. *Work, Employment and Society*, 31 (1), 36–53.

Goos, M., & Manning, A. (2007). Lousy and lovely jobs: The rising polarization of work in Britain. *The Review of Economics and Statistics*, 89 (1), 118–133.

Karahanna, E., & Straub, D. W. (1999). The psychological origins of perceived usefulness and ease-of-use. *Information & Management*, 35 (4), 237–250.

Kohli, R., & Devaraj, S. (2003). Performance impacts of information technology: Is actual usage the missing link? *Management Science*, 49 (3), 273–289.

Konradt, U., Hertel, G., & Schmook, R. (2003). Quality of management by objectives, task-related stressors, and non-task-related stressors as predictors of stress and job satisfaction among teleworkers. *European Journal of Work and Organizational Psychology*, 12 (1), 61–79.

Lee, C., Huang, G. H., & Ashford, S. J. (2018). Job insecurity and the changing workplace: Recent developments and the future trends in job insecurity research. *Annual Review of Organizational Psychology and Organizational Behavior*, 5, 335–359.

Lian, J. W., Yen, D. C., & Wang, Y. T. (2014). An exploratory study to understand the critical factors affecting the decision to adopt cloud computing in Taiwan hospital. *International Journal of Information Management*, 34 (1), 28–36.

Lokuge, S., Sedera, D., Grover, V., & Dongming, X. (2019). Organizational readiness for digital innovation: Development and empirical calibration of a construct. *Information & Management*, 56 (3), 445–461.

Lumpkin, G. T., & Dess, G. G. (1996). Clarifying the entrepreneurial orientation construct and linking it to performance. *Academy of Management Review*, 21 (1), 135–172.

Maier, C., Laumer, S., Eckhardt, A., & Weitzel, T. (2010). Analyzing the impact of HRIS implementations on HR personnel's job satisfaction and turnover intention. *The Journal of Strategic Information Systems*, 22 (3), 193–207.

Melville, N., Kraemer, K., & Gurbaxani, V. (2004). Information technology and organizational performance: An integrative model of IT business value. *MIS Quarterly*, 28 (2), 283–322.

Morgan, R. E., & Strong, C. A. (2003). Business performance and dimensions of strategic orientation. *Journal of Business Research*, 56 (3), 163–176.

Morris, M. G., & Venkatesh, V. (2010). Job characteristics and job satisfaction: Understanding the role of enterprise resource planning system implementation. *MIS Quarterly*, 34, 1.

Mukhopadhyay, T., Kekre, S., & Kalathur, S. (1995). Business value of information technology: A study of electronic data interchange. *MIS Quarterly*, 137–156.

Ngai, E.W., Law, C. C., Chan, S. C., & Wat, F. K. (2007). Importance of the internet to human resource practitioners in Hong Kong. *Personnel Review*, 37 (1), 66–84.

Nica, E. (2016). Will technological unemployment and workplace automation generate greater capital-labor income imbalances? *Economics, Management & Finance*, 11 (4), 68–74.

Nwankpa, J., & Roumani, Y. (2014). Understanding the link between organizational learning capability and ERP system usage: An empirical examination. *Computers in Human Behavior*, 33, 224–234.

Oke, A., Munshi, N., & Walumbwa, F. O. (2009). The influence of leadership on innovation processes and activities. *Organizational Dynamics*, 38 (1), 64–72.

Peters, M.A. (2017). Technological unemployment: Educating for the fourth industrial revolution. *Journal of Self-Governance and Management Economics*, 5 (1), 25–33.

Premkumar, G., & Roberts, M. (1999). Adoption of new information technologies in rural small businesses. *Omega*, 27 (4), 467–484.

Saeed, K.A., Abdinnour, S., Lengnick-Hall, M. L., & Lengnick-Hall, C.A. (2010). Examining the impact of pre-implementation expectations on post-implementation use of enterprise systems: A longitudinal study. *Decision Sciences*, 41 (4), 659–688.

Salavou, H., Baltas, G., & Lioukas, S. (2004). Organisational innovation in SMEs: The importance of strategic orientation and competitive structure. *European Journal of Marketing*, 38 (9–10), 1091–1112.

Schillewaert, N., Ahearne, M. J., Frambach, R. T., & Moenaert, R. K. (2005). The adoption of information technology in the sales force. *Industrial Marketing Management*, 34 (4), 323–336.

Stone, D. L., & Lukaszewski, K. M. (2009). An expanded model of the factors affecting the acceptance and effectiveness of electronic human resource management systems. *Human Resource Management Review*, 19 (2), 134–143.

Teo, T. S., Lin, S., & Lai, K. H. (2009). Adopters and non-adopters of e-procurement in Singapore: An empirical study. *Omega*, 37 (5), 972–987.

Torkzadeh, G., & Doll, W. J. (1999). The development of a tool for measuring the perceived impact of information technology on work. *Omega*, 27 (3), 327–339.

Trieu, V. H. (2017). Getting value from business intelligence systems: A review and research agenda. *Decision Support Systems*, 93, 111–124.

Venkatesh, V., & Davis, F. D. (2000). A theoretical extension of the technology acceptance model: Four longitudinal field studies. *Management Science*, 46 (2), 186–204.

Venkatraman, N. (1989). The concept of fit in strategy research: Toward verbal and statistical correspondence. *Academy of Management Review*, 14 (3), 423–444.

Victorino, L., Verma, R., Plaschka, G., & Dev, C. (2006). Service innovation and customer choices in the hospitality industry. *Managing Service Quality: An International Journal*, 15 (6), 555–576.

Wang, Y. S., Li, H. T., Li, C. R., & Zhang, D. Z. (2016). Factors affecting hotels' adoption of mobile reservation systems: A technology-organization-environment framework. *Tourism Management*, 53, 163–172.

Weiner, B. J. (2009). A theory of organizational readiness for change. *Implementation Science*, 4 (1), 67.

Weiner, B. J., Amick, H., & Lee, S. Y. D. (2008). Conceptualization and measurement of organizational readiness for change: A review of the literature in health services research and other fields. *Medical Care Research and Review*, 65 (4), 379–436.

Wilson, A. L., Ramamurthy, K., & Nystrom, P. C. (1999). A multi-attribute measure for innovation adoption: The context of imaging technology. *IEEE Transactions on Engineering Management*, 46 (3), 311–321.

Part 2

Country chapters

Part 2

Country chapters

3 Australia

*Roslyn Cameron, Alan Montague, Pauline Stanton,
Nuttawuth Muenjohn and Roslyn Larkin*

Introduction

This chapter will explore the overall demographic, economic and key labour market challenges and opportunities within the Australian economy in the light of the trends associated with the onset of the Fourth Industrial Revolution (4IR) and its impacts on the future of work. The chapter will first address labour market challenges for the Australian economy, including the growth industries and social and demographic issues, prior to focusing on three key sectors – healthcare; information and communications technology (ICT); and tourism and hospitality. The impact of key trends and technological advances including artificial intelligence (AI), robotics, machine learning and nanotechnology on these industry sectors will be explored, with particular attention paid to the implications for labour markets, workforces, jobs and skills.

This will be followed by the presentation of data from an online survey distributed with the support of the Australian Human Resource Institute (AHRI) which invited senior human resource managers and professionals from a range of industry sectors, including the key sectors mentioned earlier. As in other chapters in this book, survey respondents were asked questions on the nature, characteristics, implications and planning required to manage the actual and potential impacts of the 4IR and relationships between technology adoption and organisational performance. The chapter concludes with a discussion of the key issues and implications of these trends and the related issues for governments, labour market planners and human resource practitioners.

Labour market trends

Australia has a population of approximately 25 million people with an employment to population ratio of 62%. Key sector outputs in the Australian economy are health and education (13% each), finance (10%), mining and construction (8% each) and manufacturing (6%) (Reserve Bank Australia – RBA, 2019: 1). In April 2019 the labour force participation rate was 65.7%; the unemployment rate was 5.1%, with the underemployment rate at 8.3%; and the underutilisation rate was 13.4% (Australian Bureau of Statistics – ABS, 2019a). The underemployment rate is particularly disturbing, given that the 4IR is likely to result in an increase in this proportion of the Australian workforce, especially in younger and older age groups, together with overall unemployment rates of 20.5%. (ABS, 2018a).

The ABS report also found that certain industry sectors have higher rates of underemployment than others. Three sectors with high rates include: retail, healthcare and social assistance, and tourism and hospitality, which combined represent over 50% of those underemployed (ABS, 2018a; AIR, 2016). The labour market characteristics of two of these sectors (health and tourism and hospitality) together with the ICT sector, are discussed in more detail later in this chapter.

Growth industries

On the positive side, a recent report from the Department of Jobs and Small Business (2019) found growth rates for all industry sectors. Of note was strong growth for public administration and safety (up 14.6%), mining (up 10.3%) and professional, scientific and technical services (up 7.7%) whereas the manufacturing and retail sectors are decreasing (Department of Jobs and Small Business, 2019).

Demographic and social challenges

As with many countries discussed in this book (except India and Indonesia), Australia faces demographic challenges essentially driven by an ageing population and workforce, and increased life expectancy. The need to support and provide a range of services for an ageing population also places fiscal strain on governments and the services they need to supply, which, in turn, increases the cost of health care provision (The Treasury, 2010: 1). In a report compiled by the Productivity Commission in 2013 on *An Ageing Australia: Preparing for the Future*, the following projections were estimated: 'Australia's population is projected to increase to more than 38 million by 2060, more than 15 million above the population in 2012' (Productivity Commission, 2013: 3). In terms of improved life expectancy and labour force participation rates, the report found that 'the population aged 75 or more years is expected to rise by 4 million from 2012 to 2060, increasing from about 6.4 to 14.4 per cent of the population. . . . Labour participation rates are expected to fall from around 65 to 60 per cent from 2012 to 2060, and overall labour supply per capita to contract by 5 per cent' (Productivity Commission, 2013: 2).

Having outlined these economic, labour market and demographic trends and challenges, this chapter next briefly outlines the key labour force issues and technologies being introduced in three large industry sectors: healthcare, ICT, and hospitality and tourism. Selected data from a survey of human resource managers and professionals based in Australia is then presented, followed by a discussion on the implications of the 4IR for governments and labour market planners.

Three key industry sectors

The healthcare sector

The impact of ageing populations and the growth of chronic disease, as well as greater consumer awareness and expectations in relation to quality care, are creating major resource problems for governments (Bartram & Dowling, 2013; Currie et al., 2012; Mesko et al., 2018; Waring & Bishop, 2010). At the same time there are supply-based challenges in terms of major shortages in key professions. It is estimated that the shortage of healthcare workers globally is currently about 17.4 million and that there will be increasing demands on the healthcare system; not only due to ageing populations, but also due to the ageing of the medical workforce (Mesko et al., 2018). This tends to be exacerbated by burnout and exhaustion in a range of healthcare roles as professionals are under increasing strain to do more with less (Bartram & Dowling, 2013; Currie et al., 2012; Mesko et al., 2018; Stanton et al., 2014).

In recent years, health care policy makers in developed nations have introduced a range of strategies to improve productivity and create more efficient and effective health care systems. These have included the introduction of business improvement methodologies such as lean management and Six Sigma (Leggat et al., 2015; Stanton et al., 2014), new funding models, the upskilling of professionals, and the introduction of paraprofessionals in a range of areas. These initiatives have been designed to cut waste, reframe incentives, and improve labour utilisation (Leggat et al., 2015; Stanton et al., 2014). However, despite these initiatives the prospect of supply meeting demand in health care in Australia (as in other countries) is still bleak.

The Australian health workforce

According to the 2016 Australian Census, over 800,000 people were reported as working in the health services sector (Australian Institute of Health and Welfare – AIHW, 2018). Many of these are registered health practitioners who are included in one of the fourteen health professional groups regulated by the Australian Health Practitioner Regulation Agency (APHRA, 2017). These include medical practitioners, nurses, midwives and dentists. However, there are also other roles and professional groups such as social workers or ancillary staff who fall outside this regulating agency (AIHW, 2018).

The healthcare workforce is growing, up from 674,000 persons in 2011, with nurses and midwives being the largest occupational group (AIHW, 2018). Evidence suggests that demand for nurses will continue to significantly exceed supply, with a projected shortfall of 85,000 nurses by 2025, increasing to 123,000 by 2030 (Health Workforce Australia, 2014). This is exacerbated by the large number of nurses in the over 54 years age group moving towards retirement (AIHW, 2018). There are also doctor shortages – the health sector places a significant reliance on overseas born doctors – for example, in 2016 33% of medical practitioners employed in Australia had gained their initial qualification overseas. This figure rises to 41% in rural and remote areas (AIHW, 2018).

Future scenario planning for nurses suggests that, while the shortfall could decrease with better coordination between education providers, employers and governments to lower dropout rates from university courses and increase nurse retention in organisations, it will still be a significant issue in the future (Health Workforce Australia, 2014). It is also possible that different forms of service delivery could be supported with new technologies and approaches to treatment, leading to requirements for different skills and a different skill mix (Health Workforce Australia, 2014). As a result, the potential impact of artificial intelligence, robotics and machine learning technologies on the nursing and medical professionals is enormous.

Likely impacts of the 4IR?

4IR technologies have the potential to revolutionise the Australian healthcare industry through four key approaches. First, through better diagnostic decisions, thus enhancing clinical support to improve decision making and treatment outcomes and reduce medical and human errors (Jha & Topol, 2016; Mesko et al., 2018; Sensmeir, 2017). Reducing medical errors and improving decision-making lowers costs through fewer adverse events and readmissions. Furthermore, these technologies are capable of self-learning and self-correcting, hence consistently improving data accuracy (Jiang et al., 2017). Second, the ability to mine large amounts of data can aid clinicians in delivering accurate and timely care to patients, thus increasing therapeutic success rates while decreasing unnecessary medical interventions (Neill, 2013; Sheikhtaheri et al., 2014). Such technologies can act as virtual assistants in screening patients, providing diagnoses, suggesting optimal treatments and triaging patients, and responding to patient enquiries, as well as providing individualised treatment options (Pratt, 2018; Sensmeir, 2017).

Third, improved diagnostics not only leads to better decision-making but also reduced administration by eliminating repetitive routine tasks (Mesko et al., 2018; Pratt, 2018). For example, AI can simplify a range of tasks that specialists perform, such as the time spent scrolling through CT images looking for pulmonary embolus; thus leaving the specialist with more time to address the more important areas of their role, such as interpreting data and providing directions based on information gathered through AI (Jha & Topol, 2016). This can lead to significant time-savings, as the Topol Report (2018) claims that health professionals in the English National Health System (NHS) spend between 15 and 70% of their time on administrative tasks. Finally, AI has the potential to act as a screening tool for population planning, aiding policy-makers in planning, resource utilisation and decision-making. Furthermore, individuals from geographically isolated areas and remote locations can be imaged by unskilled users and directed to expert care at an earlier stage of disease recognition, leading to greater access to specialised services.

Some practical applications

Machine learning has successfully been used in the United Kingdom (UK) to help predict drug effects, identify Type 2 diabetes subgroups, and discover comorbidity clusters in autism spectrum disorder, through the use of such data (Wang et al., 2012). In the United States (US), the IBM Watson Health cognitive computing system, which is designed to mimic human thought processes and assist humans in decision-making, has been used to create a decision support system for physicians treating cancer patients, with the aim of improving diagnostic accuracy, while reducing costs associated with the large volume of patient cases (Zauderer et al., 2014). It matches individuals with a care provider, designs individual care plans and offers insights into the more effective use of care management resources (Harrow Council, 2016).

Advanced technologies have been embraced in the pathology and radiology departments, where tasks that were once performed manually, such as blood screening and cell counts, have become automated (Jha & Topol, 2016). For example, Yu et al. (2016) found that computers are capable of predicting the prognosis of lung cancer patients at more accurate and precise levels than pathologists. AI has also impacted musculoskeletal medicine, with a proven influence on the understanding of orthopaedic implant design (Kozic et al., 2010), bone tumour resection (Cho et al., 2017) and robotic surgery (Karthik et al., 2015). Machine learning has been used in the analysis of large amounts of data on patients with spinal stenosis and degenerative disc disease (Hayaahi et al., 2015), and those suffering from knee osteoarthritis (Kotti et al., 2017). Additionally, major improvements have been observed at all stages of medical imaging. For example, segmentation, which involves digitalising images into various partitions, is now more commonly used to assess cartilage lesions that were once performed manually by physicians (Pedoia et al., 2016).

In summary, AI could enable a shift from treatment to prevention and, in doing so, begin to control spiralling costs. As Mesko et al. (2018) argue, AI will eventually be evidence-based, widespread and affordable, and so could lead to a change in the doctor/patient relationship. While it is not the ultimate solution, it is advantageous in supporting care-givers by providing effective new tools. However, it also needs to be accompanied by clear strategies to engage practitioners and consumers in its best use.

Information and Communications Technology (ICT)

The ICT sector provides the infrastructure and components that enable 21st-century computing (Senkbeil, 2018; Twinomurinz et al., 2017). ICT infrastructure is the foundation that systematically supports organisations with physical and virtual resources that underpin and support the flow, storage, processing and analysis of data (Alsaad et al., 2018).

The Australian Bureau of Statistics (ABS, 2019b) is narrow in its definition of the ICT sector. The ABS (2019b, webpage) explains that the industry sector creates, enhances and stores information products 'in media that allows for . . . dissemination transmitting information products using analogue and digital signals (via electronic, wireless, optical and other means)'. The swift 'adoption of new technologies by consumers, as well as advancements in cloud technology, are set to drive growth in the ICT industry' (WEF, 2018: 16). The sophisticated techniques required include 'machine learning, natural language processing, predictive modelling, neural networks and social network mapping' (Gordon, 2013: 13).

Workforce disruption in the ICT industry is anticipated to be relatively modest compared with other industry sectors (WEF, 2016). Recruitment in this field was considered to be difficult in 2016 and is expected to be significantly more so by 2020 and beyond (WEF, 2016). Jobs within this sector have experienced growth in the areas of database and network professionals, software and application developers and analysts, and electro technology engineers, with minimal decline in mechanics and machinery repairers, electronics and telecommunications installers and repairers (WEF, 2016).

In terms of the positioning of economies which are driven by technology, Australia is lagging behind when contrasted with numerous global competitors (DAE, 2018). Improvement against international competitors is languishing in the middle range, considerably below global competitors (DAE, 2018). This position has not improved in the last five years, in an era where highly trained ICT professionals are in more demand than at any previous time across all industry sectors. The WEF (2018) forecast indicated steady growth in the ICT sector for skilled workers. In Australia, recruitment for ICT workers has expanded, but research indicates that Australia may be a poor competitor for ICT global competitiveness and digital growth (DAE, 2018). For example, DAE (2018) forecast that Australia's ICT sector will need an additional 100,000 tech-capable workers, up to 758,700 in total, by 2023:

> Our ICT workforce grew to 663,100 workers in 2017, an increase of 3.5% from the 640,800 workers reported in last year's report. Two-thirds of current ICT workers currently in Australia are in technical, professional, management and operational roles, and 51% are employed in industries outside of ICT. Demand for ICT workers is set to grow by almost 100,000 to 758,700 workers by 2023, by which time almost 3 million Australian workers will be employed in occupations that regularly use technology.
>
> (DAE, 2018: 5)

As a result, it is clear that Australia needs to develop its education system to effectively respond to technological change and develop the skills required for a labour force to initiate innovation and growth. This includes increasing the availability of skilled ICT graduates to work in 'emerging technologies and growth areas, such as AI and cyber security' (DAE, 2018: 40). A level of progress is evident, but overall, there is a lack of consistency and strategic planning to equip a hungry ICT industry due to the growing digital economy in schools, vocational education and universities (DAE, 2018).

Although it has been argued that the state of the ICT industry sector is bright, regarding opportunities (DAE, 2018; WEF, 2018), the policies regarding investment and tax concessions, and the development of more robust performances by students in science, technology, engineering and mathematics (STEM) needs to improve (DAE, 2018). The economic buoyancy of Australia is dependent on ICT performance, fuelled by the quality of the workers to fill the abundance of jobs that loom (DAE, 2018). To remain internationally competitive and take a leading role in the global digital economy, Australia needs to ensure continued investment in technology and innovation (DAE, 2018: 43).

Tourism and hospitality

In Australia, tourism and hospitality data are captured by the Australian Bureau of Statistics (ABS) under the heading of 'Accommodation and Food Services' and is published in the Tourism Satellite Account (Cat no. 5249.0). In 2017–2018, direct tourism gross domestic product (GDP) grew by 5%. This represents a 2.2% increase over national GDP for the same period, a theme consistent for some time. In response, the sector's employment levels have also experienced similar growth patterns, with the total tourism industry currently accounting for 5.2% of all employed people in Australia (ABS, 2017–2018, 2018b).

Although many factors create polarised demand patterns (for example, international terrorism, potentially fatal diseases, aviation fuel prices, geological events such as tsunamis and earthquakes and economic downturns), the sector is highly regarded for its resilience (UNWTO, 2006) and 'bounce back' after such events. That said, demand for Australian tourism and hospitality services is influenced by both international and domestic markets. Similarly, hospitality supply occurs through international operators (significantly in the form of large multi-national hotel chains – MNCs – and domestic providers – mainly small-medium enterprises and micro-businesses). The use and maturity of automation in this sector is far from uniform. This may be partly as a result of the number and composition of the industry sub-sectors and/or the nature of tasks captured within the overall sector. The 4IR's future in this sector may also be influenced by any one or more of the diverse market or customer segments.

4IR and the future of work

At the high end of the sector, predictive technology is becoming more sophisticated through reservations and bookings systems, or by capturing individual user data, where algorithms are used to predict preferences based on internet search history and social media interactions (Liu et al., 2017; Skift, 2017). Machine learning, used by travel planners, travel agents and independent travellers, captures customers' changing needs, whereby algorithms provide analytical power to immediately offer new products and services personalised to each consumer (Buhalis & Sinarta, 2019).

At the individual hotel level, automation is similarly becoming more sophisticated. Information kiosks are being located in hotel lobbies (Fesenmaier &

Kingsley, 1995), and automated check-in/check-out techniques are being developed towards e-concierge systems with built-in reasoning which engage in dialogue with guests (Cho et al., 1996; Liang et al., 2017). At the 'big end', global hotel chains are innovating through implementing voice assistants and mobile phone apps, for in-room comforts – including lighting and temperature settings and facial recognition for room access. In some countries, completely automated hotels are being trialled (Rajesh, 2015) while 'relay robots' (see for example, Ivanov et al., 2017; Rodriguez-Lizundia et al., 2015) are increasingly being used in large hotels to deliver room service items such as food, beverages and linen.

4IR and the Australian tourism and hospitality sector

So, what does this mean for the future of work in the Australian tourism and hospitality sector? While it is apparent that some jobs are being replaced by these new technologies, and will undoubtedly continue to do so, the industry is one where we are more likely to see some occupations become semi-automated rather than replaced (Fleming, 2019), and many others may be hardly affected at all, at least for some time. The rationale for this is built into the inherent characteristics of much of the work undertaken in the sector in terms of 'labour pricing', 'power relations', and the 'nature of the job' (Fleming, 2019). For example, many hospitality jobs are deemed as 'low skilled'. In some industries, those who hold power over management – for example, through threat of labour withdrawal in highly unionised industries – have already been totally replaced by technology (see for example, Waterfront Workers in Australia – Fleming, 2019). Low-skilled and contingent workers, however, hold little power over management and, in the case of the hospitality sector, workers are often employed on a casual basis and non-unionised, so they can be relatively easily replaced by other workers readily available from a large labour pool. Hospitality workers are low-paid, so therefore may be deemed as 'not worth automating' (Fleming, 2019), although it is estimated that the cost of technology to replace this workforce would currently be significant.

In addition, if real wages continue to decrease due to political pressure to remove weekend/overtime penalty rates, it may be some time before replacement becomes economically viable. It is here that the distinction between multinational corporations (MNCs) and small and medium enterprises (SMEs) operating in the sector is significant. While MNCs may be able to absorb the economic cost of 4IR investment, SMEs, which provide the bulk of employment, may struggle until the cost differential of wages and automation decreases. The impact therefore is likely to differ between operators and between service levels. However, while semi-automation can be expected, and hence overall employment will decrease, cost differentials, power relations and human elements remain part of many positions. Therefore, as Ivanov et al. (2017) assert, it is the economic efficiencies, customers and competitiveness that will determine the level of replacement of humans by 4IR technologies.

From a broader perspective (as discussed in Chapter 1), socio-technical theory, which attempts to analyse the 'interdependencies between and among people, technology and the (organisational) environment' (Appelbaum, 1997: 452), suggests that the human–technology interface is 'the most difficult task for executives . . . to execute' (ibid.). Hence, the following section of this chapter (as in other country chapters in this book) reports the findings from a study of managers' preparedness to undertake this task in the wake of the Fourth Industrial Revolution. In this case it is the perspectives of Australian human resource (HR) managers that is reported in this chapter, as they will be in the forefront of efforts to manage the human–technology interface in their organisations in the three sectors discussed previously.

Australian HR managers' perspectives

As in other country chapters, and according to the framework presented in Chapter 2, the objectives of the study were to explore:

a)   the views of managers and leaders about the nature, characteristics, implications and planning required to manage the actual and potential impacts of the Fourth Industrial Revolution and

b)   to examine the relationship between technology adoption, job satisfaction/insecurity, organisation performance, and other related outcomes.

To meet these objectives, two research methods were employed – focus groups of senior HR managers were conducted in five major Australian cities (Sydney, Newcastle, Melbourne, Perth and Adelaide). These elicited general themes that informed the subsequent online survey of an invited sample of senior Australian Human Resource Institute (AHRI) members. The focus group data were analysed using NVivo software and the survey data were analysed using the Statistical Package for the Social Sciences (SPSS) techniques. Whilst ANOVA and MANOVA statistical analyses were also conducted using the survey data, only the descriptive findings are presented in this chapter. Ethics approval was obtained from the lead university in the study (RMIT University), and research partners included Curtin University (Perth), the University of Newcastle, Cardiff Metropolitan University and the Australian Institute of Business (Adelaide).

Research sample and respondent characteristics

The focus groups attracted 19 participants, and there were 395 overall responses to the survey. Unfortunately, only 250 survey responses were useable due to incompleteness, from an invited sample of 567 (approximately 44% response). Approximately, 67% of respondents were female, and the majority of the respondents were aged between 36 and 50 (52%) and well educated (68% having postgraduate qualifications). Most of their organisations were located in Victoria and New South Wales (26%), while Tasmania and Northern Territory had the lowest number of respondents with 1.2% and 2%, respectively. This is largely representative of the relative population of the various Australian states and territories.

The results also showed that 49.2% of the respondents worked in the private sector, followed by 29.6% in the public sector. In addition, 40.8% of the respondents worked in large companies with employees more than 1,000, while companies with employees between 100 and 499 represented around 27%. Table 3.1 shows the industry sectors included.

The findings indicate that the majority of the respondents work in the professional, scientific and technical (17.2%) sector, followed by healthcare and social assistance (14.0%), public administration and safety (11.6%) and education and training (9.6%). Of the three key sectors discussed earlier in this chapter – namely, healthcare, ICT, and tourism and hospitality – healthcare is well-represented, with smaller proportions evident for ICT (information media and telecommunications – 2.0%) and tourism and hospitality (accommodation and food services – 2.4%).

Stage of automation, value and level of support for 4IR technologies

As table 3.2 shows, most of the respondents considered that their organisations were operating at the 3rd stage of automation (Computer and Automation – 64.8%), followed by the 2nd stage Mass Production (12.8%); and only 12% considered themselves to be at the 4th stage – Cyber Physical Systems/4IR.

Table 3.1 Industry Sectors

Industry	Freq.	Percent
Agriculture, forestry and fishing	4	1.6
Mining	9	3.6
Manufacturing	14	5.6
Electricity, gas, water and waste service	5	2
Construction	8	3.2
Wholesale trade	4	1.6
Retail trade	6	2.4
Accommodation and food services	6	2.4
Transport, postal and warehousing	3	1.2
Information media and telecommunication	5	2
Financial and insurance services	18	7.2
Professional, scientific and technical	43	17.2
Administrative and support services	6	2.4
Public administration and safety	29	11.6
Education and training	24	9.6
Health care and social assistance	35	14
Arts and recreation services	3	1.2
Other services	28	11.2
Total	**249**	**100**

Table 3.2 Stage of Automation

Status of industry	Freq.	Percent
1st mechanisation	10	4
2nd mass production	32	12.8
3rd computer and automation	162	64.8
4th cyber physical systems	30	12
Other	15	6
Total	**249**	**100**

Table 3.3 Current and Future Technologies

Top three technologies	Rank
Current Use	
Mobile technologies	1
Cloud technologies	2
Machine to machine communication	3
Probable Future Use	
Machine learning	1
3D printing	2
Artificial intelligence	3

Whilst the proportions of 3rd and 4th stage organisations are not surprising, the relatively high proportions of organisations identified as being at the 1st stage (4.0%) and 2nd stage (12.5%) were unexpected – especially as the Automation Readiness Index (ARI) discussed in Chapter 1 ranks Australia as number 10 on its comparative list, with a numerical rating of 70.4 against the average of 62.1 (EIU, 2018: 10) for the 25 countries included in the index.

As table 3.3 indicates, the range of current and probable future uses of 4IR technologies in the respondents' organisations is relatively conservative.

Currently, and prospectively, IT control and support for these technologies is split between centralised IT departments (66.13%) and outsourced functions (22.18%), leaving little flexibility for their use in diverse ways in different departments or sections of their organisations.

Strategy, support and perceived usefulness

Table 3.4 presents the findings concerning strategic intention, management support and perceived usefulness of the technologies. Respondents indicated that they received fairly low support from management (mean 2.99) and disagreed that their IT strategies supported and matched their business strategies (mean 2.74). However, they agreed that AI/Robotics were likely to be useful in their jobs (mean 2.08).

Table 3.4 Mean Score of Strategy, Support and Perceived Usefulness

Variable	Mean	Std. Dev.
Strategic intention	2.745	1.012
Management support	2.995	0.919
Perceived usefulness of AI/Robotics	2.088	0.842

Note: Management Support: Evaluate the degree of top management support for the use/implementation of AI/Software/Applications in your organisation. Strategic Intention: The following section concerns the strategic intentions/alignment of your organisation in the context of the usage/implementation of AI/HR Software/Applications. Please select the answer/s which best describes your opinion. Perceived usefulness of AI/Robotics: Please evaluate the following statements with respect to the usefulness of AI/Software/Applications in your organisation. Management support is measured from very low (1) to very high (5), while other dimensions are measured from strongly agree (1) to strongly disagree (5).

Table 3.5 Mean Score of Productivity, Innovation, Customer Satisfaction and Organisation Performance

Variable	Mean	Std. Dev.
Task productivity	2.02	0.726
Innovation	2.6	0.922
Customer satisfaction	2.333	0.785
Organisation performance	2.453	0.754

Note: Task productivity: Please evaluate the application of AI/Software for accomplishing tasks in your organisation. Innovation: Please evaluate the application of AI/Software for creating new ideas/innovation in your organisation. Customer satisfaction: Please evaluate the application of AI/Software for improving customer satisfaction with your organisation. Organisation performance: Please evaluate the application of AI/Software for improving organisational performance. All indicators are measured from strongly agree (1) to strongly disagree (5).

Perceived impacts of 4IR technology

Table 3.5 reports the findings concerning the impact of 4IR software on productivity, innovation, customer satisfaction and organisational performance. All scales were measured from strongly agree (1) to strongly disagree (5). The results indicated that respondents tended to agree that the application of AI/Software could improve task productivity, organisational performance and customer satisfaction, while there was a tendency to disagree that the application could improve innovation.

Job satisfaction and job insecurity

Table 3.6 reports the findings with respect to perceived job satisfaction and job insecurity for current employees. The results show that respondents tended to disagree that the use of these technologies may enhance employees' job satisfaction (mean 2.76) and were not sure that they would be able to keep their jobs, despite technological implementation (mean 2.77).

Table 3.6 Mean Score of Job Satisfaction and Insecurity

Variable	Mean	Std. Dev.
Job satisfaction	2.768	0.657
Job insecurity	2.770	0.518

Note: Job insecurity: Please indicate the item which best describes your opinion of the feelings of your employees regarding their job security due to the implementation of AI/Software/Applications. Job satisfaction: Please evaluate the following statements with respect to the likely impact of the latest AI/Software/Applications on employees' job satisfaction. All indicators are measured from strongly agree (1) to strongly disagree (5).

Table 3.7 Government Policy

Variable	Mean	Std. Dev.
Government policy	1.179	0.599

Note: From your observation, how impressed are you by the policies of government, state and federal, in Australia in preparation for the impact of Artificial Intelligence (AI) on jobs? All indicators were measured from not impressed at all (1) to very impressed (5).

Perceptions of government strategy and policy on the 4IR

Regarding government policy, the majority of respondents were not impressed by the policies of their government in preparation for the impact of 4IR technologies on jobs (mean 1.17) as illustrated in table 3.7.

Key issues and implications

The analysis of these three key sectors has illustrated some of the nuances related to the impact of the 4IR across different industry sectors in Australia. Both the health and ICT sectors have common supply-based challenges for key professionals. The ageing population is a major trend impacting the health sector which is struggling to meet the demands for medical and health professionals. An ageing nursing workforce is also anticipated to make an impact in a decade when many of the workforce will begin to retire. 4IR technologies are making an impact on diagnostics and the more productive provision of an array of health service models. The ICT infrastructure of a nation has a huge impact on their abilities to become and maintain global competitiveness. The need for more science, technology, engineering and mathematics (STEM) and ICT professionals is a key issue for competitiveness, as well as the capacity for technological innovation and adoption. The tourism and hospitality sector is not uniform in its adoption and use of 4IR technologies for several reasons (economic efficiencies, customers and competitiveness). However, when compared to the health and ICT sectors, it is more likely to have unskilled or semi-skilled workers who are prone to being replaced or having their jobs semi-automated by 4IR technologies. The bulk of this industry comprises SMEs, and due to their size, they are likely to find the introduction of new technologies to be cost prohibitive, as opposed to the MNCs in the sector.

The findings from the survey demonstrate that two thirds of respondents believe that their organisations are still in the 3rd computer and automation stage of automation with a conservative use of technologies currently evident. Nonetheless, the findings point to strong agreement that 4IR software would most likely improve innovation, organisational performance and customer satisfaction.

Implications for stakeholders

Government

According to the Productivity Commission's (PC) *Productivity Update 2017* (PC, 2017) report, the role of governments is crucial in laying the foundations for business to be able to deliver growth. These foundations relate to the drafting of laws and regulations (industry regulations, compliance with international standards and trade agreements) and other 'institutional rules of the game' (PC, 2017: 4).

In addition to this, governments provide the physical infrastructure (road, rail, maritime and air freight transport systems and hubs) and supporting social or human capital infrastructure (education, training and human capital development) that service and support businesses in their aspirations towards growth and innovation.

An earlier report from the PC was entitled *Digital Disruption: What do governments need to do?* (PC, 2016). The report examined the likely or anticipated impacts of disruptive technologies on governments and made a set of recommendations based around three main headings: Impacts of disruption on (a) markets and competition (7 recommendations); (b) workers and society (5 recommendations); and (c) how governments operate (9 recommendations). The report listed those technologies that would most likely be the most disruptive such as: digital intermediaries (digital platforms, Uber, eBay and Airtasker); advanced manufacturing (3D printing, advanced robotics and the 'internet of things'); transport technologies (autonomous vehicles, remote operated vehicles and aircraft) and energy technologies (combination of ICT advances and distributed energy generation (notably solar and wind) (Productivity Commission, 2016).

Employers and education systems

The Australian Industry Group's Survey *Workforce Development Needs: Skilling – A National Imperative* (AIG, 2018a) reported the results from a survey of its members, finding that three quarters of respondents were suffering skill shortages mainly in trades and technician positions, or had recruitment challenges in relation to STEM skills and the following occupations: Big Data, AI solutions and business automation.The survey also found that employers had higher rates of intentions to increase training for digital skills for their respective workforces. Another AIG report published in the same year considered the critical issues that need to be addressed for developing workforces in a digital future (AIG, 2018b).This report guides employers to a company action plan with key demands being the need for 4IR skills: digital, ICT and STEM skills, Industry 4.0 skills, as well as entrepreneurial skills and new management capabilities. It is proposed that company action plans need to include the reskilling of existing workers and recognise the demand for higher skilled workers. Another key element to such plans is the capacity of the education sector, and the need for the education sector to partner with government and industry towards joint investment in research and development.

Conclusion

A report by the Productivity Commission (2017) predicted that the Australian economy may be 'subject to structural pressures from an ageing population, and an unsustainable fiscal trajectory' (Productivity Commission, 2017: 4).The digital age is with us now and is rapidly impacting economies and industry sectors as well as how organisations operate currently and into the future.These factors have significant implications for human capital management and change in our education and training capabilities to meet the skills demands of a digitally-disrupted future which will impact on all sectors of the economy.

The findings/analysis reported in this chapter have focused on three large sectors in the Australian economy (health, ICT, and tourism and hospitality), finding a variety of pressures and trends impacting each sector and their respective growth and productivity. Ageing populations and workforces, national ICT infrastructures, skill shortages in key professions, and prohibitive costs of 4IR technologies for SMEs in particular, are contributing to Australia's ability to enter the 4IR in order to meet demand and build and maintain global competitiveness.

The Economist Intelligence Unit has assessed G20 nations' (and five additional nations') readiness for the next wave of automation, using an Automation Readiness Index (see Chapter 1). In assessing the existence of policy and strategy in the areas of innovation, education and the labour market, the study finds that 'little policy is in place today that specifically addresses the challenges of AI and robotics-based automation' (EIU, 2018: 5). Three countries sit at top of the list – Germany, South Korea and Singapore – with Australia sitting in 10th position.The Australian government, in partnership with industry labour market planners and the vocational and higher education systems, needs to strategize and plan for a policy infrastructure that is integrated and moves the economy and human capital towards greater readiness for the 4IR, and the rapid onslaught of digital disruption and associated technologies.These are impacting on how industries and organisations will work into the future. Human resource practitioners also play a role at the organisational level to

champion and drive the changes needed to meet future workforce readiness for
the 4IR and all that encompasses.

Acknowledgement

We would like to acknowledge the following people who supported the
research project and provided valuable support: Dr Subas P. Dhakal and
Dr Mirsad Bhatic (Curtin University); Lyn Goodear, Dana Grgas and Liz
Dunne (AHRI).

Reference list

Alsaad, A., Mohamad, R., Taamneh, A., & Ismail, N. A. (2018). What drives global B2B
    e-commerce usage: An analysis of the effect of the complexity of the trading system and
    competition pressure. *Technology Analysis & Strategic Management*, 30 (8), 1–13.
Appelbaum, S. (1997). Socio-technical systems theory: An intervention strategy for organi-
    zational development. *Management Decision*, 35 (6), 452–463.
Australian Bureau of Statistics (ABS) (2017–2018). *Tourism Satellite Account, Catalogue Num-
    ber. 5249.0.* Available at: www.abs.gov.au
Australian Bureau of Statistics (ABS) (2018a). *Labour Force, Australia, Catalogue Number
    6202.2.* Available at: www.abs.gov.au
Australian Bureau of Statistics (ABS) (2018b). *Employee Earnings and Hours, Catalogue Number.
    6306.0.* Available at: www.abs.gov.au
Australian Bureau of Statistics (ABS) (2019a). *Labour Force, Australia, Catalogue Number
    6202.2.* Available at: www.abs.gov.au
Australian Bureau of Statistics. (ABS) (2019b). *Australian and New Zealand Standard Industrial
    Classification* (ANZSIC), 2006 (Revision 2.0) Australian Bureau of Statistics. Catalogue
    No.1209.0. Available at: http://www/abs/gov.au
Australian Industry Group (2018a). *Survey Report Workforce Development Needs. Skill-
    ing: A National Imperative.* Available at: www.aigroup.com.au/policy-and-research/
    mediacentre/releases/Skilling-WFD-Survey-12Sept/
Australian Industry Group (2018b). *Developing the Workforce for a Digital Future Addressing Crit-
    ical Issues and Planning for Action.* Available at: https://cdn.aigroup.com.au/Reports/2018/
    Developing_the_workforce_for_a_digital_future.pdf
Australian Industry Report (AIR) (2016). *Economic Conditions.* Department of Industry, Inno-
    vation and Science. Available at: www.industry.gov.au/Office-of-the-Chief-Economist/
    Publications/AustralianIndustryReport/assets/Australian-Industry-Report-2016-
    Chapter-2.pdf
Australia's Institute of Health and Welfare (AIHW) (2018). *Australia's Health 2018: Australian
    Health Services*, No. 16, 221, Canberra: AIHW.
Australian Health Practitioner Regulation Agency (AHPRA) (2017). *Annual Report
    2016/2017.* Melbourne: AHPRA.
Bartram, T., & Dowling, P. (2013). An international perspective on human resource manage-
    ment and performance in the health care sector: Toward a research agenda. *International
    Journal of Human Resource Management*, 24, 3031–3037.
Buhalis, D., & Sinarta, Y. (2019). Real-time co-creation and newness service: Lessons from
    tourism and hospitality. *Journal of Travel and Tourism Marketing*, 36 (5), 563–582.

California State Board of Food and Agriculture to discuss farm labor, rural job development and workforce training needs at April 4th meeting (2017). *Targeted News Service*, 29 March. Available at: https://search-proquest-com.dbgw.lis.curtin.edu.au/docview/1882043026?accountid=10382

Cho, H. S., Park, Y. K., Gupta, S., Yoon, C., Han, I., Kim, H. S., Choi, H., & Hong, J. (2017). Augmented reality in bone tumour resection: An experimental study. *Bone & Joint Research*, 6 (3), 137–143.

Cho, W., Sumichrast, R., & Olsen, M. (1996). Expert-system technology for hotels: Concierge application. *Cornell Hotel and Restaurant Administration Quarterly*, 54–60, February.

Currie, G., Lockett, A., Finn, R., Martin, G., & Waring, J. (2012). Institutional work to maintain professional power: Recreating the model of medical professionalism. *Organization Studies*, 33, 937–962.

DAE Access Economics (DAE) (2018). ACS *Australia's Digital Pulse Driving Australia's International ICT Competitiveness and Digital Growth 2018.* Available at: www.acs.org.au/content/dam/acs/acs-publications/aadp2018.pdf

Department of Jobs and Small Business (2019). *Australian Labour Market Update*, April. Available at: www.jobs.gov.au/australian-labour-market-update-publication

EIU (2018). Automation Readiness Index: Who *Is Ready* for the *Coming Wave of Automation?* Economist Intelligence Unit. Available at: www.automationreadiness.eiu.com/static/download/PDF.pdf

Fesenmaier, D., & Kingsley, I. (1995). Travel information Kiosks. *Journal of Travel & Tourism Marketing*, 4 (1), 57–70.

Fleming, P. (2019). Robots and organization studies: Why robots might not want to steal your job. *Organization Studies*, 40 (1), 23–37.

Gordon, K. (2013). What is big data? *IT Now*, 55 (3), 12–13.

Harrow Council (2016). *IBM and Harrow Council to Bring Watson Care Manager to Individuals in the UK.* Available at: www.harrow.gov.uk/news/article/397/ibm_and_harrow_council_to_bring_watson_care_manager_to_individuals_in_the_uk

Hayaahi, H., Toribatake, Y., Murakami, H., Yoneyama, T., Watanabe, T., & Tsuchiya, H. (2015). Gait analysis using a support vector machine for lumbar spinal stenosis. *Orthopaedics*, 38 (11), 959–964.

Health Workforce Australia (2014). *Australia's Future Health Workforce – Nurses Overview*. Canberra: Department of Health.

Ivanov, S., Webster, C., & Berezina, K. (2017). Adoption of robots and service automation by tourism and hospitality companies. *Revista Turismo & Desenvolvimento*, 27–28, 1501–1517.

Jha, S., & Topol, E. J. (2016). Adapting to artificial intelligence: Radiologists and pathologists as information specialists. *Journal of the American Medical Association*, 316 (22), 2353–2354.

Jiang, F., Jiang, Y., Zhi, H., Dong, Y., Li, H., Sufeng, M., Wang, Y., Dong, Q., Shen, H., & Wang, Y. (2017). Artificial intelligence in healthcare: Past, present and future. *Stroke and Vascular Neurology*, 2 (4), 230–243.

Karthik, K., Colegate-Stone, T., Dasgupta, P., Tavakkolizadeh, A., & Sinha, J. (2015). Robotic surgery in trauma and orthopaedics: A systematic review. *Bone & Joint Journal*, 97-B (3), 292–299.

Kotti, M., Duffell, L. D., Faisal, A. A., & McGregor, A. H. (2017). Detecting knee osteoarthritis and its discriminating parameters using random forests. *Med Engineering & Physics*, 43, 19–29.

Kozic, N., Weber, S., Büchler, P., Lutz, C., Reimers, N., Gonzalez Ballester, M. A., & Reyers, M. (2010). Optimisation of orthopaedic implant design using statistical shape space analysis based on level sets. *Medical Image Analysis*, 14 (3), 265–275.

Leggat, S. G., Bartram, T., Stanton, P., Bamber, G., & Sohal, A. (2015). Has process redesign methodology been successful in changing employee practices to improve the process of care delivery in public hospitals? A systematic review. *Public Money and Management*, 35 (2), 161–168.

Liang, S., Schuckert, M., Law, R., & Masiero, L. (2017). The relevance of mobile tourism and information technology: An analysis of recent trends and future research directions. *Journal of Travel & Tourism Marketing*, 34 (6), 732–748.

Liu, Y., Teichert, T., Rossi, M., Li, H., & Hu, F. (2017). Big data for big insights: Investigating language-specific drivers of hotel satisfaction with 412,784 user-generated reviews. *Tourism Management*, 59, 554–563.

Mesko, B., Hetenyi, G., & Gyorffy, Z. (2018). Will artificial intelligence solve the human resource crisis in healthcare. *BMC Health Services Research*, 18, 545.

Neill, D. B. (2013). Using artificial intelligence to improve hospital inpatient care. *IEEE Intelligent Systems*, 28 (2), 92–95.

Pedoia, V., Majumdar, S., & Link, T. M. (2016). Segmentation of joint and musculoskeletal tissue in the study of arthritis. *MAGMA*, 29, 207–221.

Pratt, M. (2018). Artificial intelligence in primary care. *Medical Economics*, 95. Available at: https://www.medicaleconomics.com/business/artificial-intelligence-primary-care

Productivity Commission (2013). An *Ageing* Australia: Preparing for the *Future*. Available at: www.pc.gov.au/research/completed/ageing-australia

Productivity Commission (2016). *Digital Disruption: What Do Governments Need to Do?* Research Paper. Available at: www.pc.gov.au/research/completed/digital-disruption.

Productivity Commission (2017). *Productivity Update 2017*. Available at: www.pc.gov.au/research/completed/ageing-australia

Rajesh, M. (2015). Inside Japan's first robot-staffed hotel. *The Guardian*. Available at: www.theguardian.com/travel/2015/aug/14/japan-henn-na-hotel-staffed-by-robots

Reserve Bank of Australia (RBA) (2019). *Australian Economy Snapshot*. Available at: www.rba.gov.au/snapshots/economy-composition-snapshot/

Rodriguez-Lizundia, E., Marcos, S., Zalama, E., Gómez-García-Bermejo, J., & Gordaliza, A. (2015). A bellboy robot: Study of the effects of robot behaviour on user engagement and comfort. *International Journal of Human-Computer Studies*, 82, 83–95.

Senkbeil, M., 2018. Development and validation of the ICT motivation scale for young adolescents. Results of the international school assessment study ICILS 2013 in Germany. *Learning and Individual Differences*, 67, pp.167–176. https://www.sciencedirect.com/science/article/pii/S1041608018301377 accessed 21 July 2019.

Sensmeir, J. (2017). Harnessing the power of artificial intelligence. *Nursing Management*, November. Available at: https://nursing.ceconnection.com/ovidfiles/00006247-201711000-00006.pdf

Sheikhtaheri, A., Sadoughi, F., & Hashemi Dehaghi, Z. (2014). Developing and using expert systems and neural networks in medicine: A review on benefits and challenges. *Journal of Medical Systems*, 38 (9), 110.

Skift, G. (2017). *The 6 Big Trends That Are Reshaping Luxury Travel*. Available at: https://skift.com/2017/08/29/the-6-big-trends-that-are-reshaping-luxury-travel

Stanton, P., Bartram, T., Gough, R., Ballardie, R., Bamber, G., & Sohal, A. (2014). Lean management in healthcare: Work intensification or empowerment *International Journal of Human Resource Management*, 25 (21), 2926–2940.

Topol Review (2018). *Preparing the Healthcare Workforce to Deliver the Digital Future*. Interim Report NHS Education, June.

The Treasury (2010). *The 2010 Intergenerational Report*. The Treasury, Australian Government. Available at: http://archive.treasury.gov.au/igr/

Twinomurinz, H., Schofield, A., Hagen, L., Ditsoane-Molefe, S., & Tshidzumba, N. A. (2017). Towards a shared worldview on e-skills: A discourse between government, industry and academia on the ICT skills paradox. *South African Computer Journal*, 29 (3), 215–237.

United Nations World Tourism Organization (UNWTO) (2006). UNWTO world tourism barometer. *World Tourism Organization*, 4 (3), October.

Wang, Z., Shah, A. D., Tate, A. R., Denaxas, S., Shawe-Taylor, J., & Hemingway, H. (2012). Extracting diagnoses and investigation results from unstructured text in electronic health records by semi-supervised machine learning. *PLoS One*, 7 (1), 1–9.

Waring, J. J., & Bishop, S. (2010). Lean healthcare: Rhetoric, ritual and resistance. *Social Science and Medicine*, 71, 1332–1340.

World Economic Forum (WEF) (2016). *The Future of Jobs: Employment, Skills and Workforce Strategy for the Fourth Industrial Revolution*. Geneva: World Economic Forum (WEF). Available at: http://www3.weforum.org/docs/WEF_Future_of_Jobs.pdf

World Economic Forum (WEF) (2018). *The Future of Jobs Report 2018*. Geneva, Switzerland: World Economic Forum. Available at: www.weforum.org/reports/the-future-of-jobs-report-2018, accessed 27 December 2018.

Yu, K. H., Zhang, C., Berry, G. J., Altman, R. B., Ré, C., Rubin, D. L., & Snyder, M. (2016). Predicting non-small cell lung cancer prognosis by fully automated microscopic pathology image features. *Nature Communications*, 7 (7), 12474.

Zauderer, M. G., Gucalp, A., Epstein, A. S., Seidman, A. D., Caroline, A., Granovsky, S., Fu, J., Keesing, J., Lewis, S., Co, H., Petri, J., Megerian, M., Eggebraaten, T., Bach, P., & Kris, M. G. (2014). Piloting IBM Watson oncology within memorial Sloan Kettering's regional network. *Journal of Clinical Oncology*, 32 (15).

4 Singapore

*Azad Singh Bali, Christopher Vas
and Peter Waring*

Introduction

Singapore is a modern city-state, densely populated with 5.5 million people located at the end of the Malaysian peninsula. At just 700 square kilometres and with no mineral resources or permanent water supply, its sustainability was far from assured in 1965 when it became a republic. Over five decades through enterprise, trade and ingenuity, Singapore has become an advanced developed economy with one of the highest gross domestic product (GDP) per capita in the world. At the epicentre of global trade in goods, services and ideas, the Fourth Industrial Revolution (4IR) poses tremendous risk and opportunity for the country which prides itself as being a 'Smart Nation'. This chapter identifies these challenges, discusses the strategic choices of government, trade unions and industry, and presents the results of our survey on the topic.

Demographic context

Singapore has a rapidly ageing society. Sustained economic prosperity, grow-ing female labour force participation rates and a spectrum of population-control policies introduced in the 1950s–60s contributed to Singapore's total fertility rate falling below the replacement rate by the early 1970s (Yap & Gee, 2016). Coupled with declining fertility, advances in life expectancy, par-ticularly at advanced ages, has resulted in a rapidly ageing Singapore. Data from the 2019 World Population Prospects suggest that, in 2010, only 7% of Singapore's population was above the age of 65 years. That share is expected to triple by 2030. Similarly, the proportion of the population above age 80 in 2020 is expected to quadruple in the next 20 years (UNDESA, 2019). With respect to total life expectancy, in 2017 at birth it was 83.1 years with 80.7 and 85.2 for males and females respectively. The corresponding data for life expectancy at age 65 was 20.9, 19.1, and 22.5 years (Department of Statistics, 2018: Table 4.1). The Singapore government has, over the past three decades, introduced a range of socio-economic incentives and policy measures to increase fertility rates, but these have met with limited success (Lim, 2015). The nation's current fertility rate of 1.2 is one of the lowest in the world

Table 4.1 Position Level of Respondents (329 answered – 3 skipped)

Answer choices	Percentages	Responses
Staff	43.16%	142
Team leader/Supervisor	12.16%	40
Manager	20.67%	68
Senior manager	5.17%	17
Director/CEO/General manager	7.60%	25
Business owner/Entrepreneur	6.08%	20
Other (please specify)	5.17%	17
Total		**329**

(after South Korea, Hong Kong and Puerto Rico – see World Bank, 2019), and gives rise to a series of challenges for labour markets and industrial relations in Singapore.

Economic context

Singapore has enjoyed remarkable economic progress and prosperity since its independence in 1965. The city-state GDP per capita (measured in current US$) has increased manifold, from about $516 in 1965 to about $65,000 in 2018 (World Bank, 2019). This spectacular economic success, over a relatively short period of time, has been attributed to the Singapore government's deft economic management and its unfettered pursuit of a location-based growth strategy (Lim, 2015; Tan & Bhaskaran, 2015). Central to its 'location-based' growth strategy is developing a stable macroeconomic and policy environment which is conducive to capital accumulation, attracting foreign firms (multinational corporations – MNCs – in particular) and portfolio investors.

On the economic front this is enabled by relatively porous and flexible labour markets, an extensive reliance on foreign labour at all levels of the skills spectrum, lowering the costs of doing business and ensuring relatively low levels of public expenditure (Asher et al., 2015). On the political front, decades of stability, relatively shallow political competition and robust performance on most governance indices (for example, corruption, trust in government, ease of doing business) provided a steady platform for the government to implement its economic strategies. These strategies continue to serve Singapore extremely well. Over the past five years alone, amidst significant global economic uncertainty, Singapore's real GDP grew at 3.4% annually (Department of Statistics, 2018: 67). Except for extremely short recessions during notable regional and global economic crises in 1973–74, 1985–86, 1997–98 and 2008–09, Singapore has enjoyed extremely high employment rates (Pang & Lim, 2015).

Tan and Bhaskaran (2015) summarise three elements of the Singapore government's approach to economic management. First, a strong belief that the government plays a key role in the economy. This includes not only extensive regulatory frameworks, but also public investments in key strategic areas such as infrastructure, telecommunications and transport, and a presence in most areas of service delivery (such as water, electricity, waste management, commercial banking) through government-owned and/or managed corporations.

The second element concerns the unfettered pursuit of, and the primacy of, economic growth. This has required remaining economically competitive and attractive to international businesses and capital. To pursue this goal Singapore has developed extremely flexible labour markets, ensured that the cost of doing business is relatively low, supported a low-tax regime, and accrued structural budgetary surpluses to instil investor confidence. Asher et al. (2015) argue that this has meant allowing a much larger share of the national income to accrue to capital than labour (for example, the share of labour income averaged 42% between 2015 and 2017, with the corresponding capital share at 52% – Ministry of Trade and Industry, 2017). Taxes on capital income have been substantially reduced in the past two decades and, as of mid-2019, there was no income tax on interest income, dividends, most capital gains and foreign-earned income. Sustaining such a growth strategy has, however, contributed to inequalities.

A fiscal system where capital income accrues disproportionately to the upper deciles of the population and is taxed lightly is known to contribute to and perpetuates inequalities in a society (Asher et al., 2015). For instance, between 2010 and 2016 the GINI coefficient – which measures the statistical dispersion of wealth – varied between 0.458 and 0.478, and 0.402 and 0.425, after accounting for Government transfers and taxes (Department of Statistics, 2018). Since 2014 the government has introduced reforms that increase social expenditure, particularly in education (Waring et al., 2019) and healthcare (Ramesh & Bali, 2019) to reduce these inequalities.

The third element of Singapore's approach to economic management, Tan and Bhaskaran (2015) claim, is the capacity of the state to mobilise economic and political resources to meet its objectives. This has been possible after decades of political stability and a significant presence in the economy by direct participation, state-led planning and the use of interventionist policies (Lim, 2015). Singapore is also known to enjoy high levels of policy capacity (i.e. the skills and competencies in policy formulation and implementation). Cementing Singapore's policy capabilities are high performance on governance indices such as the World Bank's Ease of Doing Business Index, Bloomberg's Innovation Index and the Edelman Trust Barometer (see for example Bali et al., 2018: Table 4.1).

Labour market context

Singapore is one of the few high-income economies that relies extensively on foreign labour. Foreign workers have always played an important role in Singapore following the economic reforms introduced after the Winsemius Report in the 1960s. The total number of non-residents in the labour market grew from 20,710 in 1970 to 79,275 in 1980. By 1990, the foreign workforce in

Singapore had grown to 248,000 and to 670,000 by 2006 (Yeoh, 2007). Since 2014 about 38% of the Singapore labour force (of about 3.7 million) was comprised of foreign workers. Of these, about 14% of the foreign workforce comprised skilled and semi-skilled labour. The remaining 72% was largely unskilled (foreign domestic workers) or low-skilled labour engaged in the construction industry. The inflow of foreign labour has been beneficial to Singapore in economic and fiscal terms but, equally, as Low and Vadaketh (2014) document, it has in recent years raised a series of socio-political challenges. These challenges relate to congestion externalities, increased demand for housing, healthcare and other positional goods (Low & Vadaketh, 2014).

The domestic labour force participation rate has been relatively steady at 68%. Recent reforms in education (Waring, 2014) and skills training (Waring et al., 2019) have contributed to a higher skills-base and educational attainment in the resident labour force. For example, only one fourth of the resident workforce had a university degree in 2008, but this had increased to 36% by 2018 (Ministry of Manpower, 2019).

While the Singapore economy continues to thrive, significant labour market challenges remain. Key among them is the heavy reliance on foreign labour. Not only has this caused a series of socio-political challenges for the Singapore government, but recent studies highlight that industrial sub-sectors that relied extensively on relatively cheap foreign labour also suffered from poor labour productivity (Bali et al., 2018). Policy efforts to reduce this reliance have not been entirely successful (Bali et al., 2018; Lim, 2015). First, many businesses (especially small and medium enterprises in the manufacturing sector) derive their competitive advantage from relatively low cost foreign labour. Automating these jobs has proven to be difficult due to issues associated with scale, and raising the cost of foreign workers (through levies) has been politically challenging in some sectors. Second, in recent years the government has come under pressure to rebalance its strategy of prioritising economic growth (Low & Vadaketh, 2014). This has resulted in increased government expenditure on a range of perceived economic and social fault lines (e.g. infrastructure, transport, health, housing, education) in the society. In addition to increased spending, the Singapore government has raised the importance of harnessing technology-based solutions (such as big data, robotics, artificial intelligence and additive manufacturing) in key policy areas such as health and education, and in industrial sub-sectors such as manufacturing and services.

Key technologies currently (or likely to be) implemented

In 2014, Singapore's former Prime Minister Lee Kuan Yew launched the national 'Smart Nation' policy. Smart Nation is an ambitious strategy to harness 4IR technologies to, as PM Lee described, 'enhance our strengths, overcome our national challenges and physical limits and build new sources of comparative advantage' (Smart Nation, 2018: 1). Smart Nation focuses on plans to develop a 'Digital Economy, Digital Government and Digital Society drawing on the Internet-of-things (IOT), Artificial Intelligence, Big Data, Automation and Autonomous vehicles technologies' (ibid.). The policy provides considerable funding and resourcing for a range of initiatives. For instance, the authorities are installing new lamp posts throughout Singapore with internet-connected sensors and cameras to measure and analyse air quality and rainfall. Meanwhile, autonomous buses and taxis are being trialled at business parks and university campuses. In HealthCare, the government is also supporting an initiative to build a web-based portal for citizens to access e-Health Records and new medical services online (Smart Nation, 2018: 1).

These Smart Nation initiatives are helping Singapore to forge a reputation as a hub for innovation and technology in the Asia Pacific region. It ranked first in the 2018 Asian Digital Transformation Index (DTI): a weighted index of 23 variables across three themes (i) digital infrastructure; (ii) human capital; and (iii) industrial connectivity (The Economist, 2018). The theme *Digital Infrastructure* clusters variables that include information communication technology (ICT) product tariffs, ICT expenditure and fibre networks, amongst others. *Human capital* measures the quality of mathematics and science education, tertiary enrolment and internet penetration. Lastly, *industrial connectivity* measures technology absorption and includes publicly-available research and development (R&D) commitments from governments as part of a national AI development strategy and the availability of publicly available data. On the index it ranked first, second and sixth in these three respective categories.

Singapore was also ranked 7th globally, and 1st in Asia on the 2017 Global Innovation Index (TGII, 2017). Similar to the DTI, the index is weighted over 80 variables clustered across seven themes: institutions' (political and regulatory environments) human capital and research; infrastructure (ICTs and general infrastructure); market sophistication (level of trade, competition); business innovation (knowledge workers, innovation linkages; collaboration; knowledge and technology outputs (patents, scholarly research); and creative outputs (trademarks, cultural and creative services).

These metrics demonstrate the city-state's technology-readiness. In the following section we will focus on two key technologies that have been emphasised in recent policy documents: artificial intelligence and big data.

Artificial Intelligence (AI)

Artificial Intelligence, particularly deep machine learning, is being trialled and deployed in several sub-sectors across Singapore. In healthcare, AI is being used to improve pre-admission bill estimates at private hospitals. The proposed Model Artificial Intelligence Governance (MAIG) framework released by the government for public consultation documents a four-fold increase in the accuracy of billing estimates following the adoption of proprietary deep learning and neural network algorithms (Government of Singapore, 2018). In transport, Singapore has piloted autonomous electric buses at its university campuses and has designated public roads that can be used for testing self-driving vehicles (SNDGO,

2019; Taeihagh & Lim, 2019). In the retail sector, AI is being used in supply chains, customised shopping experiences and enabling predictive modelling. In financial services, AI-based technologies are also being trialled to automatically review legal contracts and highlight any inconsistencies.

Early in 2019 Singapore introduced the MAIG framework underpinned by two principles: decisions made by AI systems are to be transparent, and AI solutions must be human-centric (Government of Singapore, 2018). The governance framework proposes a matrix to classify the probability and potential harm to an individual as a result of a decision made by an organisation using AI about the individual. For example, if both the probability and degree of harm to an individual is considered low, then it is appropriate for automated decision-making in which a human-being is out of the loop. If on the other hand, both the probability of harm and the degree of harm is considered high, the matrix recommends active intervention in which human-beings are involved in decision-making. If this matrix were to be applied to a contemporary controversy — for instance, the idea of AI Drones for military purposes — the governance framework in Singapore would prevent their deployment.

Big data

There are three pillars that support Singapore's Big Data strategy: internet connectivity, developing business ecosystems and human capital training (EDB, 2019). Layered with this is the city state's Smart Nation Initiative that aims to develop digital capabilities in the government, society and the economy.

The Digital Economy Framework aims to (i) accelerate the digitalisation of industries, particularly SMEs, through platforms such as e-invoicing and procurement; (ii) integrate ecosystems and support companies to leverage existing digital technologies so they can discover new growth nodes; (iii) develop capabilities in four frontier technologies — artificial intelligence (AI) and data science, cybersecurity, immersive media, as well as the internet of things (IOT) and future communications infrastructure (IMDA, 2018).

The Digital Government Framework focuses on utilising data, connectivity and computing to fundamentally change how businesses and citizens interact with the government. The policy goal is to increase stakeholder satisfaction by (i) introducing services that offer e-payment options; (ii) services that are pre-filled with government-verified data; (iii) services that offer digital options for wet ink signatures; (iv) interactions that are completed digitally from end-to-end; (v) ensuring that 20,000 public officials are trained in data analytics; and (vi) increasing the use of AI for service delivery and policy making (SNDGO, 2018).

The Digital Society Framework aims to ensure that all citizens have access to technology and the skills and know-how to use it safely and confidently. This includes expanding and enhancing digital access, improving digital literacy, the widespread adoption of technology and promoting inclusive design (MCI, 2018). These policies are sophisticated in the international comparison but, illustrated from the presentation of our survey findings in the next section, they might not always match with industry or managements' expectations.

Research findings on managers' preparedness for the 4IR

Sample demographics

The Singapore survey was sent via email link to a database of 18,000 Singaporeans who are alumni of Murdoch University, Australia. The survey yielded 332 responses with 39.5% of the respondents employed at the level of manager and above, including 13% employed in director, CEO or owner positions. Male and female participants were almost equally represented in our survey. Sixty-five percent were aged between 18–35, with approximately 28% aged between 36 to 50. Sixty-seven percent held a bachelor's degree while just under 22% also held a postgraduate qualification. As table 4.1 indicates, 43% indicated that they were 'staff', while 20% stated that they were 'managers'.

More than three quarters of the respondents held undergraduate qualifications and 21% had a postgraduate degree as table 4.2 illustrates.

The key industries that were represented in the study included:

- Education and Training (17%)
- Finance and Insurance Services (13%)
- Info Media and Telecom (12%)
- Professional, Scientific and Technical (9%)
- Manufacturing (6%)
- Healthcare and Retail are 5% each.

Stage of automation, key technologies and IT structure

As figure 4.1 shows, over a quarter of respondents identified their organisation as being a participant in the Fourth Industrial Revolution (4IR). Fifty-six percent identified as being at the stage of the 3rd IR. Notwithstanding the dominance of service sector firms in the study, mobile technologies were found to be in predominant use (80%) followed by cloud technologies (70%) and

Table 4.2 Educational Attainment of Respondents (330 Answered – 2 skipped)

Answer choices	Percentages	Responses
High school or lower	0.30%	1
Diploma or trade qualification	1.52%	5
Bachelor's degree	76.36%	252
Postgraduate qualification	21.82%	72
Total		**330**

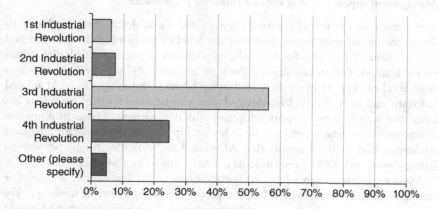

Figure 4.1 The Technological Stage of Respondents' Organisations

embedded IT systems (65%). Delving into the key technology related drivers at the firm level, it is apparent that data related security issues tend to be the key focus of firms in Singapore. Of the organisations that responded, one half indicated that they were paying close attention to data storage, communications and data exchange, with 45% already having turned to the Cloud to procure data security services. Beyond data security, a very large number of organisations (between 75% and 90%) suggest that 3D printing and artificial intelligence (AI) related technologies will dominate the near future followed by robotics and automation.

The study revealed that 56% of firms had their IT functions centralised with 23% indicating an outsourced IT function. While the high level of IT centralisation may have a bearing on the slow pace of preparation across organisations, conclusions cannot be drawn clearly which is why the study also pursued the level of alignment between firm level strategy and IT strategies.

Business and 4IR strategic alignment

The study shows that 70% of firms have their business strategies well aligned with IT strategies wherein IT is seen to support business direction, and more than three quarters acknowledged that where a misalignment might exist, IT goals and objectives are adapted and realigned. Thus, it may be fair and reasonable to suggest that IT is largely seen to be a supportive function for the organisations, as opposed to it being a driver of new processes or services that would enable firms to think and act 'technology-first'. Our results also indicate a fairly strong alignment between IT and strategy in Singapore with just under three quarters of respondents agreeing that IT strategies support and match business strategies.

Management support, ease of use and employee performance

The survey results reveal a strong view of the technologies that are likely to dominate in the near future, however the level of support, understanding and appreciation of the benefits from the application of such technologies seems to be limited. For instance, only 36% of respondents indicated there was a high level of support from their leadership towards the adoption of AI related software and only 30% acknowledged that a significant level of resources has been put in place to support adoption and deployment. These findings are symptomatic of organisations whose leadership cannot demonstrate adequate understanding of the benefits that AI related technologies might be able to bring about, and 60% of respondents confirm this to be the case.

Most respondents agreed that AI Software was useful. Just over 75% agreed or strongly agreed that AI would help employees to complete tasks more quickly. A similar majority agreed or strongly agreed with the contention that AI would improve employee performance.

Management control, innovation and customer satisfaction

Just over 70% of respondents overwhelmingly agreed that the same technologies will aid management in establishing better controls around process and performance. In addition, 60% agreed that the use of AI related technologies can also drive innovation through the creation of new ideas, although it is imperative for organisations to pilot initiatives, as this can also influence the development of new processes, products or services that can generate enhanced value for the organisation or customer. This is evident with an overwhelming 65% of respondents suggesting that AI related software can help meet customer needs and improve customer service. However, almost a third of firms are unsure whether these technologies will be able to improve customer satisfaction.

Employee satisfaction, productivity and retention

Seventy percent of respondents agreed that AI related technologies will not only enable employees to become more productive by accomplishing tasks faster and being able to multitask, but as a consequence, performance on the job is also likely to improve. Furthermore, over 60% agreed that the use of such technologies will improve employee satisfaction at work. but more importantly, they will enable employees to be more focused on important aspects of their role.

Our study, is however unambiguous about supporting the proposition that the deployment of new technologies will make roles redundant (over 60% respondents) resulting in employees having to rethink existing career trajectories; and at the same time half indicated that aside from disruption and replacement, new jobs will be created. This is in alignment with our earlier findings wherein organisations clearly identify key areas where this disruption is to take place.

Government strategies and policies

Interestingly, our study found that in Singapore, whilst over a third of the respondents were impressed with government policy and programs in this direction, conversely, close to a quarter were not or not at all impressed with government policy and strategy in this space (see table 4.3).

In relation to employee-level preparation for these changes, about a quarter of the participants suggested that employee skills were low and preparation was needed in the areas of application development, with over 70% also suggesting that in the next five years data analytics and data security will be the two key areas of skill need in organisations. Thirty percent indicated that employees are better prepared with automation technology and 36% indicate the same in the area of data analytics (see table 4.4).

Notwithstanding the importance that organisations are paying towards data security, the survey found that only 41% of respondents indicated that employees are skilled in this area. Despite this low level of skill readiness, there is overwhelming support from organisations as 75% indicated that employees will need to develop the relevant technological–related knowledge under-pinned by a positive attitude towards ongoing learning. To accomplish this successfully, employees have to demonstrate two key skills – critical thinking and teamwork.

As a result, over 65% felt that new learning and development programs had to be put in place for existing staff and that new forms of job design and new competencies would have to drive the selection and attraction of staff. What is heartening is that over half of the respondents agreed that emerging technologies, such as those related to AI, will not only be easy to use but also that learning these technologies will be easy and interaction will be flexible.

Table 4.3 Respondents Perception of Government Policy (Answered: 250 – skipped 82)

	Not impressed at all	Not impressed	Undecided	Impressed	Very impressed	Total
From your observation, how impressed are you by the policies of your government in preparation for the impact of Artificial Intelligence (AI) on jobs?	4.00% 10	19.60% 49	38.80% 97	31.60% 79	6.00% 15	250

Table 4.4 Respondents' Impressions of Employee Skill Levels

	Very low	Low	Moderate	High	Very high	Total
IT infrastructure	1.71%	5.13%	23.93%	48.29%	20.94%	234
	4	12	56	113	49	
Automation technology	1.71%	8.12%	26.07%	42.31%	21.79%	234
	4	19	61	99	51	
Data analytics	2.59%	3.45%	21.98%	44.83%	27.16%	232
	6	8	51	104	63	
Data security/ Communications security	1.28%	3.85%	18.38%	44.87%	31.62%	234
	3	9	43	105	74	
Development of application of assistance systems	3.43%	6.87%	28.33%	43.78%	17.60%	233
	8	16	66	102	41	
Collaboration software	2.14%	8.97%	29.06%	40.17%	19.66%	234
	5	21	68	94	46	
Non-technical skills such as systems thinking and process understanding	1.71%	7.69%	28.63%	42.74%	19.23%	234
	4	18	67	100	45	

Most respondents expected some level of resistance to these technological changes but suggested that the level of resistance would be moderate. Interestingly, respondents suggested that accounting and human resource management would be the departments most likely to resist the introduction of AI/Robotics (see table 4.5).

The majority of respondents believed that the proportion of jobs replaced by automation would be moderate (less than 30%); however just under a third believed that the proportion would be more likely to be high or very high. Just over a third of respondents also contended that job creation through AI and Automation would be moderate. A similar proportion believed that it would be low or very low.

Key issues

Drawing on the findings from the survey, we discuss four key issues that have emerged. In particular, we focus on the findings that reveal opportunities that are to be created as a result of the 'rising tide' of 4IR technologies.

1   New job creation and skill development

Four organisational areas were identified as being the beneficiary of technology disruption where new high value-added jobs will be created. These are information technology, marketing and sales, manufacturing and production, and research and development. In technology-mature economies such as Singapore the market has started to witness the

Table 4.5 Respondent's Perceptions of Organisational Resistance to AI/Robotics

	Very low	Low	Moderate	High	Very high	Total
Manufacturing production and operations (Product design or engineering)	13.57% 30	24.89% 55	40.72% 90	17.19% 38	3.62% 8	221
Research and development	10.36% 23	24.77% 55	41.44% 92	18.47% 41	4.95% 11	222
purchasing	7.83% 17	21.20% 46	44.24% 96	23.50% 51	3.23% 7	217
Information technology/ Data security/ Communications security	10.81% 24	22.07% 49	40.09% 89	19.82% 44	7.21% 16	222
Marketing, sales, distribution and customer support	9.91% 22	20.27% 45	44.59% 99	19.37% 43	5.86% 13	222
Human resource management	7.24% 16	21.72% 48	45.70% 101	19.46% 43	5.88% 13	221
Accounting and finance	7.69% 17	19.46% 43	47.96% 106	15.38% 34	9.50% 21	221
Transport and logistics	11.82% 26	22.73% 50	42.27% 93	19.55% 43	3.64% 8	220

creation of new jobs such as data scientists, data analysts, data governance specialists, practice managers – data and analytics, data architect, big data consultants and similar. In addition to the broad-based need for such skillsets, there are also sector-specific job creations taking place such as supply chain data scientists, regional data analysts and data leaders for banks. In the domain of marketing and sales we are witnessing the creation and increased need for digital marketing specialists and digital experience designers who can help create and evolve digital customer journeys and work to deliver superior user experiences from concept creation, ideation to prototyping. Companies such as Amazon Web Services are in the search for managers in Singapore who not only possess strong interpersonal, communication and customer relationship skills, but also the ability to lead and develop cloud based solution designers based on big data and analytics services provided by the company. Not only are such needs becoming prevalent in the for-profit sector but also in the public sector. For instance, Singapore's Ministry of Health (MoH) has recognised that for successful healthcare transformation key technologies relating to Big Data analytics, modelling techniques using statistics, artificial intelligence and machine learning will need to be leveraged.

Consequently, these high value jobs will require new forms of training provided by organisations and training institutions. The Singapore Government supports the skill development effort of its citizens and residents through its SkillsFuture program. In addition to training institutions based in Singapore, the government also funds participation in programs delivered by global learning platforms such as Coursera, Udacity and Udemy. For instance, Coursera offers data-specific courses in data management and visualisation, data warehousing, data science at scale, business metrics for data driven companies, amongst other courses, such as digital analytics for marketing, aerial robotics, internet of things and augmented reality emerging technologies.

Furthermore, the Singapore Government has also created a SkillsFuture for Digital Workplace program (Singapore Government. SkillsFuture. Available online at: www.skillsfuture.sg/digitalworkplace). The program is designed in partnership with firms such as Microsoft, enabling individuals to develop a future oriented innovation-driven and resilient mindset by understanding emerging technologies and their impact on work, while developing the capability to interpret and use data.

The Singaporean authorities are also harnessing the country's Vocational and Higher Education sectors to support the skill and knowledge requirements of the digital economy. Within Singapore's five polytechnics and at some of the public universities, there has been a shift towards offering short, modularised courses that can be micro-credentialed in areas such as the internet of things, artificial intelligence, robotics, cybersecurity and other areas of the digital economy. As Gleason (2018) notes, more than 500 such micro-courses are now available in Singapore. At the public universities there are also new undergraduate and postgraduate courses on data science, artificial intelligence and robotics, while the National University of Singapore has established overseas colleges in digital innovation hubs such as Israel, Silicon Valley, Munich Beijing, New York, Shanghai and Stockholm. These efforts are designed to deepen capabilities in the workforce while also retaining the flexibility and agility to adapt to new technological trends. The vocational and higher education sector focus has been on developing technical skills, but in relation to our survey we found it interesting that most respondents believed that soft skills (critical thinking, communication, teamwork, ethics and morality) were among the most important skills to be developed in the context of greater adoption of AI and automation.

2   Need for new forms of leadership to embrace digital and AI technologies

As we know, leadership as a practice has evolved from the periods of transactional and transformational practices to the current day forms that require authentic, people-oriented and high emotional quotient (EQ)-driven leaders. The findings from this study are unambiguous in calling for new forms of leadership to prepare and drive organisations into the

4IR. As technological advancements continue to influence changes in markets, firms and economies so will leadership practices be impacted too. What this means is that leaders will need to comprehend the impact of new technologies on organisations and their corresponding impact on society and communities. In the context of the organisation, leaders themselves will need to be digitally mature to be able to lead teams, motivate talent and manage radical change. In this scenario, digital transformation becomes an important cornerstone for organisations that want to compete across markets and improve profitability while sustaining or growing market share. Consequently, the digital transformation led by leaders has to be found across products and services, customer experience and the organisation's business model.

To this end, in Singapore training institutions are gearing up with courses in digital leadership in some cases being sector specific. For instance, Singapore Polytechnic delivers a Digital Leadership in Advanced Manufacturing program that provides learners with the skills and knowledge to develop a digital transformation strategy and a roadmap for organisations. This also includes delivery of content in the areas of business value, agile methodology, lean management, design thinking, systems thinking, human capital and change management in addition to technological content relating to cybersecurity, internet of things (IoT), AI/Robotics and big data analytics. This clearly depicts that digital leadership necessitates a certain level of digital maturity on the part of individuals, combined with what has traditionally been referred to as 'soft skills'. Finally, and following on from (1) where we discussed new high value job creation, this trend is also being witnessed in the leadership space with the creation of roles such as the Chief Digital Officer.

3   Innovation to drive customer value and create positive financial impact

Building a culture of innovation across businesses in different sectors is essential and has long been embodied in Singapore's growth and development strategy. Indeed, as early as 1998, the report of the Committee of Singapore's Competitiveness highlighted "Given our limited resources, Singapore has to compete on the basis of capabilities rather than costs. . . . As competition intensifies, Singapore needs to continually move up the technological and capabilities ladder" (Government of Singapore, 1998).

The importance of innovation across businesses and domains was also underscored by the Prime Minister in 2014 when he noted that, "Innovation does not have to be rocket-science, but companies must be willing to relook at how things are done. We will continue to work with employers and unions in all industries to raise their productivity – not just through technology, but also by transforming business processes, management, and business models" (Government of Singapore, 2014).

The process of innovation and innovative practices are key to improving productivity and ensuring that businesses remain competitive. Innovative business practices allow organisations to retain their cost competitiveness and provide flexibility to respond to challenges in the business environment. With respect to achieving innovation through the 4IR, our study suggests that the journey in Singapore is far from complete. The results of our study indicate that while over 20% of respondents felt that their organisation was at the 4IR stage, a majority (56%) believed that they were only at the 3IR stage. Thus, there remains an opportunity for the majority of organisations to innovate through the adoption of 4IR technologies. Interestingly, our survey revealed that a relatively large group of respondents (approximately 30%) either disagreed or were undecided as to whether AI software would help generate new ideas and innovation for their organisation, which perhaps suggests the continuing importance of the human mind in creativity and business innovation.

4   Technology focus

Adopting technology solutions and upgrading capital in the production process is known to drive efficiency and improve productivity (Faggio et al., 2010). Consistent with this, our survey showed that most respondents believed that 4IR technologies would improve productivity and organisational performance; however there was also a large minority (approximately 30%) who are yet to be convinced of this. A similar number also felt that the introduction of AI may not improve customer satisfaction. On the whole though, more believed that AI and automation would be positive for the commercial outcomes of their organisations than not.

The technology focus of Singaporean organisations came through clearly in our survey with respondents indicating a strong alignment between strategy and IT. This would be reassuring for the authorities who have encouraged and sometimes cajoled local businesses to update their capital vintages and explore opportunities for digitisation. Further, our survey results indicated that technologists and IT professionals have most to gain from 4IR as their role becomes more central to business success.

Implications for labour markets, workforces, jobs and skills

The results of our survey confirm that few jobs in Singapore's labour market will be untouched by the impact of 4IR. The impact of AI and automation is already being felt within a number of key industries in Singapore. In banking for instance, digitisation has had a dramatic impact on the sector, with chatbots, advanced online banking through apps, digital wallets and cashless e-payment systems reducing the need for traditional retail banking and the jobs that accompanied that business model. Artificial intelligence and data analytics are also impacting urban transport systems with bus companies drawing on commuter data to better manage bus fleets. At Singapore's Changi Airport (one of the world's busiest), new automation technologies mean that passengers are able to proceed from check-in to boarding without interacting with another person. Outside the airport, robotic parking police direct traffic and photograph errant drivers' vehicles. As a result of global competitive pressures, the large number of multinational corporations resident in Singapore, and with government encouragement, it seems very likely that that the reach of 4IR will only accelerate and transform its labour market and workforce.

One likely outcome of this transformation is the contraction of the foreign workforce (particularly in manufacturing) although construction might continue its traditional high dependency on foreign workers. Some of the trends that have been forecasted elsewhere (for example, McKinsey Global Institute, 2017) are likely to be observed in Singapore. For instance, in some cases occupations might be rendered obsolete, but what is perhaps more likely is that the 4IR will displace tasks rather than whole occupations. The results of our survey also indicate that the wave of technological change will effectively erode some jobs and professions while reinforcing others. For instance, our survey suggests that the accounting profession will be radically transformed with lower level accounting jobs destroyed, while IT is likely to be strengthened with more jobs created. In this way we see Schumpeter's (1942) cycles of creative destruction unleashed at the micro, messo and macro levels within Singapore's labour market but within shorter timeframes.

Implications for governments, labour market planners and human resource professionals

Leading a modern, agile and open economy that rides on the fluctuating winds of globalisation, the authorities in Singapore have long recognised the significance of the Fourth Industrial Revolution. They have sought to both embrace its opportunities while also inoculating the workforce from its deleterious side effects. A key pillar of the latter has been the concentrated policy focus on skills. The government's 'Skills Future' program is a significant multi-billion dollar commitment designed to upgrade the skills of the workforce and thereby hopefully preparing Singaporeans for the transformation of industry, jobs and tasks. Underpinning this initiative is an acknowledgement that automation and artificial intelligence are likely to displace certain tasks, and in some cases whole occupations.

As we have documented elsewhere (Bali et al., 2018), Singapore's productivity has lagged behind that of other developed countries over the last few decades. Automation of production processes and service delivery has therefore been encouraged by the state by increasing the costs and constricting the supply of semi-skilled foreign labour, while also providing financial and tax incentives for firms to acquire automation technologies. These strategies have proved to be partially successful but overcoming the historic and long-term dependency on foreign labour will take many years. It is likely that greater adoption of 4IR technologies will help to expedite this process and may eventually reduce the need for such a large contingent foreign labour force, which in turn would help to raise productivity and reduce urban congestion.

The prospect of a rising tide of automation represents a particular challenge in the Singapore context where there are no unemployment benefits or State provided pensions. It is typical for Singaporean men, for example, to become taxi drivers after being made redundant from a manufacturing job. Similarly, elderly Singaporeans frequently hold jobs in fast food outlets or as cleaners, gardeners or similar due to the absence of public pensions. Singaporean policy makers may no longer be able to depend upon these low or semi-skilled jobs to buttress the absence of transfer payments. Autonomous vehicles will eventually reduce the need for human drivers while greater use of automated ordering and production techniques in fast food outlets will mean fewer job opportunities for elderly Singaporeans. To address these challenges, there will need to be a renewed policy focus on task and occupational change as a result of automation. Policy-makers will need to straddle the need for Singapore to continue to be perceived as 'business friendly' while also protecting the economic interests of its citizens and especially those whose jobs are more likely to be displaced by 4IR technologies. Ideally, new employment rules will need to be commissioned which require employers to consult extensively with the tripartite partners over the introduction of such technological change and help to identify redeployment and retraining options. Beyond such measures, we would anticipate policy debate on the merits of some level of transfer payment to displaced workers or perhaps even consideration of a guaranteed minimum income scheme, though in the present political milieu that seems unlikely.

Singapore's strong emphasis on tripartism in employment relations is also likely to be an asset as it seeks to cope with the pressing challenges unleashed by 4IR. The trade union movement, which is closely aligned to the government, is unlikely to resist the introduction of new technologies, but rather can be expected to pursue negotiated change, retraining and redeployment options with businesses. For human resource professionals, the 4IR highlights the centrality of their role in business restructuring, change management and workforce planning. Further, the impact of 4IR technology on tasks and functions will draw attention to the methodology of job re-design and place a renewed onus on such professionals to (re)create meaningful jobs. To some extent, this is familiar territory, but these roles are likely to be given added piquancy as a result of the impact of these new technologies.

Conclusion

Singapore's tradition of long-term planning and strategic foresight probably places the city state in a somewhat better-prepared position than most other developed and developing nations when it comes to the impact of the 4IR. As a highly globalised nation, it has sought to ride the crest of the technological wave while also preparing its citizenry for the significant changes ahead. Our survey suggests that a reasonable level of understanding and preparedness exists within the industrial base of Singapore but it is far from perfect, and government policy in this regard (while comparatively strong) is not considered to be sufficient. The results of our study naturally indicate a level of anxiety about the future of work and employment, with many respondents recognising that the Singapore labour market and whole occupations are likely to be significantly changed as a consequence of 4IR technologies. Nonetheless, what generally emerges from our study is a sense that the technologies will be more positive than not for the commercial activities of organisations. As with globalisation, the 4IR is likely to produce 'winners and losers' in the labour market; and it will be the task of human resource professionals, trade unions and policy makers to ensure that the embrace of new technology is mediated in a way that does not create further social disruption and accentuate existing inequalities.

References

Asher, M. G., Bali, A. S., & Kwan, C. Y. (2015). Public financial management in Singapore: Key characteristics and prospects. *The Singapore Economic Review*, 60 (3), doi:10.1142/S0217590815500320

Bali, A., McKiernan, P., Vas, C., & Waring, P. (2018). *Productivity and Innovation in SMEs: Creating Competitive Advantage in Singapore and South East Asia*. London: Routledge.

Department of Statistics, Government of Singapore (2018). *Singapore Yearbook of Statistics*. Available at: www.singstat.gov.sg/publications/reference/yearbook-of-statistics-singapore

Economic Development Board (2019). *Singapore's Big Ambitions for Big Data In 2019*. Available at: www.edb.gov.sg/en/news-and-events/insights/innovation/singapore-s-big-ambitions-for-big-data-in-2019.html

The Economist (2018). *Asian Digital Transformation Index*. Available at: http://connectedfuture.economist.com/wp-content/uploads/2018/12/ADTI-whitepaper.pdf

Faggio, G., Salvanes, K., & Van Reenen, J. (2010). The evolution of inequality in productivity and wages: Panel data evidence. *Industrial and Corporate Change*, 19 (6), 1919–1951.

Gleason, N. (2018). Singapore's higher education systems in the era of the fourth industrial revolution: Preparing lifelong learners. In Gleason, N. (ed.), *Higher Education in the Era of the Fourth Industrial Revolution*, Singapore: Palgrave Macmillan, pp. 145–169.

The Global Innovation Index. *The 2017 Report*. Available at: www.globalinnovationindex.org/gii-2017-report#

Government of Singapore (1998). *The Report of the Committee on Singapore's Competitiveness*. Singapore: Ministry of Trade and Industry.

Government of Singapore (2014). *Prime Minister Lee Hsien Loong's Speech at Opening of National Productivity Month*, 7 October.

Government of Singapore (2018). A proposed model artificial intelligence governance framework. *Personal Data Protection Commission*. Available at: www.pdpc.gov.sg/-/media/Files/PDPC/PDF-Files/Resource-for-Organisation/AI/A-Proposed-Model-AI-Governance-Framework-January-2019.pdf

IMDA (2018). *Digital Economy Framework for Action.* Available at: https://www2.imda.gov.sg/programme-listing/digital-economy-framework-for-action

Lim, Y. C. (2015). *Singapore's Economic Development: Retrospection and Reflections.* Singapore: World Scientific Publishing.

Low, D., & Vadaketh, S. T. (2014). *Hard Choices: Challenging the Singapore Consensus.* Singapore: NUS Press.

MCI (2018). *Digital Readiness Blue Print.* Available at: www.mci.gov.sg/en/portfolios/digital-readiness/digital-readiness-blueprint

McKinsey Global Institute (2017). *Jobs Lost, Jobs Gained: What the Future of Work Will Mean for Jobs, Skills and Wages.* New York: McKinsey and Company.

Ministry of Manpower (2019). *Labour Force: Summary Table.* Available at: https://stats.mom.gov.sg/Pages/Labour-Force-Summary-Table.aspx

Ministry of Trade and Industry (2017). *Economic Survey of Singapore 2016.* Singapore: Ministry of Trade and Industry.

Pang, E. F., & Lim, L. Y. (2015). Labor, productivity and Singapore's development model. *The Singapore Economic Review (SER)*, 60 (3), 1–30.

Ramesh, M., & Bali, Azad S. (2019). The remarkable healthcare performance in Singapore, Chapter 3. In Compton, M., & Hart, P. (eds.), *Great Policy Successes: How Governments Get It Right in a Big Way at Least Some of the Time.* New York: Oxford University Press.

Schumpeter, J. (1942). *Capitalism, Socialism and Democracy.* New York: Harper & Brothers.

Smart Nation Digital Government Office (SNDGO) (2018). *Digital Government Blue Print.* Available at: www.smartnation.sg/docs/default-source/default-document-library/dgb_summary_june2018.pdf

Smart Nation Digital Government Office (SNDGO) (2019). *Autonomous Vehicles.* Available at: www.smartnation.sg/what-is-smart-nation/initiatives/Transport/autonomous-vehicles

Taeihagh, A., & Lim, H. S. M. (2019). Governing autonomous vehicles: Emerging responses for safety, liability, privacy, cybersecurity, and industry risks. *Transport Reviews*, 39 (1), 103–128, doi:10.1080/01441647.2018.1494640

Tan, K. S., & Bhaskaran, M. (2015). The role of the state in Singapore: Pragmatism in pursuit of growth. *The Singapore Economic Review*, 60 (3), 1550030.

UNDESA (2019). *The World Population Prospects: The 2019 Revision.* Available at: https://population.un.org/wpp/

Waring, P. (2014). Singapore's global schoolhouse strategy: Retreat or recalibration? *Studies in Higher Education*, 39 (5), 874–884.

Waring, P., Vas, C., & Bali, A. S. (2019). The transition from graduation to work: Challenges and strategies in Singapore. In *The Transition from Graduation to Work.* Singapore: Springer, pp. 161–178.

World Bank (2019). *World Development Indicators.* Available at: http://datatopics.worldbank.org/world-development-indicators/

Yap, Mui Teng, & Gee, C. (2016). Singapore's demographic transition, the labor force and government policies: The last fifty years. In Lim, L. (ed.), *Singapore's Economic Development: Retrospection and Reflections.* Singapore: World Scientific Publishing, pp. 195–219.

Yeoh, B. (2007). *Singapore: Hungry for Foreign Workers at All Skill Levels.* Working Paper. Singapore: National University of Singapore.

5 Taiwan

Min-Wen Sophie Chang

Introduction

This chapter examines the challenges of the Fourth Industrial Revolution (4IR) in Taiwan through research into government policies and industry examples. Key factors related to 4IR-readiness are also explored using a selection of case studies across the manufacturing, retail and healthcare industry sectors. The conclusions may provide some directions for managers and professionals regarding planning for or implementing 4IR technologies in Taiwanese organisations.

The 4IR can be defined as the digital transformation of the organisation and concerns the prior to management of the entire value chain process involved in the manufacturing industry (Deloitte, 2017). The 4IR an economic and political initiative proposed by the German government in attempts to transform their economy through AI, the internet of things (IoT), robotics, and other smart technologies. In response to these global trends, the Taiwanese government has proposed a range of policies with the intention of boosting the manufacturing-driven economy.

Despite the government's efforts to promote and incubate 4IR technologies, recent studies indicate that progress remains slow (Hau & Soung, 2019). A former senior vice president of the Foxconn conglomerate, which is the largest manufacturing group in Taiwan, has argued that the 4IR may not be suitable for Taiwan (Cheng, 2017). He maintains that most Taiwanese industries and manufacturers lag far behind in digitalisation when compared to their Western or Mainland Chinese counterparts. The relatively low adoption of digitalised business models and demand-driven manufacturing-services among Taiwanese manufacturers has meant that they may be unlikely to be able to act quickly enough in terms of the technological advances required to meet the demands of the end users. Deloitte (2016, 2018) also predicted that Taiwanese manufacturers will be adversely affected by their overreliance on Chinese production facilities to cut costs. As a result, Taiwan is likely to suffer in relation to its global manufacturing competitiveness, dropping from being ranked 6th in 2016 to 9th in 2020 among the top 40 manufacturing economies (Deloitte, 2018).

The results of two recent surveys tend to support Cheng's (2017) argument and Deloitte's (2016) prediction. First, *CommonWealth Magazine*, in its collaboration with a leading university, investigated 566 of the top 2000 manufacturers in Taiwan. They found that only 31 companies (5.48%) have so far reached the 3IR stage and are moving towards the 4IR through gradual technical upgrades (Hau & Soung, 2019). These authors also suggested that the 4IR may not be suitable for all types of manufacturers, especially for most family-owned and small and medium enterprises (SMEs). Most of these SME manufacturers are not in the process of digitalising their management ethos, business models, existing production facilities, and connectivity, even though there is an increasing awareness of the importance of the 4IR for their future survival (Hau & Soung, 2019). These authors also indicated that, as approximately 34% of top managers and family owners are still relying on their intuition and experience to make key decisions, while 49.7% of the 566 companies studied are still making profits with 2IR machinery, the digitalisation of management systems and equipment seems unnecessary and uneconomical in relation to large capital investment and the considerable effort that would be required to adopt it.

Similarly, Microsoft and IDC (Won, 2019) also found that more than two thirds of Taiwanese firms are shunning artificial intelligence (AI) because of conservatism, risk aversion, and the lack of any systematic planning for its impacts. They suggested that, for the 32% of the Taiwanese firms that have adopted AI, the lack of technological talent, resources and reliable AI partners, together with inadequate IT infrastructures, are still major obstacles to maximising the benefits of 4IR technologies.

Thrift, risk aversion, conservatism, a lack of technological resources and talent, seem to be the most common obstacles relating to the move towards the 4IR for the Taiwanese firms observed in these studies. Currently, most Taiwanese firms may not be ready to embrace it psychologically, culturally, methodologically, and/or financially. However, there are also other social and economic factors that may drive adoption in the future. The next section will explore societal level factors that are important for 4IR technology adoption in Taiwan.

Societal level factors influencing 4IR adoption in Taiwan

There are several key societal factors that may facilitate the 4IR. These include: (1) the ageing and shrinking population and workforce; (2) severe talent shortages; (3) sluggish economic growth and declining national competitiveness; and (4) a manufacturing-driven economy. The following section provides more details regarding each of these factors.

An ageing and shrinking population/workforce

In common with its neighbours, Japan and Korea, Taiwan is facing a population crisis due to its low birth rate and population ageing. Currently, the population stands at 23.4 million, of whom 14.56% were over 65 years old in 2019 (National Development Council, 2019). Yet, according to a recent projection, the population will move into negative growth from 2020 due to the low birth rate and declining marriage rate (National Development Council, 2018).

Taiwan's current total fertility rate and projected future total fertility rates are well below the 2.1 replacement fertility level needed to sustain the size of the population, thus its population is projected to shrink on a long-term basis.

Moreover, the National Development Council (2018) also estimated that by 2065, those aged over 65 years will account for more than 40% of the population, whereas those aged over 85 years will represent more than 10%. In other words, 4 out of 10 people will be over 65 years of age, whereas 1 in 10 will be over 85 by 2065 (National Development Council, 2018). The aging and declining population may drive companies to adapt 4IR technologies, using robotics and AI to substitute or assist older workers.

Severe talent shortages

As the population starts to shrink and many aging workers retire, it will become much more difficult for employers to fill job vacancies. The National Development Council (2018) estimated that Taiwan's working age population may drop to 8.62 million in 2065 from the all-time high of 17.37 million in 2015. This significant 50% decline in the labour supply over the next 40 years will put pressure on recruitment and retention for employers – inevitably, companies will be forced to use robotics or AI to cope with future talent shortages. Although the government has relaxed restrictions on foreign labour to ease chronic shortages, companies still have to apply for permission to hire foreign workers and follow a set of regulations to safeguard the welfare of the foreign workers and prevent them from escaping. Therefore, it might be easier and more feasible for companies to employ digital tools than hiring foreign workers to replace diminishing local workers.

In addition to the structural problems of the population, gaps between education and industry requirements, low labour participation rates, low wages, unequal labour rights for public and private sector workers are other significant factors contributing to the talent shortage (Chang & Connell, 2018). In addition, as more and more young workers are job-hopping and shunning permanent employment for non-standard forms of employment, most employers are also facing high staff turnover and difficulties in retaining talent on a long-term basis (Fong, 2017). These problems may also encourage employers to adopt robotics and AI given that labour supply is likely to deteriorate significantly in the future.

Sluggish economic growth and declining national competitiveness

In addition to its labour supply challenges, Taiwan is also suffering from sluggish economic growth, which is one of the reasons why its ranking on the IMD's National Competitiveness Index dropped from 6th in 2011 to 17th in 2018 (IMD, 2012, 2019). The economy is expected to slow even further, as the 2019 economic growth rate is projected at 2.46%, which is lower than the growth rate of 2.63% in 2018 and 3.08 % in 2017 (DGBAS, 2019). If the recent trade tensions between China and the US were to escalate, Taiwan's economic downturn is likely to worsen as these two countries are its most important trading partners. Preliminary economic data has indicated visible contractions. For example, Taiwan's manufacturing output from January to July in 2019 shrank 1.7%; while the industrial output also dropped 1.8% (DGBAS, 2019). This is in sharp contrast to the 3.6% growth for its manufacturing output and 3.6% growth for industrial output in 2018 (DGBAS, 2019).

The trade war between China and the US may hit Taiwan harder than other Asian countries. This is because many Taiwanese manufacturers have relocated their production lines to China to take advantage of the lower operational and labour costs in the past few decades. As the finished products are shipped to the US or other destinations, any heavy import duties on goods manufactured in China, will soon become unworkable for Taiwanese manufacturers. In the wake of the looming crisis, many Taiwanese manufacturers have relocated their production lines back to Taiwan or to other South East Asian countries.

The Taiwanese government and many manufacturers are also turning their attention to the 4IR as a response to the crisis, through technology upgrades, research and development (R&D), business model revamps, policy initiatives and collaborations. However, as mentioned earlier, the slow progress towards 4IR technologies, in both the private and public sectors may have already dampened Taiwan's overall manufacturing competitiveness (Deloitte, 2018; Hau & Soung, 2019).

A manufacturing-driven economy with dense industry clusters

Taiwan is still largely a manufacturing-driven economy. Even though Taiwan's manufacturing industry only accounts for a third of the nominal gross domestic product (GDP), it contributes considerably more to economic growth and the sizeable foreign reserve through exports than the service industry does (Department of Statistics of Ministry of Economic Affairs, 2019). Despite many large and medium manufacturers having relocated their production facilities abroad, they can still generate considerable overseas income. In recent years, the manufacturing industry, as the key engine of economic growth, seems to be losing its sparkle, and as a result, Taiwan's economy is also slowing down (Jang, 2019). In attempts to salvage its declining manufacturing competitiveness and keep up with intense international competition, the government has proposed some 4IR-related policies which are outlined in the next section.

Government policies and productivity 4.0

In response to Taiwan's severe talent shortages, slowing economy and declining national and manufacturing competitiveness, the government has proposed several policies that focus on enhancing productivity and upgrading city infrastructure through AI, robotics, the Internet of things (IoT), and 5G networks.

First, the "Digi 2025: Upgrade 5 + 2 Industries Through Tech Revolution" project aims to upgrade 7 selected industries, including the:

(1) aviation and high-tech industry in Taoyuan City,
(2) smart machinery industry,
(3) biotechnology industry,
(4) green energy industry,
(5) agriculture industry,
(6) circular economy industry, and the
(7) defence armour industry (Executive Yuan Digi Group, 2019).

Second, the "Productivity 4.0 Initiative" aims to enhance the productivity of the manufacturing, service and agricultural industries through technology upgrades (Executive Yuan, 2015). Third, policies have been introduced which focus on the development and implementation of state of art smart technologies, such as the "Taiwan AI project," Taiwan 5G project," and "Smart Cities project" (Executive Yuan Digi Group, 2019). Furthermore, the government has also set aside a generous 100 billion New Taiwanese Dollars (NTD) "Industry Innovation Upgrade Fund" to subsidise and encourage innovation within the private sector (National Development Council, 2015). The policy tools used in these projects includes: funding, training for talent, new infrastructure, match making, support for marketing or exports, laws and regulations, consultation, platforms, intellectual property right protection, and more research and development (National Development Council, 2019).

At a glance, these policies may make it seem as if the Taiwanese government is doing quite a lot, but on closer inspection, the scope of the various projects indicates that they are, in some cases, overlapping, ambiguous and unclear. Some of the 4IR infrastructure, which cost billions to build, is considered unnecessary and/or redundant and some have even led to speculations of abuse of power and corruption (Wang, 2017). Although there is still spare capacity in existing science parks and designated industrial zones, the government is still building more science parks and facilities at the taxpayers' expense. For instance, building a new science park for the failing green energy industry is likely to add another one to Taiwan's hundreds of "mosquito venues (蚊子館)" (Wang, 2017). These venues are public buildings or facilities that cost billions of public funds to build, but are left unused, so only "mosquitos" can be found in them instead of humans (Lin & Wang, 2017).

The selection of the key industries that will benefit from the government's resources and budget is also debatable. For example, Taiwan's green energy industry has been struggling for many years and is outperformed by its Chinese counterparts, but it has been selected as one of the seven key industries to enjoy prioritisation of public funding and resources (Lou, 2019). Policies to encourage farmers and local governments to set up solar panels on agricultural lands, natural reserves or wetlands have also raised concerns over sustainability, pollution, and the destruction of natural habitats for wildlife (Lou, 2019).

To illustrate the issues discussed earlier, this section explores case studies and challenges concerning the implementation of various 4IR technologies across the manufacturing, retail, and healthcare sectors.

Case study 1: Hota's 10-year quest towards the 4IR

Hota is a stock market listed company that produces car components, machinery, quad bikes, and medical equipment. Like many Taiwanese manufacturers, it was struggling badly after the financial crisis in 2007–2008. In order to win international orders from leading car brands like BMW, Tesla, and Mercedes Benz, the chairman turned to 4IR technologies to improve production quality and flexibility and to reduce costs. The company then started its transition to the 4IR as early as 2009 and is still building and updating smart production facilities to date.

Within a decade, Hota has incorporated AI, robotics, Internet of things (IoT), and cloud computing on its smart production lines. It has also redesigned its operational processes, the layout of the factory, and quality control mechanisms to accommodate the technology and production overhauls. Hota's employees also received training for the technology upgrade and were re-assigned with different tasks, ranging from production to quality control, problem solving, and design.

Although it cost more than 1 billion US dollars to install its smart IoT production lines, they helped the firm to reduce 71% of the manpower costs and boost the quality of their products (Business Today, 2018). The new production system also enables Hota to produce a batch of products within 90 seconds, rather than the 90 days it took through the traditional approach. Hota's production approach has also switched from semi labour-intensive to automation. The chairman believes the considerable savings in labour costs, combined with the increases in production efficiency, will create more value than the billion-dollar investment in the long run. The new approach also helps the firm to cope with problems caused by talent shortages and rising labour costs because the majority of their workers have been replaced by robots.

The smart industrial production lines also enable Hota to track the processes associated with the production of each product through smart barcodes. They can also determine the possible causes of problems by assessing the unique production regime of each product. As all the robots and equipment are interlinked through IoT technology, robotics can automatically stop faulty products from moving to the next stages of production and alert the quality control personnel as soon as a problem occurs. This helps to safeguard the quality and precision of each product and cut down defect loss and risk.

Hota's 10-year transition to the 4IR may seem to be a lengthy, complex and costly challenge, but the top managers remain committed to its continuous tech upgrade. It is still investing and altering its business models to accommodate technological advances and has been rewarded with lower labour costs and enhancements in production efficiency, flexibility and quality in return.

Case study 2: 7-Eleven's failed cashier-less store

Apart from leading manufacturing firms embracing 4IR technologies, Taiwan's leading grocer – the 7-Eleven convenience store chain – has also been keen to implement cutting edge technologies to maintain their market leadership (Lin, 2019). 7-Eleven has more than 5,300 stores across Taiwan and a market share of half of the convenience store sector (Lin, 2019). It has been leading this sector through continuous innovation in terms of products, services and technology applications. Most of the 7-Eleven stores are installed with an "i-bon" kiosk machine which allows customers to carry out their retail shopping; pay their bills or fines; book tickets for concerts, trains or flights; buy credit for games; post parcels; apply for bank loans and more. The "i-bon" kiosk machines are easy to use, and customers can get their tasks completed within minutes without going to the bank, government agencies, or train stations. For 7-Eleven, this smart system not only provides a solution to reduce manpower, improve customer service and waiting time, but it also helps to gather important consumer behaviour data. The firm can tap into information regarding what people use the machine for, when they use it and other details of their transactions. Through big data analysis, 7-Eleven is able to develop new services and adjust or upgrade existing services based on data gathered from their "i-bon" system.

In addition to this system, 7-Eleven also launched a pioneering cashier-less X store in Taiwan's capital city, Taipei, in January 2018 as a potential solution to manpower shortages. It had been having problems filling job vacancies, especially for its night shifts for some years (Kao, 2019; Yeh, 2018). Moreover, the manpower shortage is set to worsen as a result of Taiwan's fast-ageing society, extremely low birth rate, and unattractive pay-packages offered by the firm. The chain has been criticised as a sweatshop and low wage trend-setter (Teun, 2016).

4IR challenges and outcomes

In the first phase of 7-Eleven's cashier-less X store experiment, there was no human clerk present in this pioneering store, which meant that customers had to use credit cards or pre-paid store cards to pay for their shopping through the self-serve checkout machine. After six months of trial operations, the chain later launched another cashier-less X store, where the store was divided into two sections: the cashier-less section, and the section with human shop assistants. The second store also installed the latest facial recognition technology to detect if there were customers in the store and to track their behaviours.

After 15 months of trial operations of these cashier-less stores, the 7-Eleven chain decided to end this experiment in March 2019 because it was not financially viable and the business model was not replicable to existing stores (Cheng, 2019). The project leader of this experiment pointed out that, even though

7-Eleven is ready and the technology is ready, most Taiwanese consumers are just not prepared yet to embrace the novel concept of cashier-less stores and the latest 4IR technology applications (Cheng, 2019; Yeh, 2018). Taiwanese consumers are used to being served by human shop assistants and their shopping habits cannot be changed overnight. Human clerks are also useful for helping customers complete their purchases, as not everyone knows how to operate the self-check-out machines – particularly young children and the elderly, who account for a considerable proportion of 7-Eleven customers.

Another reason why the pioneering project was not viable, was the cashless payment. Because the cashier-less X store only accepted credit cards, or certain types of pre-paid store cards as the method of payment, customers without these cards were excluded from making a purchase. Once again, this was often the elderly, students, and children. If these target customers are unable to pay for their purchases, they are unlikely to shop at this concept store. In addition to the problem of the cashless payment, some consumers also felt uneasy in this cutting-edge store due to the use of facial recognition technology, surveillance cameras, and movement tracking technology (Yeh, 2018).

However, despite the experiment representing a failed attempt to embrace 4IR technologies, 7-Eleven can still apply the lessons learned to develop and upgrade their smart vending machines. Smart vending machines are linked to their nearby stores through IoT technology that enables the stores to obtain data without time lags. For example, 7-Eleven uses these smart vending machines to sell fresh food, milk, pre-packed ready meals, and sandwiches in schools, factories, and more. The nearby 7-Eleven branches can refill these vending machines quickly if the demand is high, or they can remove food which may be reaching its use-by date. The smart vending machine may also be used to replace night shift staff in the future, similar to the ATMs machines used by banks outside opening hours.

Case study 3: smart technologies in leading hospitals

In addition to the manufacturing and service industries, the Taiwanese healthcare industry is another sector where smart technologies are being adopted by leading firms. Taiwan's national health care system is renowned for offering high quality healthcare with a low-price tag (Roberts, 2014). However, it is also suffering from talent shortages and high staff turnover due to the incredibly long working hours, stressful work environments, and lack of labour rights protection affecting healthcare workers. Currently, most doctors and nurses are not included under the current labour laws, so they are not protected by limitations related to working-hours and they are not entitled to labour pensions. They also do not have paid leave or the public holidays that ordinary workers enjoy either.

In attempts to address manpower shortages and boost work efficiency, smart technologies are increasingly being used in Taiwan's healthcare industry. There are two main types of smart technology usage in the healthcare industry: (1) medical or professional aspects and (2) administrative/supportive functions. In terms of medical or professional aspects, many of Taiwan's leading hospitals have installed robotics or cutting-edge smart medical machines, such as the da Vinci System for Surgery, to carry out keyhole surgery. The government provides funding for both the robotic equipment and the surgeries through this system. Many hospitals have also employed IoT technology in the inpatient wards, for example using tablets to replace the old-fashioned call buttons. Patients can select what they need from the menu on the tablets, such as controlling the lighting and air-conditioning in their hospital rooms, notifying the nurses about empty drips, or requesting assistance.

In terms of administrative or supportive aspects, 4IR technologies are increasingly being used to carry out manual or administrative tasks in hospitals. For example, many hospitals use robotic vacuum cleaners to sweep hospital floors. Digital check-in-boards and self-service systems are widely used in large medical centres. When arriving at hospitals for appointments, outpatients have to insert their national healthcare identity (NHI) cards into the smart boards outside the consultation rooms to alert the staff of their arrival. Outpatients can also see their status in relation to the waiting list just by looking at the smart check-in board, which is also linked to the hospital's registration system and each clinic consultation room's desktop medical record system. This allows doctors and nurses to retrieve patients' medical records from the national healthcare cloud. For hospitals, the digital check-in boards help to enhance administrative efficiency, and reduce waiting times and administrative errors through IoT technology.

Many hospitals also use smart robotics with built-in satellite navigation systems to move equipment, documents, and medical supplies in the hospital to relieve workloads and boost efficiency. The use of self-check-out machines, automatic-ticketing machines for queuing, and tablets to gather customer satisfaction data are also common in large medical centres.

Overall, Taiwan's health care industry is embracing the latest smart technologies, but this is not enough to prevent doctors and nurses from being overworked and experiencing stressful work conditions. Although 4IR technologies and equipment are widely adapted by most hospitals, doctors and nurses still have to cope with long hospital outpatient hours from 8:30am to 9:00pm. As a result, some resident and trainee doctors are often forced to work up to 20–30 hours continuously without sleeping, and up to 100 hours in a week (Hwang, 2019). The government has decided to cap the maximum working hours for certain types of doctors to 80 hours a week after several residential doctors died from overwork, while many others also suffered from major illness, including cancer and stroke, which may have been caused by the stressful long working hours (Hwang, 2019). However, this limit is still double most workers' 40 hours per week, even after the labour law restrictions on some doctors' working hours came into effect in September 2019.

Implications for industry managers

From these case studies it is evident that there are several common themes which may provide insights for industry managers: (1) robotics cannot replace human workers completely, especially in the services sector; (2) digitalisation towards the 4IR can be a costly, lengthy, and complex process; and (3) business model revamps are necessary for successful digitalisation. These themes are now discussed in more detail.

Robots are unlikely to be 'labour terminators' in the services sector

Talent shortages are perhaps one of the most important driving forces behind the introduction of robots to replace workers across some Taiwanese industries. As observed in the case studies presented here, using robotics to replace human workers may work better in manufacturing sectors to carry out repetitive tasks than it does in the services sector. In sectors such as retail and healthcare, robots and smart systems operating as "task-terminators" can help workers and organisations to alleviate heavy workloads and boost work efficiency. Yet, they may not be sufficient to address the fundamental causes of talent shortages or replace human workers completely. For instance, consumers shunned 7-Eleven's pioneering cashier-less store because they prefer to be served by humans rather than robots. Conversely, the use of smart medical equipment in hospitals does very little to reduce the hours worked by doctors and nurses which can be attributed to understaffing and the long hospital opening hours.

Costs of progressing towards the 4IR

Moving towards the 4IR may entail a costly, lengthy, and complex process for Taiwan. Even with careful planning and a sizeable budget, there is no guarantee for success, as observed in the case of 7-Eleven's cashier-less store. Moreover, a long-term perspective may work better than short-term approaches when it comes to upgrading organisations with 4IR technologies. This may be because current technologies, tools, and equipment may not yet be mature enough to succeed; therefore, it is suggested that managers allow sufficient time and contingency funding for development, adjustment, trials, and modifications to support effective implementation.

Business model makeovers are necessary

Finally, another lesson evident from the case studies is that business model overhauls are necessary for the successful implementation of these new technologies. In the case of Hota, the company has changed its business models, management systems, and work processes to accommodate the hardware and software upgrades, in order to support successful implementation. In contrast, 7-Eleven trialled cutting-edge new technologies without changing much of the existing business model, but later abandoned the project when they realised it was not financially feasible or replicable.

For managers, planning and executing a business model revamp to accommodate smart technologies can be the key for successful transitions to the 4IR. However, changing mindsets and the traditional ways of doing things is difficult for most family owners of Taiwanese SMEs who may be unwilling to change because of their cost-cutting mentality, conservatism and risk avoidance (Hau & Soung, 2019). Yet, without top management support for business model and management system overhauls, it is very unlikely that workers at the bottom of the hierarchy will be able to push through a successful 4IR upgrade. This is perhaps why most Taiwanese organisations remain largely inactive at the moment when it comes to 4IR technologies and smart technology upgrades.

Conclusion

After considering the cases of 4IR technology upgrades across the manufacturing, services and healthcare industries, it appears that some large Taiwanese firms seem capable and ready to install robots, smart hardware and equipment. Large manufacturers are perhaps more likely to adjust their business models and management systems to support radical technology upgrades when compared with the service sector, where concerns over customers' responses, feasibility or profitability, may deter firms from making changes. This may be one of the reasons why these sectors have so far been less successful in terms of their transitions. Once again, this reflects Cheng's (2017) argument that the majority of Taiwanese firms are not suitable for 4IR technological implementation because they do not have the right business models to support the digitalisation. Merely installing the latest technology is unlikely to work effectively without changing mindsets and the traditional way of doing things to support them. Yet, as cultural values of thrift, uncertainty avoidance, and conservatism continue to shape management practices in Taiwan and obstruct progress towards the 4IR, it seems unlikely that the country as a whole will be able to turnaround quickly to adopt widespread smart upgrades and digitalisation.

Moreover, although embracing 4IR technologies and robotics may help to boost productivity, enhance product quality and precision, improve work efficiency, and reduce workload and manpower; the implementation of smart technologies does not automatically lead to these benefits. It takes effort to bring about change, for consumers to become comfortable with their usage, and for efficiencies to become evident over time. Even with careful preparation and execution, managerial support and investment, attempts to incorporate 4IR technologies may still fail like the 7-Eleven's cashier-less X store. Hence, business owners and managers need to assess capital investments, tech competence, organisational strategies, management systems, and operational redesign thoroughly prior to commencement of adaption and adoption projects.

References

Business Today (2018). Car components produced in 90 seconds for Tesla – the new winner of smart production. *Business Today* (in Mandarin), 9 May. Available at: www.businesstoday. com.tw/article/category/80392/post/201805090028/, accessed 3 August 2019.

Chang, M-W. S., & Connell, J. (2018). Graduate work-readiness in Taiwan: Stakeholder perspectives and best practices. Chapter 11. In Dhakal, S., Prikshat, V., Nankervis, A., & Burgess, J. (eds.), *The Transition from Graduation to Work: Challenges and Strategies in the Twenty-First Century Asia Pacific and Beyond.* Singapore: Springer, pp. 179–202.

Cheng, I-H. (2019). 7-Eleven to discontinue cashier-less stores and refocus on smart vending machines, *Business Next* (in Mandarin). Available at: www.bnext.com.tw/article/52631/7-11-self-service-store, accessed 3 June 2019.

Cheng, T-Z. (2017). 32 management advice for entrepreneurs: Turnaround struggling firms. *Business Weekly* (in Mandarin), Taipei.

Deloitte (2016). *2016 Global Manufacturing Competitiveness Index.* Available at: https://www2. deloitte.com/content/dam/Deloitte/global/Documents/Manufacturing/gx-global-mfg-competitiveness-index-2016.pdf

Deloitte (2017). *Industry 4.0: The Birth of the Smart Factory.* Available at: https://www2.deloitte. com/content/dam/Deloitte/cy/Documents/innovation-and-entrepreneurship-%20cen tre/CY_IEC_Industry4.0_Noexp.pdf

Deloitte (2018). *Analyze Smart Manufacturing* (in Mandarin). Available at: https://www2. deloitte.com/content/dam/Deloitte/tw/Documents/manufacturing/tw-2018-smart-mfg-report-TC.pdf

Department of Statistics of Ministry of Economic Affairs (2019). *Key Economic Statistics* (in Mandarin). Available at: https://dmz26.moea.gov.tw/GMWeb/common/Common Query.aspx, accessed 8 September 2019.

Directorate General of Budget, Accounting and Statistics (DGBAS) (2019). *National Accounts*, 31 May. Available at: https://eng.stat.gov.tw/np.asp?ctNode=1539, accessed 7 September 2019.

Executive Yuan (2015). *Taiwan Productivity 4.0 Initiative* (in Mandarin). Available at: www. nchu.edu.tw/~class/bulletin/MOE/105_MoE_re_allr.pdf, accessed 30 September 2019.

Executive Yuan Digi Group (2019). *DIGI Policies.* Available at: www.digi.ey.gov.tw/Con tent_List.aspx?n=194E61A960269E4B, accessed 8 September 2019.

Fong, M. (2017). Graduates are job-hopping. *China Times* (in Mandarin). Available at: www. chinatimes.com/newspapers/20170823000049-260202?chdtv

Hau, K-F., & Soung, I-S. (2019). The first ever survey of 566 manufacturers: Who's the best industrial 4.0 role model? *CommonWealth Magazine* (in Mandarin), 665, 72–86.

Hwang, T-Z. (2019). Doctors are working 20 hours a day, liable for patients' death – can labor law revision really solve the problem of residential doctors' overworking? *Business Today* (in Mandarin), 27 March. Available at: www.businesstoday.com.tw/article/category/80392/post/201903270056

IMD (2012, 2019). *IMD World Competitiveness Ranking.* Available at: www.imd.org/wcc/world-competitiveness-center/, accessed 1 June 2019.

Jang, J-R. (2019). Manufacturing industry fallen 10.5%, the worst in 7 years. *Financial Times* (in Mandarin), 24 April. Available at: https://money.udn.com/money/story/5648/3773438

Kao, J-Y. (2019). No cashier-less stores, not attempted with cutting edge new technology, the futuristic continent stores projected by Family Mart. *Business Next* (in Mandarin). Available at: www.bnext.com.tw/article/52969/Family Mart-tech-strategy, accessed 3 June 2019.

Lin, B-C., & Wang, S-U. (2017). Tracking mosquito venues in Taiwan: Why Taiwan has become a kingdom of mosquito venues. *Business Today* (in Mandarin). Available at: www.businesstoday.com.tw/article/category/156651/post/201712270004, accessed 8 September 2019.

Lin, P-S. (2019). Can 7-11 create another revenue all-time high? *Global Views Monthly* (in Mandarin). Available at: www.gvm.com.tw/article.html?id=60137, accessed 1 June 2019.

Lou, S-W. (2019). Is green energy industry really a eco-friendly business? *The Storm Media* (in Mandarin). Available at: www.storm.mg/article/1103762, accessed 6 September 2019.

National Development Council (2015). *Industry Innovation Transformation Fund* (in Mandarin). Available at: www.ndc.gov.tw/cp.aspx?n=8FF439709596F872&s=7C0CA8982E163402&upn=CEC92759D6B06B2D, accessed 8 September 2019.

National Development Council (2018). *Taiwan's Population Projections 1960–2065* (in Mandarin). Available at: https://pop-proj.ndc.gov.tw/, accessed 8 September 2019.

National Development Council (2019). *Policies for Industry Innovation*. Available at: www.ndc.gov.tw/Content_List.aspx?n=9D024A4424DC36B9&upn=6E972F5C30BF198F, accessed 8 September 2019.

Roberts, E. (2014). Taiwan tops the expat health care charts. *The Telegraph*, 28 October. Available at: www.telegraph.co.uk/news/health/expat-health/11190870/Taiwan-tops-the-expat-health-care-charts.html, accessed 1 June 2019.

Teun, Mong-Sen (2016). Taiwan has the highest density of convenient stores – but at what cost? *CommonWealth Magazine* (in Mandarin). Available at: www.cw.com.tw/article/article.action?id=5077792, accessed 3 June 2019.

Wang, S-F. (2017). If the old bad habits are not dealt with, the foresight project will turn into building mosquito facilities again. *New Talk* (in Mandarin). Available at: https://newtalk.tw/news/view/2017-07-03/91020

Won, C-Z. (2019). IDC and Microsoft to investigate AI adaptation across Asia – the result of Taiwan: Only 30% Taiwanese firms embraced AI because conservatism is the greatest obstacle for AI adaptation. *iThome* (in Mandarin). Available at: www.ithome.com.tw/news/129871, accessed 6 September 2019.

Yeh, G-W. (2018). 7-Eleven reflected on its 6 months experiment on the cashier-less X store: We have ignored three important things. *Manager Today* (in Mandarin). Available at: www.managertoday.com.tw/articles/view/56420

6 China

Yi Liu, Zengke An and Haiyue Xiu

Introduction

The Chinese government has designed its own strategy to address the challenges of the Fourth Industrial Revolution (4IR) called "Made in China 2025" and released in May 2015 (Ling, 2017). However, due to its economic structure (by industry and across regions) and its relatively low independent innovation capability, China is still unable to take a leading role in confronting the 4IR. However, over the past 40 years, China has been developing rapidly and making progress in these endeavours. The process of technological development in China can be divided into three stages – the first, from 1978 to 1991; the second, from 1992 to 2001; and the third, from 2002 to the present. In order to adapt to these changes and gradually take the lead in the 4IR, China is taking proactive actions to improve the quality of economic development and advance domestic reforms.

This chapter focuses on these three development stages since 1978 in order to show the historical events China has experienced and to explain how they have influenced the Chinese labour market, and, thus, to indicate where China is currently in terms of its preparation and positioning for the 4IR. Following the historical outline, the findings from an empirical study are presented with subsequent discussion of their implications for China. Following the presentation of the research findings, suggestions are proposed to assist China towards building on its unique advantages in addressing the challenges posed by the 4IR.

First stage: 1978–1991

In December 1978, the 11th Communist Party of China (CPC) Central Committee Third Plenary Session was held in Beijing. The meeting made a decision to implement reform and implement an "opening-up" policy, which marked a historical turning point and the beginning of the modernisation of the Chinese society and economy. China's domestic reforms are geared towards comprehensive and integrated political, economic and social systems. After 1978, China began to transition into a market economy system, of which the main direction of the reform is the "planned commodity economy" based on the foundation of public ownership (Brødsgaard & Rutten, 2017).

To this end, China carried out price reforms in 1979, changing from a single national unified pricing system to a dual pricing system in which national unified pricing and market regulation prices coexisted. This reform promoted the transformation of the price formation mechanism and accelerated the formation of the market economy. It also paved the way for the introduction of foreign investment and the development of new domestic enterprises. The other development was to promote the institutionalisation, legalisation and democratisation of politics (Yao, 2018; Zheng, 2009), building a modern state that is more aligned with economic and social progress goals.

China's "opening-up" policy successfully attracted foreign investment, and from the mid-1980s until the 1990s, this was a period of full development of foreign direct investment (FDI) and China's foreign investment projects developed rapidly (Fetscherin et al., 2010; Ye, 2009). Together with foreign investment there was a national program of industry and infrastructure development. Following these reforms China began to introduce Western advanced production technologies and imported technology and equipment to boost national productive capability. Such actions were intended to narrow the technological gap between China and the rest of the world.

China's independent innovation capability was limited during this period. In April 1985, the Patent Law of the People's Republic of China decreed the protection and encouragement of inventions and creations. In 1988 the government proposed that "science and technology are the primary productive forces" and the reform of the science and technology system began (Li et al., 2018; Tse, 2018). Opening up the technology market saw scientific and technological work supported by marketisation (Fan et al., 2013). However, from 1978 to 1991, the state-owned science and technology units were still the main drivers of technological innovation, and new enterprises and other social organisations failed to occupy a place in the national technological innovation landscape (Kou, 2008; Fang & Liu, 2004).

The major changes in the labour market were associated with large scale migration from rural areas to the emerging coastal cities that required labour in the emerging manufacturing industries driven by foreign investment and the global demand for goods (Yuan & He, 2012).

Second stage: 1992–2001

During this second stage, China's opening up to the outside world steadily advanced, and matching domestic reforms became the top policy priority. Following the policy and economic preparations in the 1980s, in 1992 the 14th National Congress of the Communist Party of China, formally proposed the reform goal of establishing a socialist market economic system, and the socialist market economy construction was officially launched. Enterprises were expected to become financially independent and market oriented in order to improve their competitiveness to proactively meet the requirements of the market and global economy (Zhou & Tao, 2018). During this period the proportion of the working population increased significantly, and the social dependency ratio showed a significant downward trend. Throughout the 1990s, China experienced a population dividend (Xie, 2017), with abundant labour resources and relatively low labour costs, which provided human resources support for the economic development, especially in coastal cities. Supportive education reforms (Zhou et al., 2017), including the nine-year compulsory education system which was introduced in 1986, began to show their effectiveness during this period, and the basic quality of workers in terms of education levels increased (OECD, 2016). The improvement in the quality of education in the 1990s provided a rich talent pool for the country's future technological innovation and economic development.

By accelerating the introduction of international advanced technology, China's independent innovation capability gradually improved during this period. In 1995, the strategy of rejuvenating the country through science and education was formally proposed (Wang, 2017). Chinese macroeconomic policies strongly supported independent innovation activities, and research and experimental development expenditures accounted for an increasing proportion of gross domestic product (GDP) research and experimental development funding intensity. The research and development (R&D) expenditure in 2001 nearly tripled that of 1995, the average R&D investment growth rate exceeded 20%, and the R&D expenditure intensity nearly doubled in seven years (Hu & Jefferson, 2009).

With the establishment of the market economic system, China's domestic technology market began to form (Hu, 2013). At this stage, enterprises began to actively participate in the process of technological innovation and used their technological advantages to occupy a more favourable market position. In 1995, the Internet era began in China (Yang, 2003), and in 1991 China's three major World Wide Web portals (Netease, Sohu, and Sina.com) were established and dominated the portal market. In 2000, the three major portal companies were listed on NASDAQ in the US and China ushered in the Internet era (Zhang et al., 2017). Between 1998 and 2000, companies that led the technological and economic changes in the Internet age, represented by Tencent, Alibaba and Baidu, were established (Jiang, 2012).

The changes that took place in Chinese society in the 1990s had a huge impact on the labour market. First of all, it was characterised by large-scale labour mobility. Economic development, especially in the south-eastern coastal areas, increased the demand for labour in these coastal areas (Fan et al., 2013). The surplus rural labour in neighbouring areas and central and western China continuously compensated for the shortages in the urban labour market, leading to the formation of a "migrant workers' tide" in the south-eastern coastal areas (Ning & Ye, 2016). This workforce migration increased the economic gap between the coastal areas and the central and western regions. Secondly, the reform of the economic system brought changes in the supply of labour and the structure of labour demand. The reform of state-owned enterprises caused large-scale redundancies for former state employees (Chen & Tang, 2016). Except for workers who chose to start a business, most joined the labour exodus to the emerging coastal cities with their high labour demand (Peng & Tu, 2017). Furthermore, as many of the laid-off state-owned workers were over 40 years of age with low education and limited skills, a large proportion of them had no choice but to enter labour-intensive industries. However, with the transformation of the economy and the adjustment of the industrial structure, the emergence of new industries such as sunrise and high-tech industries increased demand for high-quality labour, together with technical, management, and knowledge-based talent (Qiu, 2011). As more Chinese organisations developed global operations, there was increasing demand for technical and international skills to support the competitiveness of these multinational enterprises.

Third stage: 2002 to the present

From the beginning of the 21st century the process of institutionalisation and legalisation of Chinese politics has been accelerating (Garnaut et al., 2018), and "ruling the country according to law" has become an important political concept of the Chinese government. The reform of the political system has actively promoted the decentralisation of power. At the same time, China officially joined the World Trade Organisation in 2001, marking the new stage of closer linkages to the rest of the world. There have been significant increases in foreign investment and in technology imports and increased international trade and growth in a number of multinational Chinese enterprises (Xie, 2017; Zhang et al., 2016). From product exports to greenfield investments, Chinese enterprises actively participated in the global market and continuously improved their international competitiveness. Domestically, the economic reforms are also advancing. For example, the state-owned enterprises have accelerated the adjustment of their operational and product structures through the process of restructuring, joint venturing and mergers to improve market competitiveness (Chen & Tang, 2016).

In 2015, China began supply-side structural reforms to balance market demand and promote the upgrading of industrial structure (Zhang, 2017). In the same year, the proposal of the "One Belt, One Road", the modern Silk Road linking China to the rest of Asia initiative was a significant boost for China's industrial restructuring and global exposure, and it also brought new development opportunities for the central and western regions. With the popularity and broad development of the Internet, new processes of business and communication emerged including the platform, shared and social economies; blockchain technology and new media operations linked to the developments of the web (Wang & Tian, 2017).

The development of the market economy has led to the transformation of the national science and technology innovation system. Before the establishment of the market economic system, China's technological innovation was almost entirely dominated by the government, relying on state funding. The mainstays were the state-owned science and technology units which restricted national innovative ability (Hu, 2013). However, enterprises from the private sectors have gradually become the backbone of technological innovation. From 2002 to 2016, the proportion of R&D expenditures of enterprises to the total R&D expenditures increased, while the proportion of the government's R&D expenditures has shown a downward trend (Showstack, 2018), and China's technology introduction capability has been greatly improved (Hu, 2013). From 2004 to 2016, the number of patents of industrial enterprises in China increased by more than 24 times. By 2016, more than 760,000 patents had been developed across industry (National Bureau of Statistics of China, 2017).

The development of the Internet and AI technology and the displacement of labour through industrial and sectoral adjustment have resulted in significant unemployment levels for low skilled workers (Vermeulen et al., 2018). However, at the same time as the tertiary sector has expanded, surplus labour from the primary and secondary industries has moved into the tertiary sector (Xie, 2017).

The next section of the chapter explores the responses from Chinese managers' concerning the perceived impact of the 4IR within the context of the economic and labour market developmental stages outlined previously.

Chinese managers' perceptions of the 4IR

Methodology

Subjects and site

Research respondents included business owners, senior and middle managers as well as the general staff of organisations in China. The survey scope and respondent positioning provide a comprehensive perspective on the impact of the 4IR on future workplaces and workforces. In order to incorporate a wide range of geographical and industrial factors, questionnaires were distributed across all regions in mainland China. Given that "conducting empirical research in China is uniquely challenging, due to China's size, culture, and recent economic and social history" (Peng et al., 2010: 161), a snowball sampling method through the use of interpersonal relationships was employed (Liu et al., 2019). The survey generated responses from more than 20 industries, including the financial and insurance services, manufacturing, professional, and scientific and technical services. A total of 204 respondents participated in an online survey, and after screening the responses, there were 164 useable questionnaires.

Research design

The research was conducted in three phases. First, a comprehensive examination of the existing local literature regarding the 4IR and its potential impacts on the workforce in China was conducted. Specifically, a review of the stages of economic development in relation to China's economic and technological development (as previously) was undertaken which facilitated the design of a questionnaire in English to obtain relevant data. Second, in order to validate the translation of the survey instrument from English to Mandarin a "back-translation" procedure was employed by the research team. Prior to administering the Mandarin version of the survey in China, a pilot study was conducted to ensure the representativeness and suitability of the questionnaire. In the third phase, a modified questionnaire was used, and the survey data were collected through an online survey platform called Sojump. A letter that introduced the researchers, clarified the study purposes and emphasised voluntary participation, was provided at the beginning of the online survey. Eligible respondents were invited by the researchers to participate in the study. A snowball sampling method, through personal social networks and offline interpersonal networks was used in this process to increase the response rate. Participants were asked to complete the online survey either via the Internet or using their smartphones.

Research findings

Sample demographics

Amongst the 164 valid respondents, the proportion of males and females was approximately equal with 48.2% males and 50% females. Another 1.8% of respondents chose not to provide their gender. More than half the respondents were aged between 18 and 35 years, and 81.1% had a bachelor's degree or above. Younger, educated respondents, who have access to and use digital technologies, might be expected to have a more comprehensive and accurate understanding of 4IR technologies. The distribution between management and non-managerial staff was as follows: 56.7% being managers across all levels (supervisors, managers, senior managers and CEOs) and 43.3% being non managerial staff. The sample covered a range of organisational types including government, business enterprises, private-domestic/national organisations, private-subsidiaries of multi-national corporations (MNCs) and state-owned enterprises. Private enterprises accounted for 76.2% of the sample, which is representative of the composition of enterprise types in China.

Alignment of corporate and IT strategies

Table 6.1 indicates that the strategic intention of implementing new technologies is positively related to ease of use, innovation and customer satisfaction as well as improving management control; while strategic intention appears to have little or no impact on usefulness and task accomplishment. Chinese organisations can establish a competitive advantage through the combination of information technology (IT) and corporate strategic needs. You and Liu

Table 6.1 Managers Strategic Intentions/Alignment

Statements	Strongly disagree	Disagree	Undecided	Agree	Strongly agree	Mean	SD
Our IT strategies support match our business strategies	7	17	74	62	4	3.24	.835
We adapt and align our IT strategy to business strategic change	7	13	59	79	6	3.39	.855
We adapt our IT goals and objectives to our business goals and objectives	6	25	60	70	3	3.24	.864
Our IT strategies and business strategies correspond to each other	6	10	67	76	5	3.39	.803

(2008) suggest that the combination of IT strategies and corporate strategies can further improve the efficiency of information systems. Indeed, effective IT strategies can promote application systems to support the development strategies of enterprises (Yu et al., 2015). Melville et al. (2004) argued that integration of enterprise and IT strategies is a regulating variable of IT and corporate performance. Henderson and Venkatraman (1993) examined the relationship between enterprise/IT strategies integration and corporate performance and drew similar conclusions.

Top management support

According to the respondents, management support is positively connected to the usefulness, ease of use, innovation and improvement in management control but not to task accomplishment or customer satisfaction. Table 6.2 indicates that managers are aware of the support of top management for AI and digital applications; however, this is tempered by the large number of undecided responses.

Usefulness and ease of use of 4IR technologies

In terms of the usefulness and ease of use of 4IR technologies more than 75% of respondents agreed or strongly agreed that they would enable employees to accomplish tasks more quickly, improve employee performance and make it easier for employees to do their jobs. In terms of the ease of use, while over half of the respondents either agreed or strongly agreed, about a third of respondents were undecided whether the technologies would be easy to use, clear and understandable and flexible to interact with.

Table 6.2 Top Management Support

Statements	Strongly disagree	Disagree	Undecided	Agree	Strongly agree	Mean	SD
Top management enthusiastically supports the adoption of AI/Software/ Applications in different departments	9	11	82	56	6	3.24	.850
Top management has allocated adequate resources for the adoption of AI/ Software/Applications in different departments	8	13	74	61	8	3.29	.872
Top management is aware of the benefits of implementing AI/Software/ Applications in different departments	7	9	67	71	10	3.41	.857
Top management actively encourages employees to use AI/Software/ Applications in their daily tasks	6	9	81	54	14	3.37	.859

Organisational and employee performance

In terms of organisational and employee performance there was a positive endorsement that the new technologies would improve employee and organisational performance, enhance innovation, improve customer satisfaction, increase profitability and enhance managerial control within the organisation. Management was viewed as supportive the new technology developments. There was also support for the propositions that the new technology will improve the job satisfaction of employees. However, the views were not all positive and optimistic. There was a correspondingly strong perception that the new technology would increase job insecurity and lead to redundancies (see table 6.3).

In terms of the future skill needs associated with the new technology there was strong support for the propositions that highlighted key skill needs for current and future employees (see tables 6.4 and 6.5). Skills linked to data analytics, data security and collaboration were rated as being the most important immediate skills needs, while for future employees, communications, ethics,

Table 6.3 Employees' Job Security

Statements	Strongly disagree	Disagree	Undecided	Agree	Strongly agree	Mean	SD
Employees are very confident that they will be able to keep their jobs despite the implementation of AI/Software/ Applications	11	81	55	13	4	2.50	.833
Employees think that they will be able to continue working in the organisation despite increases in the use of AI/Software/ Applications	11	77	60	13	3	2.51	.810
Employees fear that they might be made redundant due to increases in the use of AI/Software/ Applications	4	28	57	68	7	3.28	.883
Employees worry about the continuation of their careers due to increases in the use of AI/software/ Applications	2	24	51	79	8	3.41	.842

Table 6.4 Organisational Skill Needs – Current and for Next 5 Years

Statements	Very low	Low	Moderate	High	Very high	Mean	SD
IT infrastructure	3	4	51	67	39	3.82	.886
Automation technology	3	4	47	71	39	3.85	.876
Data analytics	4	7	34	72	47	3.92	.940
Data security/ Communications security	5	5	32	68	54	3.98	.962
Development of application of assistance systems	8	5	51	64	36	3.70	1.004
Collaboration software	4	3	46	69	42	3.87	.903
Non-technical skills such as systems thinking and process understanding	6	3	59	59	37	3.72	.956

Table 6.5 Proposed Organisational Skill Needs by 2025

Statements	Very low	Low	Moderate	High	Very high	Mean	SD
Communication	1	3	23	78	59	4.16	.778
IT knowledge	1	4	46	66	47	3.94	.849
Team work	2	2	19	83	58	4.18	.775
Critical thinking/ Problem	1	7	34	72	50	3.99	.862
Ethics/Morality	1	4	21	73	65	4.20	.800
Positive attitude to ongoing learning of new skills	1	1	24	78	60	4.19	.748
Other: Please specify	3	1	39	54	41	4.26	1.118

Table 6.6 AI/Robotics Technologies – The Impact on Different Organisational Functions

Statements	Very low	Low	Moderate	High	Very high	Mean	SD
Manufacturing production and operations (Product design or engineering)	3	6	36	76	43	3.91	.889
Research and development	3	4	43	71	43	3.90	.884
Purchasing	5	5	55	64	35	3.73	.936
Information technology/Data security/Communications security	3	5	30	76	50	4.01	.883
Marketing, sales, distribution and customer support	3	4	49	71	37	3.82	.872
Human resource management	4	5	51	69	35	3.77	.904
Accounting and finance	2	6	42	71	43	3.90	.877
Transport and logistics	3	4	36	70	51	3.99	.893
General administration	3	5	56	61	39	3.78	.907
Other: Please specify	5	3	48	55	30	4.04	1.179

teamwork and learning were all rated as key attributes which are presumably intended to include the skills included under current needs.

In terms of the sections of organisations that are most likely to be affected by AI and robotics, table 6.6 presents the responses. The sections that are considered to be most likely to be high or very high impact areas include manufacturing, R&D, IT, accounting and logistics. Nearly two thirds of the respondents indicated that there would be moderate to very high resistance to the changes. The sections identified as having the highest levels of resistance included manufacturing, purchasing, marketing, accounting and human resource management.

The reasons for the resistance were not identified (possibilities include job loss, increased job insecurity, additional training).

Applying multivariate analysis to the survey results reveals that the usefulness and ease of use of 4IR technologies will not significantly predict the organisation's demand for employees' relevant skill levels in the next five years. The usefulness and ease of use of these technologies can only partly explain why companies employ them and has little to do with the organisation's future skill needs. Similarly, the effect of using such technologies on accomplishing tasks and ensuring customer satisfaction in the workplace is not significantly related to the skills of the employees which the organisation needs to recruit in the next five years. The use of 4IR technologies is predicted to have a positive effect on the innovation and management control of the enterprise, which in turn will have a significant impact on the skills of the employees which the organisation needs to recruit in the next five years.

Innovation and improving management control are both comprehensive and long-term processes, which include multiple contents such as talent training. Hence, there is no surprise that these two factors can directly influence how organisations judge and select employees. It can also explain why innovation can significantly impact the type of skills the organisation needs when recruiting new staff while usefulness, ease of use, accomplishing tasks, and customer satisfaction have no influence. The impact of these new technologies on improving management control is mainly reflected in assisting the management control of workflows, management process and performance, but has little effect on their communication skills when recruiting new employees.

In the era of the 4IR, organisations will need to pay more attention to the creative thinking and experimental abilities, data analysis and interpretation, and the strategic development capabilities of managers.

Implications for government, industry and the education sector

In this chapter, we examined the possible effects of the 4IR on a range of workforces in the Chinese context. Specifically, we explored the path of technology development that was embedded in the economic and social development and designed a survey to gain further insights accordingly. We found that China's economy and society have achieved significant growth and development levels since the 1970s. Although China will adapt to and actively participate in the 4IR, there are still some areas of concern. For example, the regional imbalance of the economic structure (China Daily, 2016) and talent structure remain unsolved, which holds back economic sustainability and social development. Second, there has been a lack of investment and outputs in basic research leading to the limitation of independent innovation. Indeed, most of the scientific and technological achievements are concentrated in the field of applied technology (Chen, 2017), lacking basic and core creative capabilities. With the advent of the 4IR, a large number of traditional jobs are facing unemployment risks, but employees are unaware of the relationship between job loss and the implementation of new technologies. Meanwhile, the existing labour market is unable to meet the demand required by the emerging industries (Manyika et al., 2017; Rotman, 2013).

In order to minimise the gap with developed countries and gradually play the role of leader in adaptation to the 4IR, China has taken proactive measures to solve existing social problems and enhance its economic strength. First, between 2000–2010, in order to balance the development gap between coastal areas and the central and western regions, the Chinese government proposed a "Western Development" strategy aimed at attracting capital, technology and talents to the western region (Wang & Tian, 2017). The construction of the western region was mainly focused on the improvement of infrastructure and the cultivation of featured industries (SIC, 2005; Ye, 2006). At the same time, it actively introduced high-quality talents and created a favourable economic development environment (Lu & Deng, 2013). After 2010, the "Western Development" strategy was accelerated, and the industrialisation and marketisation of the western economy was enhanced. The introduction of the "One Belt, One Road" initiative in 2015 provided assistance for the economic development of the western region, and it became China's, Asia's and Europe's important land ports (Ghiasy & Zhou, 2017; Lokhande, 2017). A large number of international cooperation projects were undertaken in the western part of China, followed by the government and enterprises with strong capital and technology investments, and the western region experienced unprecedented development opportunities

Second, the Chinese government continues to increase its support for technological innovation. In 2006, the government formulated the National Medium- and Long-Term Science and Technology Development Program (2006–2020), proposing that China should continuously enhance its original innovation and integrated innovation capabilities (Zhang et al., 2016). The nation will develop its ability to innovate and create innovative national goals by 2020 and realise the transformation from "the world's largest technology country" to "the world's science and technology power". At the end of 2012, the 18th National Congress of the Communist Party of China further proposed the "Innovation-Driven Development Strategy" (Zhang & Qin, 2015), placing the innovation-driven economic structural adjustment and upgrading at the core of national development. In 2016, the government released "Made in China 2025", reaffirming the "innovation-driven" policy and creating its own 4IR path towards technological innovation (Sui et al., 2015). In addition to such policies, the government's financial support for technological innovation activities remained firm. From 2001 to 2016, national R&D expenditures continued to expand and there was an increase from 0.94% to 2.11%, marking China as an important power in global R&D (OECD, 2017).

In addition, it is necessary for China to actively promote education reform to match the new labour demand brought about by the 4IR. On the one hand, emerging occupations require higher education and vocational education systems to respond to the needs in a timely manner and to fill the gap in labour supply. At the same time, due to technological upgrading, unemployed labour requires professional vocational training to adapt to new labour market needs, and, thus achieve re-employment. From the perspective of the labour market, the essence of the 4IR is to empower people who will not be replaced by machines (Keywell, 2017). Indeed, assistance provided by the technological advancements gives people the opportunity to liberate themselves from manual or mechanical work in order to discover their potential and obtain more high-level career choices. China's education reform should focus on cultivating high-quality talent with high skills levels, global thinking and innovation abilities in order to support the transformation of the industrial structure and the progress of industry 4.0 (Anderson, 2012; Marsh, 2013; Rifkin, 2011).

Conclusion

Since the reforms discussed earlier in the chapter, the development of Chinese society can be roughly divided into three stages, facing different political, economic, social and technological environments. The political environment has remained relatively stable for economic development during these stages. The improvement of the living standards together with the advancement of technological innovation capability has led to China's economic and social changes. The Chinese government has always firmly grasped the development opportunities brought by the 4IR and insisted on seeking higher quality economic development. This phenomenon is mainly reflected in China's active adjustment of development modes, the cultivation of technological innovation capabilities and the emphasis on high-quality talents.

References

Anderson, C. (2012). *Makers: The New Industrial Revolution*. New York: Random House.

Brødsgaard, K. E., & Rutten, K. (2017). *From Accelerated Accumulation to the Socialist Market Economy in China: Economic Discourse and Development from 1953 to the Present*. Brill China Studies, No. 38. Leiden: Brill.

Chen, N. (2017). *China Concentrates on Sci-Tech Innovation*. Available at: http://english.cas.cn/newsroom/news/201709/t20170921_183341.shtml, accessed 6 March 2018.

Chen, Y., & Tang, Z. H. (2016). Discussion on mode features of China's economic growth and macro-economic management since the reform and opening – also study on the meaning of supply-side structure reform. *Economist*, 10, 5–12.

China Daily (2016). *China Five-Year Plan Brings Hope to China's West*. Available at: www.chinadaily.com.cn/business/2016-12/27/content_27786244.htm, accessed 12 May 2018.

Fan, B. N., Duan, Z. X., & Jiang, L. (2013). On independent innovation policy's evolution, effects and optimization in China. *Forum on Science and Technology in China*, 1 (9), 5–12.

Fang, C., & Liu, S. (2004). Retrospect and prospect of China's science and technology system reform. *Qiushi*, 5, 43–45.

Fetscherin, M., Voss, H., & Gugler, P. (2010). 30 years of foreign direct investment in China: An interdisciplinary literature review. *International Business Review*, 19 (3), 235–246.

Garnaut, R., Song, L., & Fang, C. (2018). *China's 40 Years of Reform and Development 1978–2018*. Australia: Australian National University Press.

Ghiasy, R., & Zhou, J. Y. (2017). *The Silk Road Economic Belt: Considering Security Implications and EU-China Cooperation Projects*. Sweden: Stockholm International Peace Research Institute.

Henderson, J. C., & Venkatraman, H. (1993). Strategic alignment: Leveraging information technology for transforming organizations. *IBM Systems Journal*, 32 (1), 472–484.

Hu, A. G. Z. (2013). China's featured independent innovation (1949–2012). *Bulletin of Chinese Academy of Sciences*, 2, 8–13.

Hu, A. G. Z., & Jefferson, G. H. (2009). A great wall of patents: What is behind China's recent patent explosion? *Journal of Development Economics*, 90 (1), 57–68.

Jiang, M. (2012). *Internet Companies in China: Dancing Between the Party Line and the Bottom Line*. Pairs, France: The Centre for Asian Studies, IFRI (Institut Français des Relations Internationales).

Keywell, B. (2017). *The Fourth Industrial Revolution Is About Empowering People, Not the Rise of the Machines*. World Economic Forum, 14 June. Available at: https://www.weforum.org/agenda/2017/06/ the-fourth-industrial-revolution-is-about-people-not-justmachines/

Kou, Z. L. (2008). Thirty years of China's scientific and technological system reform. *World Economic Papers*, 1, 77–92.

Li, J., Li, M. Y., Dang, A., & Song, Z. W. (2018). The spatial and temporal evolution of innovative function of science and technology of Beijing based on the analysis of enterprise data. In Shen, Z., & Li, M. (eds.), *Big Data Support of Urban Planning and Management*. Advances in Geographic Information Science. Cham: Springer, pp. 193–217.

Ling, L. (2017). *China's Manufacturing Locus in 2025: With a Comparison of "Made-in-China 2025" and "Industry 4.0"*. Technological Forecasting and Social Change, in press. Available at: www.sciencedirect.com/science/article/pii/S0040162517307254

Liu, Y., Chan, C., Zhao, C. H., & Liu, C. (2019). Unpacking knowledge management practices in China: Do institution, national and organizational culture matter? *Journal of Knowledge Management*, 23 (4), 619–643, doi:10.1108/JKM-07-2017-0260

Lokhande, S. A. (2017). *China's One Belt One Road Initiative and the Gulf Pearl Chain*. Available at: www.chinadaily.com.cn/opinion/2017beltandroad/2017-06/05/content_29618549.htm, accessed 7 June 2018.

Lu, Z., & Deng, X. (2013). Regional policy and regional development: A case study of China's Western development strategy. *Annales Universitatis Apulensis Series Oeconomica*, 15 (1), 250–264.

Manyika, J., Lund, S., Chui, M., Bughin, J., Woetzel, J., Batra, P., Ko, R., & Sanghvi, S. (2017). *Jobs Lost, Job Gained: Workforce Transitions in a Time of Automation*. London: McKinsey & Company: McKinsey Global Institute.

Marsh, P. (2013). *The New Industrial Revolution: Consumers, Globalization and the End of Mass Production*. New Haven: Yale University Press.

Melville, N., Kraemer, K., & Gurbaxani, V. (2004). Review: Information technology and organizational performance: An integrative model of IT business value. *MIS Quarterly*, 28 (2), 283–322.

National Bureau of Statistics of China (2017). *China Statistical Yearbook 2017*. Beijing: China Statistical Publishing House.

Ning, X., & Ye, J. Z. (2016). Peasant-worker transformation since the reform and opening: A review of domestic research. *China Review of Political Economy*, 7 (1), 43–62.

Organization for Economic Co-operation and Development (OECD) (2016). *Education in China: A Snapshot,* Paris, France: OECD Publishing. Available at: www.oecd.org/china/Education-in-China-a-snapshot.pdf, accessed 22 May 2018.

Organization for Economic Co-operation and Development (OECD) (2017). *OECD Economic Surveys: China 2017.* Paris, France: OECD Publishing. Available at: https://doi.org/10.1787/eco_surveys-chn-2017-en, accessed 6 April 2018.

Peng, J., Moffett, S., & McAdam, R. (2010). Knowledge management in China: A review. *Journal of Technology Management in China,* 5 (2), 158–175.

Peng, S., & Tu, Z. (2017). China's market-oriented reform and employment changes in industrial enterprises: 1998–2008. *Inquiry into Economic Issues,* 4, 26–38.

Qiu, X. Y. (2011). *Information Technology Fusion and Its Empirical Research on Organizational Performance.* China: Jilin University.

Rifkin, J. (2011). *The Third Industrial Revolution. How Lateral Power is Transforming Energy, the Economy, and the World.* New York: Palgrave Macmillan.

Rotman, D. (2013). How technology is destroying jobs. *MIT Technology Review.* Available at: www.technologyreview.com/s/515926/how-technology-is-destroying-jobs/, accessed 6 March 2018.

Showstack, R. (2018). *China Catching Up to United States in Research and Development.* Available at: https://eos.org/articles/china-catching-up-to-united-states-in-research-and-development, accessed 9 April 2018.

SIC (China State Information Center). (2005). *Extraordinary Five Years: The Five – Years Progress of Western Development Strategy.* Special Report of Five – years Western Development. Available at: www.chinawest.gov.cn/, accessed 17 March 2018.

Sui, J., Bi, X. K., Yang, C. J., & Liu, G. (2015). Research on the impact mechanism of MNCs' technology transfer on green innovation performance of green innovation system in China's manufacturing. *China Soft Science,* 1, 118–129.

Tse, E. (2018). *R&D Driving China's Innovation Speed.* Available at: http://africa.chinadaily.com.cn/weekly/2018-02/16/content_35707128.htm?from=groupmessage&isappinstalled=0, accessed 11 July 2018.

Vermeulen, B., Kesselhut, J., Pyka, A., & Saviotti, P. P. (2018). The impact of automation on employment: Just the usual structural change. *Sustainability,* 10, 1161–1188.

Wang, S. (2017). Science, technology, and mathematics education. In Morgan, W. J., Gu, Q., & Li, F. L. (eds.), *Handbook of Education in China.* Cheltenham: Edward Elgar Publishing Limited, pp. 391–416.

Wang, X. J., & Tian, X. (2017). Shifting toward the West? An analysis of sectoral employment growth across China's countries, 2000–2010. *Journal of Emerging Markets Finance and Trade,* 53 (9), 2082–2103.

Xie, X. N. (2017). The historical significance and enlightenment of restoring the college entrance examination system. *New Horizons from Tian Fu,* 5, 5–8.

Yang, G. B. (2003). The co-evolution of the internet and civil society in China. *Asian Survey,* 43 (3), 405–422.

Yao, J. W. (2018). The conflict and integration of China's political system reform and western political system model – based on the perspective of the complexity of modern democratic system. *Jianghai Academic Journal,* 1, 132–137.

Ye, M. (2009). Policy learning or diffusion: How China opened to foreign direct investment. *Journal of East Asian Studies,* 9 (3), 399–432.

Ye, X. (2006). China Increases western development investment. *People's Daily Overseas Edition,* 4, 6 September.

You, J., & Liu, W. (2008). IT strategies planning process combining strategic matching with IT application analysis. *Technological Progress and Countermeasures*, 25 (6), 44–47.

Yu, D. H., Huang, L. H., & Shi, G. H. (2015). Research on the path and method of establishing IT strategy adapted to enterprise strategy-a case study of strategic matching between UPS and FedEx. *Journal of Industrial Engineering and Engineering Management*, 19 (1), 24–29.

Yuan, Y. M., & He, L. (2012). Investing in foreign capital in special economic zones, industrial transformation and employment of poor labourers: Taking Shenzhen as an example. *Studies on China's Special Economic Zones*, 70–86, 228–249.

Zhang, G., Jiang, W., Wang, Y., & Liu, S. (2017). *Research on Multifunctional Integrated Internet Platforms*. Proceedings of the 17th International Conference on Electronic Business, 4–8 December, ICEB, Dubai, UAE, pp. 215–221.

Zhang, H. (2017). *Supply-Side Structural Reform: New Practice Under the "New Normal"*. Available at: www.chinatoday.com.cn/english/spc/2017-07/31/content_747684.htm, accessed 8 March 2018.

Zhang, L. Z., & Qin, Z. L. (2015). Innovation-driven development strategy since the eighteenth national congress of CPC: A literature review. *Journal of Sichuan University of Science & Engineering (Social Sciences Edition)*, 30 (4), 83–90.

Zhang, Y., Kang, J., & Jin, H. (2016). A review of green building development in China from the perspective of energy saving. *Energies*, 11 (2), 334, doi:10.3390/en11020334

Zheng, H. S. (2009). Thirty years of reform and opening up: Theory of social development and theory of social transformation. *Social Sciences in China*, 2, 10–19.

Zhou, K., Liu, T., & Zhou, L. (2017). *Industry 4.0: Towards Future Industrial Opportunities and Challenges*. 12th International Conference on Fuzzy Systems and Knowledge Discovery, pp. 2147–2152.

Zhou, M., & Tao, R. (2018). State-owned enterprises reform in China: Experience, problems and solutions. *Economic Theory and Business Management*, 37 (1), 87–97.

7   India

Sanjeev Kumar, Verma Prikshat and J. Irudhaya Rajesh

Introduction

The Indian economy can be characterised as fast-growing, reflecting its young workforce, infrastructure and the development of the construction sector. The speed of adoption of emerging technologies by diverse industries has been observed as one of the key determinants of the Fourth Industrial Revolution (4IR) and the Future of Work (FoW) in the Indian economy. The resultant automation has the potential to transform highly disorganised sectors such as transportation, maintenance, food catering and software development services into organised ones (FICCI et al., 2017). That said, government spending to date indicates there will be relatively modest potential for automation over the next 15 years (McKinsey, 2017).

The Indian service sector in particular has experienced remarkable growth, playing a critical role in enabling the country to become one of the fastest-growing economies in the world. The service sector accounted for 55.2% of the country's Gross Value Added (GVA) rate of $2.038 billion. In 2017–18 it was up 40% from that of 1980, exceeding the shares of both the agricultural and manufacturing sectors (Economic Survey, 2016–17). It is also the second highest employer, at around 31% (after agriculture) which employed 47% of the population between 2016–2017 (GOI, 2018). India's service sector can be categorised into three groups. The first group consists of education, health and defence; the second includes trade, transport and hotels; and the third comprises business services, including banking and insurance, information technology (IT) services, such as software and communication, and legal services. The third group in particular has demonstrated rapid growth emphasised by the service requirements of high technology-oriented manufacturing firms (Balasubramanyam & Virmani, 2018).

India's service sector comprises both large organisations (airlines, telecoms, IT companies, banks and insurance companies) and an estimated 10–50 million micro-small-medium enterprises (MSMEs). These MSMEs include accountants, caterers, car cleaners, yoga instructors, flooring contractors, roof leak repairers, interior decorators, movers and packers among others (GOI, 2007). Given that MSMEs face various problems such as lack of capital, unsustainable businesses and excessive regulations in relation to start-ups, the running and closure of businesses (Economic Times, 2018), any discussion concerning the adoption of convergent technologies as part of the 4IR is inherently problematic. However, given the scale of MSMEs and the 'teething problems' they face, a recent survey covering 2250 MSMEs across different industries in 34 cities in India found an encouraging trend towards technology adoption. The results of the study indicated that 35% of MSMEs have already adopted business management software; and of these, more than 40% already use digital banking and payment services, with another 40% likely to adopt them soon (Goenka, 2019).

In such a context, there is a strong rationale for exploring the level of adoption of the latest 4IR technologies in the Indian service sector, as well as identifying how technology adoption may impact organisations and their organisational performance. While there is an abundance of literature on the adoption of technology relating to the various services provided by the service sector in India, there is a paucity of empirical studies which have investigated the perceived impact of new technologies on work and the resultant organisational performance. This study seeks to fill this void by investigating the perceptions of Indian managers on the impact of convergent technologies on work and organisational performance in the Indian service sector.

The chapter begins by reviewing literature on the potential adoption of 4IR technologies in the service sector in India, followed by discussion of the potential impacts of adoption and applications of these technologies. The next section provides a brief snapshot of the proposed conceptual framework (see Chapter 2), followed by the research design adopted and an analysis of the results. Finally, the findings arising from this research, the implications and recommendations are outlined.

Technology adoption in the Indian service sector

It has been observed that in OECD countries service sectors are typically the most intensive users of information technology (Pilat & Devlin, 2004). This predominance has been attributed to the fact that they are information-intensive in nature and require well-developed IT systems to enable improved service performance (Uwizeyemungu & Raymond, 2011). India is on the verge of the rapid diffusion and adoption of the latest technologies – such as mobile internet (with a potential reach of 700 million to 900 million Indians by 2025), cloud-based services, the automation of knowledge work, digital payments, and verifiable digital identity, that can transform the Indian services sector (McKinsey, 2014). As a key example, the Indian government's 'JAM trinity' strategy:

. **Jan Dhan Yojana** – a 'banking for all scheme'
. **Aadhaar number** – a unique identification number for each citizen, and
. **Mobile phones**

has transformed the financial landscape of India, thus acting as an enabler for the foundation of a digital service economy (IBEF, 2015; McKinsey, 2019).

The penetration of telecommunications technology and the potential for upgrading broadband technology, are additional tools for service industry providers that can affect changes to help make the Indian service industry technology-compliant (Saran & Sharan, 2018). Moreover, as a 2017 joint report prepared by FICCI, NASSCOM and Ernst and Young (EY) suggests, the rapid adoption of 4IR technologies in the advanced markets, and the subsequent impact on off-shoring, increasing/shrinking overseas job markets for the Indian workforce, and the level of foreign direct investment (FDI) flows among others, is referred to as one of the 12 megatrends that will impact the future of jobs in 2022 (FICCI et al., 2017). New business service models are increasingly relying on e-commerce and mobile based e-tailing, creating new job profiles in logistics, warehousing, web and app design, system integration, customer service, big data and machine learning (ET Retail, 2017).

Scholars and industry managers are still debating strategic and tactical approaches with regard to the successful adoption and use of information technology. As a result, a plethora of studies have investigated the categories of adoption, utilisation or success at the organisational and individual levels (Ul-Ain et al., 2019). Although there is considerable research assessing the success of the implementation of information technology within organisations (see for example, DeLone and McLean's IS Success Model, Technology Acceptance Model –Davis, 1989; DeLone & McLean, 2016), there are fewer studies which investigate the impact of the adoption of information technology on the nature (or future) of work. Torkzadeh and Doll (1999) developed explicit definitions for four impact dimensions based on an extensive review of the information technology literature. The four impact dimensions identified were task productivity, task innovation, customer satisfaction and management control – taken together, they describe 'how' technology adoption and its application may impact employees in an organisational context. The conceptual framework underpinning this study and including these dimensions is outlined in detail in Chapter 2. This chapter (in common with others in this book) uses these four dimensions to investigate the perceptions of Indian managers in the service sector in relation to the adoption and application of these 4IR technologies.

Research findings: Indian managers' perspectives

As discussed earlier, this study used the conceptual framework and survey questionnaire described in Chapter 2. Data collection was restricted to organisations that had either already adopted some of the latest technologies or were using business intelligence systems for their business activities. Data were collected in person using the standard questionnaire, as well as through online Google forms, to obtain wider reach and speed. The on-line survey technique was used in earlier studies as both single and additional survey methods (Elbashir et al., 2008). The survey was conducted during November and December 2019 with the assistance of Master of Business Administration (MBA) students studying a business research methods course in a university in the northern region of

India. Each student was asked to collect three responses from three different organisations in the service sector in the region. A total of 118 usable responses were received.

Sample demographics

Table 7.1 outlines the survey respondents' demographics based on organisation type, number of employees and type of industry. From the sample of 118 respondents, 22 (18.64%) were companies operating at the local level, whereas 40 (33.90%) had units/ offices across India, and 56 (47.46%) were functioning at the international level. Based on the *number of employees*, 42 (35.59%) enterprises employed between 1 and 99 employees; 33 (27.97%) represented 101–500 employees, and 43 (36.44%) employed over 500 employees. Although the sample varied across different industry types, the majority of respondents were from banking, financial and insurance companies, and the IT sector, which represented 22.03%, and 17.80% respectively. Although the data were based on an organisation sample from the northern region of India, given the importance of the region and its contribution (6 states and 1 union territory) of around 25%

Table 7.1 Sample Demographics – Organisation Type, Employees and Industry

Organisation type	Frequency	%	Cumulative %
Local	22	18.64	18.64
National	40	33.90	52.54
International	56	47.46	100.00
Number of Employees			
Between 1 and 100	42	35.59	35.59
101–500	33	27.97	63.56
501–1000	43	36.44	100.00
Type of Industry			
Aviation	1	0.85	0.85
Banking/Financial/Insurance	26	22.03	22.88
Communications	3	2.54	25.42
Education and research	11	9.32	34.75
Medical tourism	4	3.39	38.14
Hospitality	5	4.24	42.37
Housing and infrastructure	4	3.39	45.76
IT	21	17.80	63.56
ITES	2	1.69	65.25
Media	4	3.39	68.64
Public relations	2	1.69	70.34
Real Estate and construction	3	2.54	72.88
Retail	1	0.85	73.73
Transportation	2	1.69	75.42
Travel and tourism	2	1.69	77.12
Other	27	22.88	100.00

of the national GDP, the service sector distribution and sample can be considered to be representative of the rest of India.

Concerning the various stages – technological (or automation) stage – almost half of the respondents (51.69%) considered their organisations to be in the third technological stage, as shown in table 7.2.

These findings imply that the respondent organisations may be attempting to advance towards the fourth stage, so understanding how prepared they are to embrace the 4IR will be of great relevance to them. Twenty-three respondents (19.49%) reported that their organisations have already adopted proactive approaches to new technologies and moved into stage four, beginning to leverage the benefits of these new technologies. Interestingly, 28.82% of organisations were still operating at the first or second stages, which suggests that there is a significant need to address this gap by informing organisations about the changing technologies, and how they can be leveraged to improve operations for the enhancement of their organisations.

When asked about information technology (IT) management in their organisations, most respondents reported that their organisations have a centralised IT department (see table 7.3).

The centralisation of IT has been an ongoing trend in Indian organisations as it offers a value proposition for investment, especially for organisations which do not have big IT budgets. With changing technologies and the emergence of the 4IR, it has become imperative for organisations to increase their IT budgets to leverage new technologies and gain competitive advantage, as better flows of information and specialised IT systems enhance organisation capabilities and offer greater efficiency.

Table 7.2 Stage of Technology/Automation

Status of industry	Freq.	Percent	Cum.
1st Mechanisation	17	14.41%	14.41%
2nd Mass production	17	14.41%	28.81%
3rd Computer and automation	61	51.69%	80.51%
4th Cyber physical systems	23	19.49%	100.00%
Total	**118**	**100**	

Table 7.3 Organisation of IT functions

Organisation of IT	Freq.	Percent	Cum.
Central IT department	49	41.53%	41.53%
No in-house department/Contracted out	19	16.10%	57.63%
IT experts attached to each department	7	5.93%	63.56%
Local IT departments in each functional	16	13.56%	77.12%
Other	27	22.88%	100.00%
Total	**118**	**100**	

Organisational strategy and the 4IR

This study attempted to understand the strategies that organisations are adopting to move from their current phase to the 4IR, as well as to investigate how they are aligning their strategic intentions. These strategies are underpinned by issues such as the usage/implementation of 4IR technologies; the level of top management support; the usefulness of the technologies; and their impacts on organisational performance. The study captured this through a set of statements which were measured on a five-point Likert 'agree – disagree' scale.

Concerning strategic intentions (table 7.4) the analysis suggested that most organisations adopt IT and business strategies that correspond with each other (M=3.84, S. D=0.92), and adapt IT goals and objectives to suit their business goals and objectives (M=3.80, S. D=0.97).

Effective strategic alignment is not possible without the support of top management, as it requires major investment, recruitment and operational decisions about the implementation of technological change in an organisation. The study findings (see table 7.5) suggest that top management is generally aware of the benefits of implementing these technologies in different departments (M=3.52, S. D=1.13), and actively encourages employees to use them in their daily tasks (M=3.49, S. D=1.04).

Concerning the usefulness of 4IR technologies in their organisations, the majority of respondents reported that they would be useful to employees in performing their tasks (table 7.6) and would be likely to enhance performance (M=3.73, S. D=1.08), and enable employees to accomplish tasks more quickly (M=3.66, S. D=1.11).

Table 7.4 Strategic Intentions/Alignment

Statement	Strongly disagree	Disagree	Undecided	Agree	Strongly agree	Mean	SD
Our IT strategies support match our business strategies	6	7	22	68	15	3.67	0.95
We adapt and align our IT strategy to business strategic change	4	7	21	67	19	3.76	0.91
We adapt our IT goals and objectives to our business goals and objectives	4	10	15	65	24	3.8	0.97
Our IT strategies and business strategies correspond to each other	4	5	22	62	25	3.84	0.92

Table 7.5 Top Management Support

Statement	Strongly disagree	Disagree	Undecided	Agree	Strongly agree	Mean	SD
Top management enthusiastically supports the adoption of AI/Software/Applications in different departments	4	21	34	42	17	3.4	1.05
Top management has allocated adequate resources for the adoption of AI/Software/Applications in different departments	5	25	33	44	11	3.26	1.03
Top management is aware of the benefits of implementing AI/Software/Applications in different departments	6	16	33	37	26	3.52	1.13
Top management actively encourages employees to use AI/Software/Applications in their daily tasks	5	14	36	44	19	3.49	1.04

When respondents were asked about the impact of 4IR technologies on organisation performance (table 7.7), most of them believed that it is useful in their jobs (M =3.5, S.D =1.14), and they are flexible to interact with (M=3.33, S.D =1.17). Most respondents also reported that the adoption of 4IR technologies is likely to lead to increased revenues, reduce lost sales, enhance profit margins and provide an improved competitive advantage. Conversely, the findings shown in table 7.8 indicate that 68% of organisations have low to very low levels of preparedness for the anticipated changes concerning AI and other 4IR technologies. This is of concern and needs immediate attention from policymakers, because if it is not addressed in a timely fashion then it may result in loss of competitiveness, squeezing of profit margins and possibly even closure for some organisations. With technological change already starting, the fact that 40% of organisations in this sample have only moderate preparation should also be a cause for concern and attract the attention of policymakers.

Impact on jobs

Table 7.9 shows respondents' views on the impact of 4IR technologies on employee satisfaction and perceived job security, indicating that that most believed that using AI software would improve employees' job satisfaction.

Table 7.6 Usefulness of 4IR Technologies

Statement	Strongly disagree	Disagree	Undecided	Agree	Strongly agree	Mean	SD
Using AI/Software/ Applications in jobs would enable employees to accomplish tasks more quickly	6	14	21	50	27	3.66	1.11
Using AI/Software/ Applications would improve employees' job performance	6	14	22	51	25	3.64	1.1
Using AI/Software/ Applications would make it easier for employees to do their job	3	16	31	44	24	3.59	1.04
Employees will find AI / Software/ Applications useful in their jobs	4	15	19	51	29	3.73	1.08

Table 7.7 Impacts of 4IR Technologies on Organisational Performance

Statement	Strongly disagree	Disagree	Undecided	Agree	Strongly agree	Mean	SD
Learning to operate AI/ Robotics would be easy for employees	6	27	32	43	10	3.2	1.05
Employee's interaction with AI/Robotics would be clear and understandable	10	18	29	46	15	3.32	1.14
Employees would find AI/Robotics to be flexible to interact with	10	21	23	48	16	3.33	1.17
Employees will find AI software/application useful in their jobs	9	13	27	48	21	3.5	1.14

Table 7.8 Level of Organisational Preparedness

Organisational preparedness	Freq.	Percent	Cum.
Very Low	31	26.27%	26.27%
Low	50	42.37%	68.64%
Moderate	26	22.03%	90.68%
High	6	5.08%	95.76%
Very High	5	4.24%	100.00%
Total	**118**	**100**	

Table 7.9 Employees' Job Satisfaction

Statement	Strongly disagree	Disagree	Undecided	Agree	Strongly agree	Mean	SD
Use of AI/Software/ Applications will enhance employees' satisfaction with their jobs	8	28	30	44	8	3.14	1.07
AI/Software/Applications will not affect the way employees work	15	32	36	28	7	2.83	1.11
Using AI/Software/ Applications will help to enhance employees' satisfaction with the important aspects of their job	10	26	28	43	11	3.16	1.13

Respondents did, however, report mixed feelings regarding job security (table 7.10). Some respondents indicated that they believe they will be able to continue working in the organisation despite increases in the use of the new technologies, and some had fears that they might be made redundant. Others were worried about the continuation of their careers. This mindset signals the need for organisations to create positive environments for the adoption of 4IR technologies and also to train/retrain the existing workforce so that they are prepared for the coming changes.

Resistance to change

Resistance to technological changes can play a major role in the adoption of new technologies (Joachim et al., 2018). This study found that employees are willing to adopt new technology (if with some resistance) as 53% of respondents showed very low to low resistance, whereas 23% showed

Table 7.10 Employees' Job Security

Statement	Strongly disagree	Disagree	Undecided	Agree	Strongly agree	Mean	SD
Employees are very confident that they will be able to keep their jobs despite the implementation of AI/Software/Applications	7	23	29	46	13	3.3	1.09
Employees think that they will be able to continue working in the organisation despite increases in the use of AI/Software/Applications	5	20	31	47	15	3.4	1.05
Employees fear that they might be made redundant due to increases in the use of AI/Software/Applications	5	23	27	48	15	3.38	1.07
Employees worry about the continuation of their careers due to increases in the use of AI/Software/Applications	7	17	30	52	12	3.38	1.05

Table 7.11 Resistance to Change

Organisational preparedness	Freq.	Percent	Cum.
Very low	28	23.73	23.73
Low	46	38.98	62.71
Moderate	32	27.12	89.83
High	8	6.78	96.61
Very high	4	3.39	100.00
Total	**118**	**100**	

moderate resistance (table 7.11), which could be the result of job insecurity issues.

The future of jobs

Respondents were asked what skills will be needed to perform anticipated jobs in the next five years. Interestingly, non-technical skills such as systems-thinking and process understanding were reported as likely to be the sought-after skills

Table 7.12 Extent of Likely Job Changes

Job change	Freq.	Percent	Cum.
Very high	87	8.19	8.19
High	278	26.18	34.37
Moderate	346	32.58	66.95
Low	235	22.13	89.08
Total	**1062**	**100**	

in the next five year period. Further, when asked about technical skills required, the majority emphasised automation technology, IT infrastructure and data analytics. These observations gel well with the technological transformation of Indian industry, where demand for data analytics skills is increasing, together with an understanding of the specific tools and techniques, and many companies have shifted to data-driven decision making, given the importance and abundance of data that prevails today.

When asked about the likely percentage of jobs that will change significantly concerning different functions in the next decade, due to the impact of artificial intelligence and automation in their organisations, respondents generally believed that the impact will be on all functional areas, but that manufacturing production and operations (product design or engineering) and information technology, data and communications security will experience the major changes. Since the major functions of business will be automated in future, most functions will be interconnected and breaches of data security will be a major concern, so information technology, data and communications security will be the areas that will undergo the most changes.

Concerning jobs that are likely to be replaced in the next decade due to the impact of artificial intelligence and automation, the respondents were of the opinion that the nature of jobs will change rather than these jobs disappearing completely. This is probably the reason why, when asked to estimate the percentage of jobs overall likely to be created within their organisations as a result of these technologies, most respondents were of the view that existing jobs will not vanish but will undergo major shifts in the way they are presently carried out, as shown in table 7.12.

Key issues

Although the findings suggest that all the dimensions discussed earlier in this chapter positively influence organisational performance, the roles of IT governance mechanisms and the strategic alignment of information systems (Wu et al., 2015) were the key areas of concern that managers need to tackle to achieve the desired task productivity, innovation, customer satisfaction and management control outcomes. The adoption and application of 4IR technologies without proper IT governance mechanisms and an absence of strategic alignment are the most likely to result in negative consequences. IT governance is 'the process for controlling an organisation's IT resources, including information and communication systems and technology' (Spremić, 2009: 906). In the information age, new ways of working, and the increasing availability of these technologies could significantly impact task productivity, innovation, customer satisfaction and management control in the Indian service industries.

Thus, the results of this study are likely to be particularly important for managers in the Indian service industry to assist their understanding of the significance of the adoption and application of 4IR technologies in business service processes.

Given that some of the respondents from the Indian service organisations represented here expressed concerns about their jobs being made redundant due to the integration of new technologies, it is also essential that managers in service organisations create a positive environment for their adoption. Another key issue needing attention is the lack of organisational preparedness with regard to 4IR technologies at work. As evidenced in this study, a significant percentage of managers reported very low to low levels of preparation for the anticipated technology changes. As noted earlier, these concerns may be detrimental in the longer term for organisations in terms of reduced productivity, profit, loss and sustained competitiveness.

Policies and interventions

Relevant policies and suitable intervention mechanisms are key to capitalising on the 4IR wave in Indian service organisations. The findings reported here shed light on those areas where relevant policies and suitable intervening mechanisms can be introduced to maximise organisational performance in the context of the 4IR.

First, as noted earlier, there needs to be effective policies and processes in place for controlling the organisation's IT resources, including appropriate information, communication and technology. In this regard, IT governance mechanisms need to be set up in all the service organisations in India for the effective direction and control of IT resources in order to achieve enterprise goals. With respect to the other key issues identified, suitable intervention mechanisms are required in Indian service organisations to enhance their preparedness for the impact of the 4IR technologies. This will enable employees to be suitably prepared for the challenges ahead and will facilitate appropriate training of the workforce as well as help to reduce the potential of resistance to future changes. Fear of job redundancies is one of the unavoidable challenges of AI and 4IR technology. In light of this, it is important that service organisations in India engage in transparent communication with their employees and provide suitable upskilling of their employees with training programs that will reduce fear and promote greater adoption of 4IR technologies.

Conclusion

The Fourth Industrial Revolution (4IR) provides huge opportunities for the Indian service sector. With the help of the latest technologies, Indian service organisations can make inroads into optimum customer experiences and service efficiency. The findings clearly demonstrated high levels of perceived impact on all the four dimensions (i.e. task productivity, task innovation, customer satisfaction and management control). Further, these impact dimensions have a positive influence on the resultant organisation performance. Given that the service sector is a mainstay of the Indian economy, and most MSMEs demonstrate encouraging trends towards technology adoption, the results of the study confirm that this will facilitate the enhancement of task productivity and innovation, customer satisfaction, management control and the potential for improved organisational performance.

References

Balasubramanyam, V. N., & Virmani, S. (2018). *The Enigmatic Services Sector of India.* Available at: https://mpra.ub.uni-muenchen.de/89174/

Davis, F. D. (1989). Perceived usefulness, perceived ease of use, and user acceptance of information technology. *MIS Quarterly*, 13 (3), 319–340.

DeLone, W. H., & McLean, E. R. (2016). Information systems success measurement. *Foundations and Trends in Information Systems*, 2 (1), 1–116.

Economic Times (2018). *Most Powerful Engine of India's Growth: Service MSMEs.* Available at:// economictimes.indiatimes.com/articleshow/62670137.cms?utm_source=contentof interest&utm_medium=text&utm_campaign=cppst

Elbashir, M. Z., Collier, P. A., & Davern, M. J. (2008). Measuring the effects of business intelligence systems: The relationship between business process and organizational performance. *International Journal of Accounting Information Systems*, 9 (3), 135–153.

ET Retail (2017). *Maximum Impact of Technology Adoption Will Be in Warehouse.* Available at: https://retail.economictimes.indiatimes.com/news/industry/maximum-impact-of-technology-adoption-will-be-in-warehouse-management-report/62264808

FICCI, NASSCOM, & Ernst & Young (2017). *Future of Jobs in India: A 2022 Perspective.* Available at: www.ey.com/Publication/vwLUAssets/ey-future-of-jobs-in india/%24FILE/ey-future-of-jobs-in-india.pdf

Goenka, T. (2019). *Changing Digital Behaviour and Technology Adoption of SMEs.* Available at: //economictimes.indiatimes.com/articleshow/69886442.cms?from=mdr&utm_source=contentofinterest&utm_medium=text&utm_campaign=cppst

Government of India (GOI) (2007). *Micro, Small and Medium Enterprises in India: An Overview.* New Delhi: Government of India – Ministry of Micro, Small and Medium Enterprises, Office of the Development Commissioner.

Government of India (GOI) (2018). *National Sample Survey Organisation, Surveys on Employment.* Government of Labour and Employment.

IBEF (2015). *Jam Trinity. India Brand Equity Foundation.* Ministry of Finance, Department of Expenditure.

Joachim, V., Spieth, P., & Heidenreich, S. (2018). Active innovation resistance: An empirical study on functional and psychological barriers to innovation adoption in different contexts. *Industrial Marketing Management*, 71, 95–107.

McKinsey (2014). *India's Technology Opportunity: Transforming Work, Empowering People.* Available at: www.mckinsey.com/~/media/mckinsey/industries/high%20tech/our%20insights/indias%20tech%20opportunity%20transforming%20work%20empowering%20people/mgi%20india%20tech_full%20report_december%202014.ashx

McKinsey (2017). *Jobs Lost, Jobs Gained: Workforce Transitions in a Time of Automation.* Available at: www.mckinsey.com/~/media/mckinsey/featured%20insights/Future%20of%20Organizations/What%20the%20future%20of%20work%20will%20mean%20for%20jobs%20skills%20and%20wages/MGI-Jobs-Lost-Jobs-Gained-Report-December-6-2017.ashx

McKinsey (2019). *Digital India: Technology to Transform a Connected Nation.* Available at: www.mckinsey.com/~/media/McKinsey/Business%20Functions/McKinsey%20Digital/Our%20Insights/Digital%20India%20Technology%20to%20transform%20a%20connected%20nation/Digital-India-technology-to-transform-a-connected-nation-Full-report.ashx

Pilat, D., & Devlin, A. (2004). The diffusion of ICT in OECD economies. In *The Economic Impact of ICT: Measurement, Evidence and Implications.* Paris: OECD Publishing, doi:10.1787/9789264026780-3-en

Saran, S., & Sharan, V. (2018). *The Future of the Indian Workforce: A New Approach for the New Economy.* Available at: www.orfonline.org/research/the-future-of-the-indian-workforce-a-new-approach-for-the-new-economy/

Spremić, M (2009). IT governance mechanisms in managing IT business value. *WSEAS Transactions on Information Science and Applications,* 6 (6), 906–915.

Torkzadeh, G., & Doll, W. J. (1999). The development of a tool for measuring the perceived impact of information technology on work. *Omega,* 27 (3), 327–339.

Ul-Ain, N., Giovanni, V., DeLone, W. H., & Waheed, M. (2019). Two decades of research on business intelligence system adoption, utilization and success – a systematic literature review. *Decision Support Systems,* 125, 113.

Uwizeyemungu, S., & Raymond, L. (2011). Information technology adoption and assimilation: Towards a research framework for service sector SMEs. *Journal of Service Science and Management,* 4 (2), 141.

Wu, S. P. J., Straub, D. W., & Liang, T. P. (2015). How information technology governance mechanisms and strategic alignment influence organizational performance: Insights from a matched survey of business and IT managers. *MIS Quarterly,* 39 (2), 497–518.

8 Indonesia

*Saskia P. Tjokro, Matheus S. N. Siagian
and Soegeng Priyono*

Introduction

This chapter reports on the findings of the Fourth Industrial Revolution (4IR) research study within the Indonesian context. It begins with a country profile; followed by analyses of its current labour market and productivity levels; and finally, a discussion of government, industry and educational strategies towards the 4IR. The findings from the research study are then outlined, together with commentary on their implications for the government, industry and higher and vocational education systems.

Country profile

Indonesia is now classified as a middle-income country with slow but consistent economic growth over the last two decades. Its current growth rate hovers around five percent, with a labour force of nearly 129 million people and overall unemployment around 5.5% (approximately 7 million – ILO, 2016). It is the fourth most populous country in the world, spread over an archipelago of more than 17,000 islands with three hundred different ethnic groups, and it has the 7th largest global economy as measured by relative purchasing power parity (Rajah, 2018; World Bank, 2018a: 1–4). The re-elected President Joko Widodo government's imperatives have been on the development of infrastructure (roads, public transport, airports, ports and sanitation systems), fiscal reform, and limited economic programs designed to encourage foreign direct investment. There is also a plan for 1000 new start up digital companies by 2020 as part of a Smart City initiative (Anggraini, 2015).

Infrastructure development projects have focused on easing Jakarta's notorious traffic congestion through light rail and elevated toll roads as well as another 245 planned infrastructure projects nationwide between 2014–2019 (Faisal, 2018). The re-elected Widodo government has also announced plans to relocate the capital, Jakarta, to a new site away from Java island, at least in part to further reduce traffic congestion and associated pollution. To date, only 26 of these projects have been completed (Rajah, 2018), due to Indonesia's complex geography, the myriad of natural disasters which frequently beset it (earthquakes, volcanoes, tsunamis and landslides) and political will. As an example of the latter, the former infrastructure-focused mayor of Jakarta was removed from office due to concerns about the adverse effects of his infrastructural initiatives on local residents, as well as for religious reasons.

The World Bank's (2018a) perspective is that Indonesia 'needs to boost its global competitiveness to increase (its) resilience to shocks and to reap the opportunities of the current global environment' (p. 37), including improving its present 5% economic growth rate. Rajah (2018) suggested that slow economic growth is the 'new normal' for Indonesia, and that it needs to more effectively embrace the burgeoning e-commerce industry and the growing cohort of middle-class consumers; further reduce red tape; and encourage innovation, creativity and foreign direct investment (FDI), especially in the context of declining export commodities (coal, palm oil, base metals, natural gas, crude oil and rubber). Currently, Indonesia's FDI is only 2% of gross domestic product (GDP), and is half that of Malaysia's GDP and a third of Thailand's (Rajah, 2018).

The labour market

Currently, the employment proportions of Indonesia's key industry sectors are agriculture (32%), industry (21%) and services (47%) (World Bank, 2018a), with numbers increasing in the services (up by 14.2 million) and industry (7.1 million new jobs) sectors, and declining in the agriculture sector (by approximately a million) during the last decade (Allen, 2016: 4). The workforce participation rate is 68% (compared with 83.5% in 2014) which is lower than most other Asia Pacific countries and accompanied by significant gender and rural inequalities, together with a disparity in incomes across jobs and provinces (ILO, 2016: 4–5). As examples of the inequities, the female participation rate has stagnated around 48.9% (cv. 82.7% males – Allen, 2016: 5), which may be explained by religious, cultural and gender role restrictions, rural or remote locations, and different education levels between men and women. What is perhaps of more concern is the disproportionate representation of informal work, without employment protections or job security (estimated to be between 50–72% of the workforce – ILO, 2016; Rajah, 2018) and workers on short-term contracts with below minimum wages (Allen, 2016: 2). Contrary to the relatively low overall unemployment level, youth unemployment levels remain consistently high, affecting approximately a third of those aged between 15–24 years (Allen, 2016: 11). The very limited number of employees with post-secondary education qualifications (9% – ILO, 2016: 5) is also problematic, given the new skill requirements of the 4IR, which include a combination of data analytics, ICT, digital marketing and social media skills, together with higher levels soft skills than before (ILO, 2016: 6).

Context of the study

The Indonesian economy thrives on micro-entrepreneurs and freelancers (www. bps.go.id/subject/6/tenaga-kerja.html), and most of them are private domestic companies (80.09%). Most of the early adopters of cyber physical system technology are spread across the services and tourism and hospitality sectors - 37.61% of respondents work within accommodation & food services and

22.12% in transport, postal and warehousing sectors. The manufacturing and consumer goods sectors are still largely in the 3IR or 2IR automation phase. Alongside the ever-expanding IT infrastructure development of the country, most companies now have an IT function.

The central government in Indonesia has committed to developing *Smart Cities*, where IT infrastructure is deliberately prepared as a strategic intervention across the country. Indonesia's workforce readiness is tied to work-skills related education, by providing IT skills-based education in public vocational high schools. In addition to that, the government has allocated paid training for youth through vocational training centres which offer programming training, graphic design, and general administration and computing skills. From small rural towns such as Tuban or Malang to large cities such as Yogyakarta, Indonesia is trying to rapidly integrate into the fast-moving ecosystem of the 4IR. However there has been criticism that the IT infrastructure is still centralised in Java rather than the rest of the country.

In fact, only one in seven businesses in Indonesia today has implemented artificial intelligence in their business, according to a recent study by Microsoft and research firm IDC, titled "Future Ready Business: Assessing Asia Pacific's Growth Potential Through AI." (Yasmin, 2018).

Labour productivity, education and government strategies

In addition to the earlier issues, whilst large companies (including multinationals) in Indonesia produce around 80% of value-added productivity they only employ 30% of the workforce. (Allen, 2016: 6). Conversely, small and medium size organisations (including state-owned enterprises) employ around two thirds of the workforce and contribute 10% of value-added productivity (Allen, 2016: 6), thus providing a potentially significant threat to Indonesia's future economic growth and sustainability in the wake of the 4IR due to their low productivity levels. The World Bank suggested that 'the problem of labor skills is consistent with the need to improve the quality of the domestic education system and limited on-the-job training, especially for skilled employees' (World Bank, 2018b: 43). In response, the government has significantly increased secondary school enrolments and the average years of education and has taken some steps towards coordinating research and higher education programs associated with artificial intelligence and machine learning skills development, as discussed in the following sections of this chapter.

The current Indonesian government has taken some steps towards addressing these economic and labour market concerns to modernise the country and attempt to prepare it for the forthcoming 4IR; especially in relation to infrastructure, economic liberalisation, workforce development, secondary education completions and, importantly, basic employment protections. For example, recent amendments to the Law on Manpower include provisions for minimum wages, worker dismissals, severance pay, trade unions and industrial relations dispute resolution (Allen, 2016: 13). These government initiatives have been obstructed by a series of intractable conundrums, including political instability, the growth of Islamic opposition to some of the initiatives, the fragmented geography of Indonesia and the frequency of natural disasters and distortions in the labour market. It might be argued that more comprehensive strategies are required to effectively respond to some of the key economic and labour market challenges it faces in the wake of the 4IR.

Challenges and opportunities for Indonesia in the 4IR era

Allen (2016) suggests that the relatively poor quality of science, technology, engineering and mathematics (STEM) education at both vocational and higher education levels is not conducive to a 'tertiary education system that allows the labor force to develop high quality cognitive and technical skills' (p. 10), posing serious problems for a post-4IR society. She further emphasises the need to expand the opportunities for 'quality' jobs, to provide incentives for organisations to conduct more on-the-job training 'in support of structural transition' (p. 35), to make the labour market more flexible, and to develop sustainable wage policies. The key challenge for the Indonesian government and employers is to achieve its goal of becoming one of the key technology 'giants' of Southeast Asia (Chopra, 2017; Tao, 2018).

In practical terms, the development of automation, internet of things, big data and artificial intelligence provide many opportunities and new choices for businesspeople in running their businesses and for consumers in making their choices. That is also true in relation to Indonesia.

However, the baseline is lower when compared with other developed countries. On the downside, it might be harder to catch up for certain industry sectors, such as manufacturing, due to investments already made that have not fully returned on those investments. However, because information technology is not only progressing but also changing, on the upside it opens up broad and immediate opportunities for startups to jump-start their operations. They can quickly adopt the latest technologies, as the Indonesian 'unicorns' – start-up businesses, usually e-commerce services, with greater than US$1billion in market capitalisation – (Despardins, 2019) have achieved within the past three years or so (see for example, Gojek, Tokopedia, Traveloka, and Bukalapak – Tao, 2018). Smaller startups such as Gilkor have invested in the latest technologies to undertake data analytics which record and interpret customer behaviour, preferences and buying patterns in 13 super-malls in Indonesia (www.gilkor.com).

The Global Innovation Policy Center's (GIPC) International Intellectual Property (IP) Index 2018 ranked Indonesia in the 45th position in the world for innovation. The report, "Inspiring Tomorrow," analyses the 'innovation policy' (IP) climate in 50 world economies. Here they rank economies on 45 unique indicators that are critical to an innovation-led economy supported by robust patents, trademarks, copyright and trade secrets protection. The ranking is a slight improvement on its previous 47th position (Dutta et al., 2018: 267). Meanwhile, for the ASEAN region, Indonesia is in the 4th place behind Singapore, Malaysia and Thailand, presenting a challenge for Indonesia to immediately upgrade its ranking.

However, Indonesia also ranks last on the Automation Readiness Index (EIU, 2018) which rated 25 countries. To improve this ranking, all stakeholders will need to collaborate to develop joint strategies, policies and programs. To date, new fiscal policies have been announced by the government to support Indonesia's 4IR readiness including the development of digital infrastructure.

In relation to the manufacturing sector, in 2018 the government set ten priorities that it is intended will be followed up with more programs going forward. The intention of these priorities is to:

1   Fix the flow of materials to strengthen material production at the upstream level.
2   Redesign the industrial zone by building a map for the national industrial zone and to overcome the problems that are faced by several industrial zones.
3   Accommodate sustainability standards through global trends such as electric powered vehicles (EV), biofuel, and renewable energy sources.
4   Empower the 3.7 million small and medium-sized enterprises (SMEs) through technological funding.
5   Build a national digital infrastructure supported by latest technologies.
6   Attract global renown manufacturing companies to invest in Indonesia through an attractive incentives scheme.
7   Redesign academic curricula to adopt 4IR standards.
8   Develop innovation-based research, development, and demonstration centres
9   Introduce tax exemption and or subsidies for companies to adopt specific technologies.
10 Harmonise regulations and policies among state governments (Ministry of Industry, Ministry of Manpower, Ministry of Trade, and President's strategic decisions) and regional governments.

(Gorbiano, 2019; Priyono – interview with Ministry
of Industry, 2019)

Indonesian leaders' and managers' preparedness for the 4IR

Research method

In common with the other countries featured in this book, the Indonesian study was based on the conceptual framework outlined in Chapter 2 concerning the adoption of technologies by organisations in the wake of the Fourth Industrial Revolution (4IR). Due to reportedly low response rates to online surveys in Indonesia, administered surveys were conducted by face-to-face interviews, based on the standard survey instrument used in the other countries in this study. Research assistants were employed for this purpose.

To analyse the responses, a thematic content analysis approach was adopted to explore leaders' and managers' perspectives of the 4IR and Indonesia's future workforce dynamics. Braun and Clarke (2006) view thematic content analysis as a technique to identify, examine and report patterns or themes within data. A total of

226 managers were interviewed between January and May 2019. Responses were collated manually and then entered into the computer by the research assistants. The respondents are managers whose companies reside in three provinces in Indonesia:

1 DKI Jakarta in Java island (48 managers)
2 Bali in Bali island (79 managers)
3 East Nusa Tenggara – Flores Island (99 managers).

The three provinces were chosen to represent three different economic contexts in Indonesia – Jakarta represents the capital city and the financial centre of Indonesia; Bali is the tourism and hospitality – driven region; and East Nusa Tenggara is a traditional agricultural region based on the Republic of Indonesia Presidential Regulation No. 4 year 2011 concerning the Nationwide Master Plan for the Acceleration and Expansion of Indonesian Economic Development (MP3EI) for 2011–2025.

Whilst respondents from broader industry sectors, including tech-oriented companies, were contacted for the study, the response was relatively low. Respondents from the tourism and hospitality and services sectors therefore constituted the majority of the sample.

Research findings

Alignment of IT and business strategies

As figure 8.1 shows, most respondents felt that their IT/4IR strategies are closely integrated with their overall business strategies. However, in this and the following figures and tables, 'undecided' responses are relatively high, suggesting that some managers are adopting a 'wait and see' approach rather than proactively preparing for the impact of 4IR technologies.

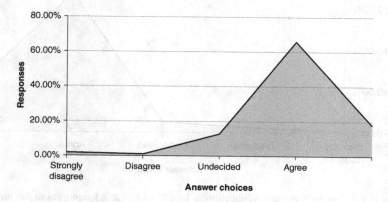

Figure 8.1 Strategic Intentions/Alignment IT Strategies Support and Match Our Business Strategies

AI usefulness

Managers generally agree that 4IR technologies will enable employees to accomplish tasks more quickly, and in general will be useful to increase employees' individual work performance. This implies that job-seekers with IT ability are likely to be favoured by many employers. Based on the findings, more than half the managers reported that these technologies will be useful, easy to use, and will assist in increasing employees' individual work performance (as seen from figures 8.2 to 8.4).

The 4IR and Customer Service and Experiences Management

Managers in the agriculture and tourism and hospitality sectors believe that the human touch is still important, especially to differentiate them from other parts of the world where labour is more expensive and tourism is less crucial to their economies. For instance, various hotels based on 'tourism experiences' require their employees to smile more, and actually sell the idea that they employ real 'sailors' and 'traditional' timber boats, which requires more traditional boatmen as workers, rather than using modern fibre boats and automated global positioning systems (GPS). Based on the study, there is a significant degree of doubt about whether 4IR technologies will provide competitive advantage. This possibly explains the significant proportion of 'undecided' responses. Managers seem to be acting pragmatically in the use of these technologies – adopting wait and see attitudes. Nevertheless, figures 8.5–8.8 show significant support for positive impacts on indicators such as revenue, reductions in the number of lost sales, profit margins and competitive advantage.

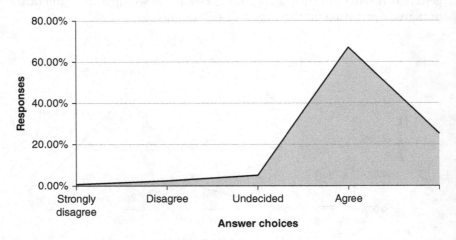

Figure 8.2 Using AI/Software/Application in Jobs Would Enable Employees to Accomplish Tasks More Quickly

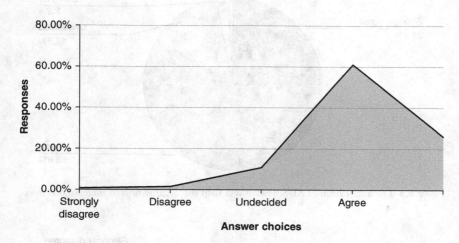

Figure 8.3 Using AI/Software/Applications Would Make It Easier for Employees to Do Their Job

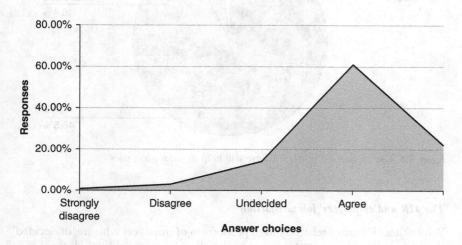

Figure 8.4 Employees will find AI/Software/Applications useful in their jobs

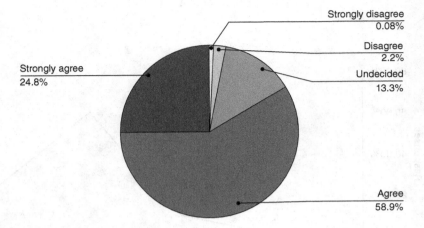

Figure 8.5 The application of AI/Software will help the organisation to increase revenues

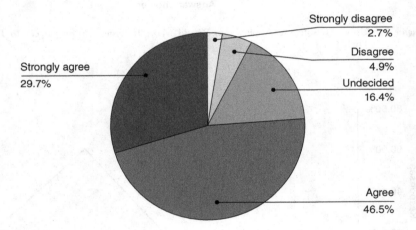

Figure 8.6 The application of AI/Software will help to reduce lost sales

The 4IR and employees' job satisfaction

Whilst there is again a relatively high proportion of managers who are 'undecided' about the effects of the 4IR on employee job satisfaction and job changes (figures 8.9 & 8.10), a majority of the respondents felt that job satisfaction would be enhanced, but there were (more or less) equal views about the need for changes to existing jobs. In the case of the tourism and hospitality sector, most managers felt that the technologies will not affect their business-as-usual approach as they sell tailored human interactions, while the manufacturing sector respondents believe that there will be significant changes to the nature of work in that sector.

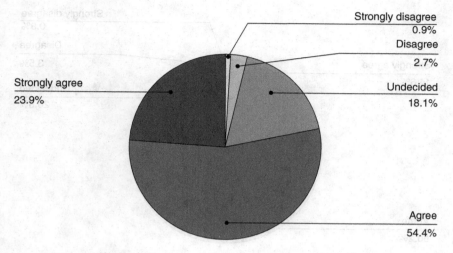

Figure 8.7 The application of AI/Software will help to enhance profit margins

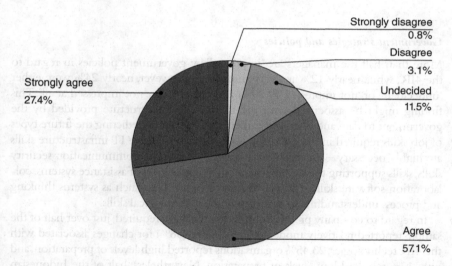

Figure 8.8 The application of AI/Software will help to improve competitive advantage

The 4IR and employee job security

With regard to employees' job security, more than half the managers believe that their employees are confident that they will keep their jobs, continue working in their current organisations, and will not be made redundant as a consequence of the 4IR, at least in the short-term. However, they are more divided about whether increases in the use of associated technologies will threaten their careers into the future (figures 8.11–8.14).

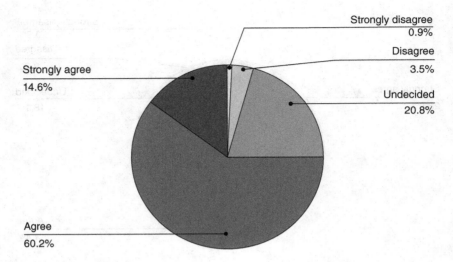

Strongly disagree
0.9%

Disagree
3.5%

Undecided
20.8%

Strongly agree
14.6%

Agree
60.2%

Figure 8.9 Use of AI/Software/Applications will enhance employees' satisfaction with their jobs

Government strategies and policies

More than half the managers are 'impressed' by government policies in regard to the 4IR, while nearly 12% are 'very impressed'. However, nearly 24% were either 'undecided', or 'not impressed' (9.29%) and 6.64% were 'not impressed at all'. This finding might be associated with the uneven IT infrastructure provided by the government to date and discussed earlier in the chapter. Predicting the future types of job skills required in the next five years, managers believe IT infrastructure skills are highly necessary – especially, data analytics skills, data/communication security skills, skills supporting the development of the application of assistance systems, collaboration software skills – as well as non-technical skills such as systems thinking and process understanding, to accompany the technological skills.

In regard to company preparedness for the changes required, just over half of the sample reported relatively moderate preparation (58%) for changes associated with the 4IR technologies, 23.45% organisations reported high levels of preparation, and only 12% reported low levels of preparation. Nevertheless, half of the Indonesian managers anticipate resistance to the forthcoming changes. Predictions of the proportion of new jobs created varied between 30% – 40% within their organisations.

Key current and future technologies

According to some sources, Indonesia 'ranks first in the Asia Pacific region in implementing artificial intelligence', with 65% of respondents (sample of 260 including the retail, IT, telecoms, financial services and insurance sectors) saying

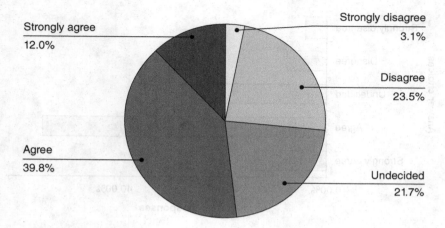

Figure 8.10 AI/Software/Applications will not affect the way employees work

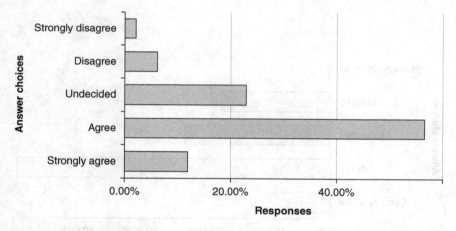

Figure 8.11 Employees are very confident that they will be able to keep their jobs despite the implementation of AI/Software/Applications

that they had 'either implemented AI in their businesses or were expanding or upgrading their AI capacity' (Tao, 2018). Another report emphasised the key sectors for AI technology expansion in Indonesia as retail, IT/telecoms, financial and insurance companies (Yuncarin, 2018). However, in that study of the more than 500 respondents, one quarter reported that they had already adopted 4IR technologies and a further two thirds indicated that they were preparing to do so (Yuncarin, 2018). Some examples provided by the survey included Go-Jek (a ride-share company), and Kaskus (a web forum), and Jakarta's Smart

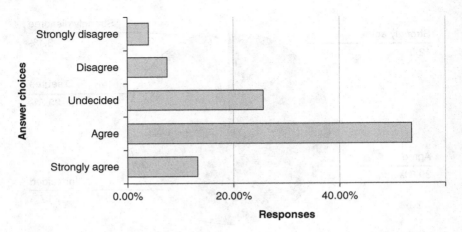

Figure 8.12 Employees think that they will be able to continue working in the organisation despite increases in the use of AI/Software/Technologies

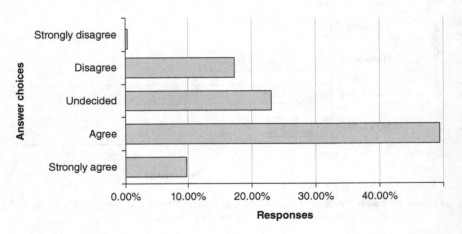

Figure 8.13 Employees fear that they might be made redundant due to increases in the use of AI/Software/Applications

City initiative which featured the replacement of 90,000 streetlights with LED globes, promoted to result in energy savings of more than 70% (Yuncarin, 2018).

Aligned to that, a study conducted by Microsoft Indonesia showed that AI can help Indonesian companies grow their innovation and employee productivity at a faster rate compared to their counterparts in the Asia Pacific (IDC,

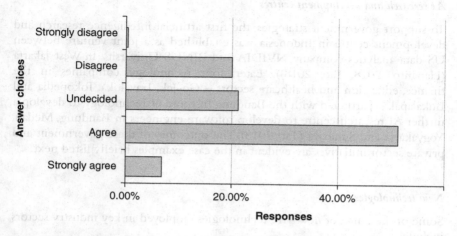

Figure 8.14 Employees worry about the continuation of their careers due to increases in the use of AI/Software/Applications

2019). The study predicted that Indonesian companies can expect to see their innovation rate increase by 56% in 2021 from 41% in 2019 if they implement artificial intelligence now than if they do not. Based on this prediction, employee productivity is also expected to be 46% higher (Yasmin, 2018).

Strategies, policies and practices

Government strategies

The present government's 1000 Start-Ups Movement (2020) has developed momentum during 2018–2019 by convening workshops, hackathons, boot-camps and 'incubation programs' across Indonesia as a 'strategic partnership' between the government, the technology company Kibar and the private sector. It has been successful in forming 200 new start-ups across ten cities to date (Anggraini, 2015) and has also established Hub ID to assist peer-to-peer communication between entrepreneurs and investors which has been coordinated by four government ministries. The program is similar to the entrepreneurship program formulated by the Malaysian government with dual imperatives – to fast-track the adoption of new online technologies, and to attempt to reduce high youth unemployment rates. In addition, business-friendly government policies – such as permission for full foreign ownership of e-commerce companies; a dedicated section of the stock exchange for such enterprises; a new 'technology board'; and incubator programs for start-ups are now operational in four local universities – Bandung (manufacturing), Bogor and Brawijaya (agriculture) and Surabaya (creative technologies) – all of which are designed to stimulate and support such entrepreneurial activities (Anggraini, 2015).

AI research and development centres

To support government strategies, the first artificial intelligence research and development centre in Indonesia was established as a joint venture between US data analytics company NVIDIA and BINUS University in West Jakarta (Hananto, 2018; Tao, 2018)). Later, four technology companies in the finance, education and healthcare sectors – Go-Jek, Traveloka, Tokopedia and Bukalapak – partnered with the Bandung Institute of Technology to develop a further AI research centre to develop software engineers in Bandung, Medan, Yogyakarta and Surabaya (Tao, 2018). The outcomes of these government and private sector initiatives are evident in the case examples briefly listed next.

New technologies

Some of the range of new 4IR technologies employed in key industry sectors include:

- *Public Transport & Water Services:* Microsoft has partnered with the Transjakarta public transport system, using artificial intelligence software to help predict customer demand and thence to provide appropriate numbers of buses at suitable times; and with the city's water department to predict potential flooding and take appropriate remedial actions
- *Entrepreneurs:* Kata.ai has developed the Kata Bot Platform which 'helps developers to create and deploy chatbots for start-ups – Botpreneurs', thus supporting the government in its goal of encouraging 1000 new start-ups
- *Banking & Finance:* DBS Bank has set up Digibank, which uses biometric user authentication and mobile interfaces' in both Bahasa Indonesia and English as part of an AI assistant platform which facilitates 'paper-less and signature-less' banking
- *Internet & Social Media:* The Indonesian Communications Technology Ministry is using AI and machine learning technologies to monitor and block explicit gambling, terrorism, fraud and pornography websites
- *Agriculture:* Habibi Garden employs sensors to monitor plant growth and outputs, prevent crop failure, improve yield productivity and improve costs and efficiency; Helien uses wi-fi balloons to connect rural and remote residents to the internet and 'bring people back after disasters'; Kumparan provides community-based digital media
- *Retail:* radio frequency identification, AI and facial recognition systems are used by X-Mart retail stores to 'monitor customer traffic flow, product selection and customer profiles' for marketing, product placement and inventory control purposes; Matahari Mall, Q0010 Indonesia, East Ventures, 500Startups and Indosat all use various forms of artificial intelligence
- *Healthcare:* CekMata is an online ophthalmologist robot which can detect cataracts – 'can tell the difference between cataract-infected and healthy eyes early on by simply looking at photos'

- Philanthropy & Social Causes: KitaBisa.com is an online fundraising platform, Indonesia's crowdfunding focused on social causes.

(Compiled from: Anggraini, 2015; Chopra, 2017; Hananto, 2018; Haupter, 2018; Lie, 2017; Liu, 2017; Lukman, 2013; Marzuki, 2017; Rahmadiani, 2018; Woo, 2018)

Conclusion

In summary, the Indonesian government and the private sector have made significant steps towards building an economy and the infrastructure necessary for the country to become one of the most successful adopters of 4IR technologies in the Asia Pacific region. In some sectors it has demonstrated the capability of its best and brightest human capital to leverage technologies for future economic and social benefits. Further the government has allocated paid training for youth through vocational training centres where subjects include programming training, graphic design, and general administration and computing skills.

Indonesia is currently in a unique state of 4IR preparedness with, on the one hand, very enthusiastic and well-prepared managers and leaders in Jakarta and Yogyakarta (Java island), supported by the government through its workforce education in government-paid training institutions. On the other hand, there are very pessimistic managers and leaders in East Nusa Tenggara (Flores Island) where sectors such as agriculture and tourism have become part of the central government's regional strategic intervention. Overall, Indonesian managers see AI and robotics technologies as a challenge. Some managers act defensively, stating that there needs to be a balance between human and non-human technology. They also suggest that the Indonesian workforce in general is not fully ready, ability-wise and mindset-wise, to work in a 4IR world. On the other hand, there is optimism from the private sector. AI is estimated to raise employees' productivity, despite the challenges faced by the sectors today. It is estimated that the rate of innovation and employee productivity will be raised in Indonesia as the 4IR will cultivate competitiveness among companies to innovate their businesses even further.

In Indonesia, AI adoption is currently led by tech startups such as the e-commerce platform Bukalapak and the finance technology company Crowdo Indonesia. There are also startups that develop AI for specific purposes that can be implemented in conventional businesses. These are likely to be at the forefront in tackling Indonesian managers' perceptions of considering the 4IR as a positive opportunity for the future rather than a negative challenge.

References

Allen, E. R. (2016). Analysing trends and challenges in the Indonesian labour market. *ADB Papers on Indonesia*, No. 16, March.

Anggraini, E. (2015). Indonesia's vision: 1000 start-ups by 2020. *Digital News Asia*, 27 November. Available at: www.digitalnewsasia.com/indonesias-vision-1000-startups-2020, accessed 12 August 2019.

Braun, V., & Clarke, V. (2006). Using thematic analysis in psychology. *Qualitative Research in Psychology*, 3, 77–101.

Chopra, A. (2017). Indonesia's Tech Sector: A look at government policies promises to buoy the emerging economy. *InFocus*, 6 January.

Despardins, J. (2019). *The Ten Biggest Unicorns in the World – Mapped*. Geneva: WEF. Available at: weforum.org/agenda/2019/05/visualizing-the-unicorn-landscape-in-2019, accessed 30 July 2019.

Dutta, S., Lanvin, B., & Wunsch-Vincent, S. (eds.). (2018). *Global Innovation Report 2018*. Cornell University, INSEAD & WIPO.

EIU (2018). *The Automation Readiness Index: Who Is Ready for the Coming Wave of Automation?* London: EIU Ltd.

Faisal, M. (2018). Four key trends to watch in Indonesia's economy in 2018. *The Australia-Indonesia Centre*. Available at: www.australiaindinesia centre.org/commentary/four-key-trends-to-watch-in-Indonesias-economy, accessed 15 February.

Gorbiano, M. (2019). Manufacturing sector to drive Indonesia's economy. *Jakarta Post*, 11 February. Available at: www.thejakartapost.com/news/2019/02/11, accessed 12 August 2019.

Hananto, A. (2018). *Indonesia to Develop Its First AI Research Centre*. Available at: www.seasia.com/2018/10/28/indonesia-to-develop-its-first-AI-research-centre, accessed 12 August 2019.

Haupter, R. (2018). Welcome to 2018, the year of AI. *Microsoft Asia News Center*, 3 January.

IDC (2019). *Future Ready Business: Assessing Asia Pacific's Growth Potential Through AI*. Jakarta: Microsoft Indonesia.

ILO (2016). *Indonesian Labour Market Outlook*. Geneva: ILO.

Lie, T. (2017). 5 new Indonesian tech companies to watch in 2017. *Business Property*, 16 January.

Liu, C. (2017). AI is on the rise in Southeast Asia helping everyone from fashion designers to rice growers. *This Week in Asia*, 5 November. Available at: www.scrp.com/week-aia/business/article/2118345/ai=is-on-the-rise-in southeast-asia, accessed 28 July 2019.

Lukman, E. (2013). KitaBisa is Indonesia's kickstarter for social causes. *Tech in Asia*, 25 September.

Marzuki, Y. (2017). Indonesia's Kata.AI launches Kata Platform. *Digital News Asia*, 20 December. Available at: www.digitalnewsasia.com/business/indonesias-katai-launches-chat-bot-platform, accessed 28 July 2019.

Rahmadiani, A. (2018). 100 smart cities between Indonesia and India. *Center for Digital Society*. Available at: www.cfds.fisipol.ugm.ac.id/article/373/100-smart-cities-indonesia

Rajah, R. (2018). *Indonesia's Economy: Between Growth and Stability*. Sydney: Lowy Institute.

Tao, A. L. (2018). *Indonesia Leads ASEAN in AI Adoption*. Available at: www.computerweekly.com/news/252444634/, accessed 12 August 2019.

Woo, J. (2018). DBS launches digibank in Indonesia. *The Straits Times*, 30 August. Available at: www.straitstimes.com/business/companies-markets/dbs-launches-digibank-in-indonesia, accessed 27 July 2019.

World Bank (2018a). Towards inclusive growth. *Indonesian Economic Quarterly*, March, p. 1–4.

World Bank (2018b). Strengthening competitiveness. *Indonesian Economic Quarterly*, December, p. 43.

Yasmin, N. (2018). Only one in seven companies in Indonesia use AI today. *Jakarta Globe*. Available at: https://jakartaglobe.id/context/only-one-in-seven-indonesian-companies-use-ai-today/

Yuncarin, S. (2018). Yitu Tech sees Indonesia as a significant market as the country has been showing a willingness to embrace AI. *Jakarta Globe*, 25 October.

9 Malaysia

Noorziah Mohd Salleh and Badariah Ab Rahman

Introduction

This chapter discusses the challenges and opportunities emanating from the Fourth Industrial Revolution (4IR) in the Malaysian context. Currently, there is broad understanding of the significant changes taking place as a consequence of these new technologies, especially in relation to industry sectors, the contemporary labour market, workplaces, jobs and skills. However, despite government investment in proactive strategies and policies, Malaysia faces many of the same challenges that confront other countries considered in this book. The chapter begins with an overview of the economy; labour market; government, industry and educational strategies; and the key current and future technologies likely to have the most impact on industry and the economy. Subsequent sections of the chapter present and analyse the findings from the research study conducted and highlights the resultant implications for governments, industry managers, human resource professionals and educational systems, in order to address the challenges and maximise the opportunities posed by the 4IR.

Country profile

Malaysia is a multiracial country located in Southeast Asia, with a population of more than 32 million people (Department of Statistics Malaysia, 2019). It is a rapidly developing country demonstrating stable economic growth averaging between 4.5% to 5.5% over the last few years. With gross domestic product (GDP) reaching US$314.5 billion in 2017, Malaysia is on par with other neighbouring countries such as Singapore, Thailand and the Philippines (World Bank, 2019). Its main contributing economic sectors are services (55%) and manufacturing (22.5%), which together represent approximately 77.5% of the country's GDP (Department of Statistics Malaysia, 2019). Prime Minister Mahathir Mohamad's government, which held power from 1980 to 2013 and then again after the 14th historic election in 2018, maintains that Malaysia needs to reform in order to recover from the previous government, competing at the highest level possible to succeed. In pursuit of these objectives, a strategic plan referred to as the Malaysia 11th Plan 2016–2020 (MP11) has been promulgated.

The MP11 focuses on three key industries – namely, electrical and electronics (E&E), mechanical and electrical (M&E), and chemicals – together with other sectors such as aerospace, medical devices, automotive, petrochemicals, and textiles and services (Rosli, 2019).

As Malaysia is currently facing high levels of debt, the government intends to reduce the country's expenditure and encourage export and foreign direct investment (FDI) to spur economic transformation for greater prosperity. The majority of investment in the Malaysian economy comes from the top five investors: China (16.7%), Singapore (12.9%), the United States (8.3%), Japan (7.1%) and Thailand (5.6%). Its main markets, which contribute 51.3% of its exports, are China (13.9%), Singapore (13.9%), the United States (9.1%), Hong Kong (7.5%) and Japan (6.9%) (MATRADE, 2019). Under Mahathir's leadership, Malaysia is now pursuing economic and infrastructure development (for example, the Pan Borneo Highway and East Coast Rail Link -ECRL), but these have been problematic due to high debt levels incurred by the previous government. The 29 billion Ringgit (US$7.05 billion) Pan Borneo project, a road connecting two eastern Malaysian states (Sabah and Sarawak); and an East Coast Rail Link (ECRL) with an estimated cost of RM55 billion (US$13.3) (Mahalingam, 2019), are designed to attract foreign investment. The outcome of these rapid advancements requires investment in human capital to boost the country's socio-economic infrastructure and will also support industrial growth, serving as a strong backbone of the country's developmental plans, and more importantly, acting as a catalyst for the acceleration of the Fourth Industrial Revolution (4IR).

The labour market in Malaysia

Consistent economic growth, a high labour participation rate (68.4%), and a low unemployment rate (3.3% – Department of Statistics Malaysia, 2019) have partly contributed to Malaysia's ranking as the 17th most competitive country in the global manufacturing sector (Deloitte Touche Tohmatsu's Global Manufacturing Competitiveness Index 2016 – Deloitte.com). The latter report also projected that Malaysia would climb by four notches to 13th place by the year 2020. From the perspective of technology and innovation, Malaysia was ranked in 37th place globally amongst 127 countries, and 8th in Asia in the Global Innovation Index 2017 designed by Cornell University, INSEAD and WIPO (The Star Online, 2019). Furthermore, the Readiness for the Future of Production Report (2018) highlighted that Malaysia was well-positioned to benefit from the future of the 4IR (MITI, 2019). Hence, the Malaysian economy is likely to support preparation for the 4IR. Malaysia will not, however, be likely to face a significant lack of jobs but will face a lack of skills needed for future jobs (Monash Malaysia, 2018).

The MP11 plan discussed earlier promotes the journey towards realising Vision 2020. The main aim of Vision 2020 is to be a developed country, strengthening the government's commitment to achieve future growth by focusing on the GDP and wellbeing of its people. To realise the aim of Vision 2020, according to the World Bank, a developed country should have a national per capita income of at least US$12,236 per year, but in 2018 Malaysia's gross national per capita income was estimated at only US$10,321 (MIDA, 2019a). Thus, Malaysia needs to increase its labour force output and carefully calibrate the development of its human capital in line with the demands of the labour market (ICEF Monitor, 2017) to achieve this goal.

Labour productivity, education and government strategies

Small Manufacturing Enterprises (SMEs) represent 98.5% of all businesses, have contributed more than 37% of Malaysia's GDP, and are a critical source of employment in Malaysia (42.1%), together with 57.9% from large firms in the manufacturing sector. The government realises the attractiveness of the sector and thus provides incentives for it to flourish. In 2018, RM2.3 billion (US$470, 000) was spent on training for female entrepreneurs (Raj, 2019). However, to increase labour productivity through employment enhancement plans are required, as the productivity level dropped by 0.1% in the first quarter of 2019 from 2.3% in the previous year (Labour Productivity of First Quarter, 2019). SMEs need to transform to be more knowledge-intensive and innovation-led, as they are expected to grow and contribute 56.5% to the GDP in 2020, and to provide 9.3 million jobs (Department of Statistics, 2019).

Addressing the economic issues and the current labour situation is imperative for the Malaysian government, especially in the 4IR era which is likely to significantly affect both employment and unemployment due to the replacement of low and medium-skilled jobs by robots. However, the 4IR agenda is not being currently monitored by any specific ministry, leaving it to be primarily managed by industry representatives. Nonetheless, the Malaysian Industry-Government Group for High technology (MIGHT) under the Ministry of International Trade and Industry (MITI), is leading an initiative to promote the optimisation of innovation for the benefits of the people (Abdullah et al., 2017). The 4IR era is expected to affect business activities and human resource management policies and functions; there will be communication via networks and software over the entire value chain. This will generate a production system with autonomous optimisation and control (Deloitte, 2015). To face the consequences that will affect human resource skills, particularly at mid-levels, Malaysia is actively promoting the 4IR (Abdullah et al., 2017) and encouraging industrialists to capitalise on industry opportunities.

Some local businesses are also showing a positive response to the 4IR, with many increasing their collaboration with foreign investors in ways that are more efficient and effective. Some examples include: Keretapi Tanah Melayu Berhad (KTMB) – tickets sold online through an online e-ticket system, or Mobticket smartphone applications (Might.org.my, 2018). The Aerospace Malaysia Innovation Centre (AMIC) is trying to accelerate progress in making the country the hub for supplying aerospace products or services, in areas such as original equipment manufacturers (OEM), aerospace manufacturing, engineering services, precision parts, components, education and training, as well as maintenance repair and overhaul (MRO) services. To support these initiatives, there is a need for future workforces to increase their skills and knowledge in engineering and information technology.

Despite the opportunities provided by the 4IR, there are also significant challenges and concerns. Many of the SMEs in Malaysia are still unaware of it, and this lack of awareness could weaken their competitive advantage (Mohd Yatid, 2019). The government provides consultation and financial assistance to SMEs and others to make the most of the opportunities provided by the 4IR.

Strategies and opportunities for Malaysia in the 4IR era

Malaysian manufacturing and service industries have been the main contributors to the country's economic growth. Industry capability in stimulating jobs, attracting investment and creating business opportunities is essential, and needs to be developed in the context of the 4IR. As such, the government has outlined 13 strategies under its national policy to transform industry over the next ten years (Zakariah, 2018). The strategies will be supported through five strategic enablers – namely, funding, infrastructure, regulation, skills and talent, and technologies (FIRST) – along with action plans created to address other areas related to the 4IR (Raj, 2019). As discussed earlier, actions to address the skill deficits in Malaysia's workforce are included in the 13 strategies and plans to create new talent and address skills development.

It has been reported that Malaysian SMEs are generally unaware of the opportunities brought by the 4IR (Mohd Yatid, 2019), and accordingly, the Ministry of International Trade and Industry is creating Readiness Assessment Guidelines that will enable businesses to assess their performance and create their plans to embrace the 4IR in order to be more competitive. Currently, an e-Commerce Strategic Roadmap or Digital Free-Trade Zone (DFTZ) is an incentive to provide a proper platform for SMEs to reinvent themselves and implement the latest technologies for these purposes (Mydftz.com, 2018). The DFTZ was created to capitalise on the exponential growth of the internet economy and global e-Commerce activities. The DFTZ has three components: a Fulfilment Hub, designed to assist entrepreneurs' export activities; a Satellite Services Hub, mainly designed for services (for example, financing, last-mile fulfilment and insurance); and the element of DFTZ called the e-Services platform, which is designed to assist businesses with cargo clearance management. Thus, the DFTZ digitally connects users with government and business services to support cross-border trade. In the future, this digital platform can be connected to similar platforms in other countries to facilitate global trade processes. Malaysia is among the first countries to embark on such a digital services platform (Mydftz.com, 2018).

According to the Malaysian Productivity Corporation (2018), the government has allocated RM210 million from 2019 to 2021 to support the transition to the 4IR. In this project, the preparedness of 500 SMEs will be evaluated to help them in assessing their capabilities to adapt (Adilla, 2019). According to the Executive Vice-President (Yong Yoon Kit) of the Malaysia Performance Management and Delivery Unit (PEMANDU), manufacturing companies that have adopted new technological practices were found to perform 26% better than their peers which did not have a digital strategy. He also stated that much of industry is still averaging at Industry 2.5 level, which lies between the utilisation of electricity and automation in mass production (Toh, 2019). To further galvanise the Malaysian economy through innovation and technology towards becoming a key player in the 4IR, an allocation of RM210 million for a Readiness Assessment Programme, and RM3 billion for an Industry Digitalisation Transformation Fund were tabled in the 2019 budget presentation in November last year (Adilla, 2019; New Straits Times, 2018).

According to Market Research Malaysia (2019) which surveyed 200 companies from three key industries in Malaysia – manufacturing, logistics and healthcare – the level of the expected impact of the 4IR was 30% in manufacturing, 25% in logistics and 25% in healthcare (Duhamel, 2019). The manufacturing and logistics sectors perceived that the biggest challenge would be with funding and talent, and healthcare respondents perceived that talent was the most challenging issue to tackle.

The government has plans to embrace the 4IR through developing Malaysia's people's skills. The Ministry of Higher Education has developed initiatives that encourage public universities to design new courses that will enable job creation. The new courses are designed to work with industry and will provide industrial exposure for university students. It is proposed that a *2u2i* (two years at a university, and another two years in industry) could be built into higher education programs (Asma, 2019). The government also encourages industry to develop the scope of their talent to drive business growth, particularly in areas such as information technology (IT), computing, digital marketing and research and development (R&D). Many organisations have reinforced their innovation and technology capabilities to capitalise on growth, and they need skilled talent to support their business growth (Mahpar, 2019). The Malaysian government is also aiming to capitalise on the opportunities brought about by the 4IR and has outlined strategies to embark on the new industrial wave (National Policy on Industry 4.0, 2019). Many sectors will reap the benefits of the transformation of industry as well as open up completely new possibilities, including additive manufacturing, artificial intelligence (AI) and supplementing smart factories. Customer experience and product quality will be improved by using big data techniques; efficiency will be achieved by using advanced material and nanostructures and better-quality products will be provided with minimal capital investment and by using many of the 4IR technologies (MITI, 2019).

Key current and future technologies

The 4IR will affect many, if not most, businesses, governments and people. At the moment, the Ministry of International Trade and Industry (MITI) under The National Policy on Industry 4.0 is the most active ministry pursuing associated research. Its responsibility is to design methods to transform the manufacturing sector and its related services to become smarter, more systematic and resilient (New Straits Times, 2018). The main aim of MITI is to create a platform or mechanism to help the sector (especially SMEs) to assess and develop their business operations in order to face 4IR-related challenges and opportunities. Efforts are also being actively undertaken to study and profile the local manufacturing industry's state of readiness in adapting to the associated challenges. For example, as mentioned earlier, the Malaysia Productivity Corporation (MPC) is currently undertaking a readiness assessment programme to help approximately 500 medium-sized enterprises to make the change. The government is also establishing an RM3 billion-Industry Digitalisation Transformation Fund to encourage industries to utilise artificial intelligence, is offering scholarships to engineering and technology students at the technical, degree and diploma levels (New Straits Times, 2018).

Research findings on managers' preparedness for the 4IR

The data collection for this study was carried out from January–May 2019. Respondents were asked to participate in the study prior to sending questionnaires through WhatsApp or electronic mail. More than 500 questionnaires were sent to various organisations either by using Google form or via printed questionnaires. Three hundred and seventeen questionnaires were returned – a response rate of 63.4%. Survey respondents' profiles are shown in table 9.1. Respondents were equally male (114) and female (115). Respondents were

Table 9.1 Description of Respondents

Item	Description	Frequency (n=317)	Percentage
Gender	Female	114	35.9
	Male	115	36.2
	Prefer not to say	88	27.8
Age	Between 18 until 35	222	70.0
	Between 36 until 50	87	27.4
	Between 51 until 65	8	2.5
Education background	High School or lower	30	9.5
	Vocational education	30	9.5
	Bachelor's degree	220	69.6
	Postgraduate qualification	36	11.4
Position level	Staff	188	59.3
	Team leader/ Supervisor	71	22.4
	Manager	20	6.3
	Senior manager	9	2.8
	Director/CEO	7	2.2
	Business owner/entrepreneur	22	6.9

mostly from organisations that had between 1 and 99 employees (54%), or between 100 and 499 employees (38%); the lowest number of responses was received from organisations that had more than 1000 staff (6%) (figure 9.1).

As the table shows, a large majority (69.6%) of the respondents have a bachelor's degree, with 9.5 % holding only a school certificate. Respondents were mainly middle management (59.3%), but 40.6% were top management (team leader, manager, senior manager, Director/CEO and business owner). They worked in administrative and support services (26.8%), followed by agriculture, forestry and fishing (21.7%); and the third largest was the education and training sector (12.3%) (figure 9.2).

Figure 9.3 shows that overall, respondents reported that Malaysia was still in the era of the second (36%) and third (53%) industrial revolution (computer and automation) stages. Despite the government initiatives discussed earlier in the chapter, only 3% reported that Malaysia had reached the 4IR technological stage.

Top management support for the adoption of 4IR technologies was perceived as moderate and the majority of respondents agreed that their use in jobs would enable employees to accomplish tasks more quickly. More than half of the respondents (74%) agreed that the use of such tools would enhance their satisfaction with their tasks (figure 9.4), with 64% stating that learning some of the technology was relatively easy (figure 9.5).

The earlier responses may explain why 75% of respondents showed confidence in their ability to keep their jobs (figure 9.6)

■ Between 1 and 99 ■ Between 100 and 499 ■ Between 500 and 999 ■ 1000 and over

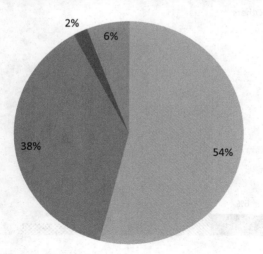

Figure 9.1 Respondent's Size of Organisation (by employee)

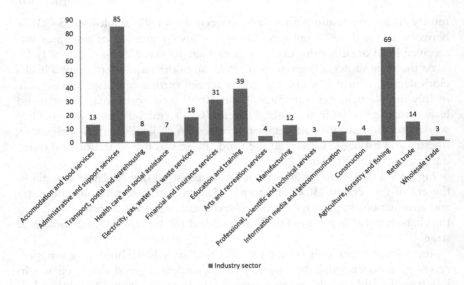

Figure 9.2 Industry Sectors Represented by Respondents

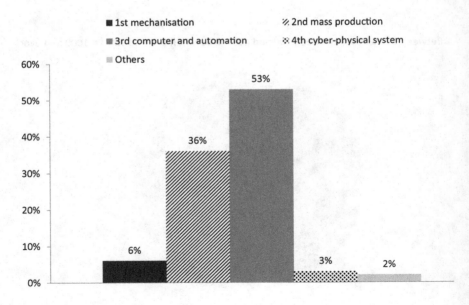

Figure 9.3 Malaysia's Technological Stage

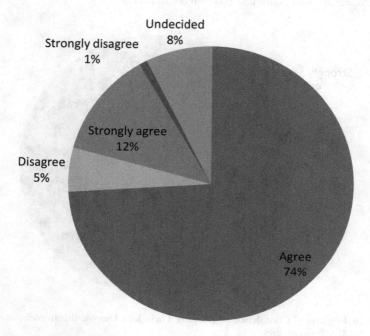

Figure 9.4 Use of 4IR Technologies Will Enhance Employees' Satisfaction With Their Tasks

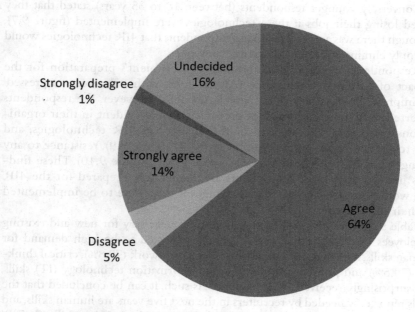

Figure 9.5 Learning to Operate 4IR Technologies Would Be Easy for Employees

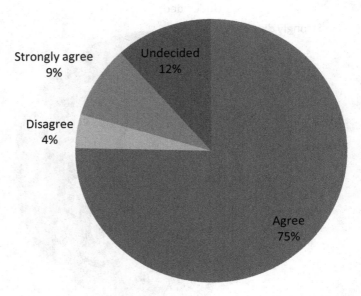

Figure 9.6 Employees' Confidence in Keeping Their Jobs Despite the Implementation of 4IR Technologies

Conversely, younger respondents (between 18 to 35 years) stated that they feared losing their jobs if these technologies were implemented (figure 9.7), although there was agreement among respondents that 4IR technologies would not only eliminate jobs but also create new ones.

Respondents were positive about the government's preparation for the impact of Artificial Intelligence (AI) on jobs, with 83% 'very impressed' or 'impressed' with their initiatives (figure 9.8). However, the respondents reported only moderate levels of preparation were evident in their organisations in terms of acceptance of the changes in 4IR technologies, and due to the moderate preparation levels (81%) (figure 9.9), resistance to any changes was likely to be moderate as well (83%) (figure 9.10). These findings indicate that most respondents are moderately prepared for the 4IR and would possibly accept related changes if they were to be implemented in their organisations.

Table 9.2 shows the skills anticipated to be necessary for new and existing employees in the next five years. There is expected to be high demand for human skills, namely: communication (77%), teamwork (79.8%), critical thinking (79.5%) and positive attitude (80.4%). Information technology (IT) skills, not surprisingly, received 78.2% support. As such, it can be concluded that the skills reportedly needed by recruiters in the next five years are human skills, and higher requirements are anticipated in relation to IT knowledge/skills (76.7%).

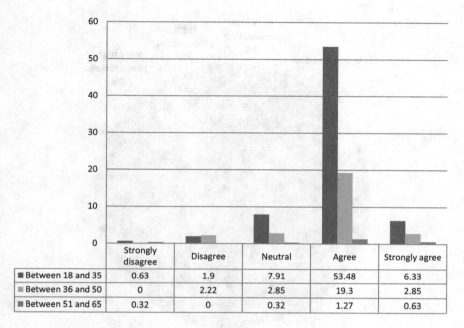

	Strongly disagree	Disagree	Neutral	Agree	Strongly agree
■ Between 18 and 35	0.63	1.9	7.91	53.48	6.33
■ Between 36 and 50	0	2.22	2.85	19.3	2.85
■ Between 51 and 65	0.32	0	0.32	1.27	0.63

Figure 9.7 Employee Concern About Job Loss Due to 4IR Technologies

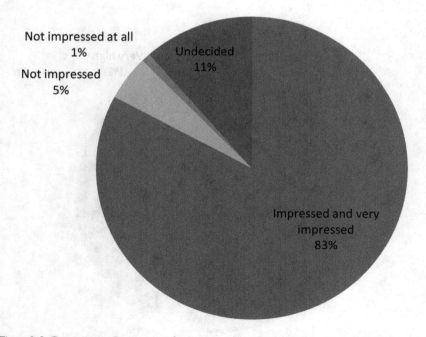

Figure 9.8 Government Preparation for Impact of Artificial Intelligence (AI) on jobs

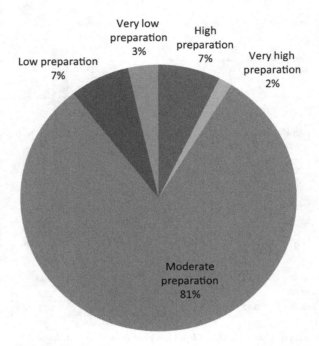

Figure 9.9 Organisation Preparedness

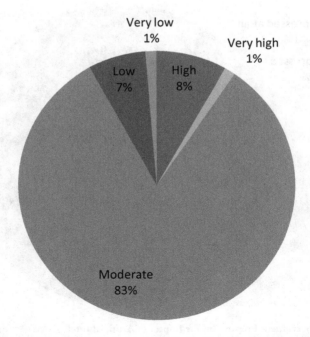

Figure 9.10 Resistance Anticipated due to AI/Robotic Technological Change

Table 9.2 Skills Needed to Recruit in the Next Five Years

	Communication	IT (Knowledge)	Team work	Critical thinking	Ethics	Positive attitude to ongoing learning of new skills
Skills needed in the next 5 years	77	78.2	79.8	79.5	80.4	80.4
Skills need to recruit in the next 5 years	77.3	76.7	78.3	78	76.4	76.3

Key issues

The study and the associated literature suggest that many Malaysian organisations are keen to embrace the 4IR, but there are factors hindering their preparedness. Malaysia is still far behind many developed and intermediary countries and appears to still be in the 2nd and 3rd technology stages across many sectors. The new government is trying to support knowledge-intensive enterprises that leverage science and technology in order to take the economy to the next level. However, knowledge-intensive enterprises are challenging to create when the human capital is not readily available. As the 4IR is not just about technology, the education sector and human resource ministry need to play primary roles in educating and upgrading current levels of human capital in both numbers and skills.

The majority of organisations in Malaysia are aware of the rapidly developing areas such as software development, big data analytics and automation technologies. This is partly due to the government's efforts in disseminating the opportunities and challenges associated with the 4IR to the populace. Such efforts include: persuading businesses to embark in business online, encouraging factories to adopt smart factories, and educating and offering incentives to businesses so they can be ready for new industries and jobs. As such, more job opportunities are arising from IT and automation streams. Although new technologies have been introduced, it may be predicted that non-repetitive blue-collar jobs will survive at least for another decade. In this study, one of the main skills identified was a positive attitude; together with the skills to adapt quickly, be versatile, and willing to learn. As more jobs are becoming data-oriented, employees are expected to possess strong data analysis and ethics skills. The skills to interpret data and make sound recommendations are increasingly in demand.

In general, it appears that the government and the labour market are preparing for the future. Despite this, there are some limitations. Firstly, the implementation of new 4IR technologies requires skilled management and learning processes. Secondly, fear of job loss and resistance to change is likely to occur in some workplaces. The fear of job loss was identified among young workers, possibly due to their employment status, while resistance to change may occur due to the need for reskilling which demands effort, time and resources. With the advent of AI/robotics/applications, some relevant supportive measures are required to assist organisations and their workers to become more aligned with the government's aspirations. Hence, the Ministry of Human Resources and Education need to introduce initiatives that foster areas that are in constant demand in order to be effectively integrated in the workforce.

Implications for labour markets

The main findings of this research show that the 4IR will lead to substantial increases in the demand for high-skilled workers and low demand for low-moderately skilled workers. The study identified that the main skills needed to recruit and redevelop employees in the next five years are information technology, knowledge and human skills (communication, ethics, creative thinking, teamwork and positive attitude). As mentioned previously, the service sector accounts for 55% of the GDP in Malaysia and provided more than 68,838 places for employment in 2018; and the sub-sector that offered the most employment places was the distributive trade segment (MIDA, 2019b). This segment comprises all linkage activities that channel goods and services down the supply chain to intermediaries for resale or final buyers – for example, wholesalers and retailers. Based on the data and activities required in the sector, IT knowledge is necessary to secure jobs. Malaysian organisations have shown a positive response to the 4IR by expressing their willingness to accept changes and they generally appear to be motivated to move forward. However, respondents indicated concerns about the future loss of jobs.

There is, however, a positive perspective concerning the consequences of the 4IR. More advanced technologies are going to be introduced in the market which will require a significant number of workers who have expertise in more specialised technical skills, while eventually eliminating low-skilled jobs. This scenario is supported by the data shown in this study that workers are willing to accept changes and prepared to learn new things despite the challenges of time, effort and resources. As job tasks become automated and digitalised, management activities are expected to become more standardised and perhaps more efficient. However, in Malaysia, human intervention is still considered important and is not likely to be eliminated in the next decade. In fact, this study shows that managers believe in the growing importance of human skills: teamwork, ethics and having a positive attitude. The reduction of repetitive, manual and standardised jobs may become highly problematic, as in the Malaysian labour market much of the workforce possess low to moderate skills. Accordingly, change management initiatives are necessary to avoid the labour market being swamped with a high number of unemployed workers.

Implications for government, labour market planners and human resource professionals

The majority of respondents were impressed with the Malaysian government's efforts to date in strengthening policies and frameworks through the participation of various public–private agencies as key stakeholders. Along with these aspirations, a strong manufacturing sector with a focus on SMEs would pave the way to enhancing productivity, job creation, innovation capability, higher skills, economic prosperity and societal well-being. These research findings indicate that many workplaces are generally ready to embrace the 4IR to achieve organisational objectives. The majority of the management respondents also agreed that the 4IR has significant potential benefits for their respective organisations in terms of increasing productivity and profitability. As a result, in the next decade, it is expected that there will be significant changes particularly in the fields of IT, communication and automation.

However, in preparation for the 4IR, some unforeseen challenges and issues are likely to arise among the workforce in Malaysia. Respondents in this study were mostly working in the manufacturing sector and their skill levels ranged from low to moderately skilled, and most had a secondary school education qualification. However, future engineers, for example, will need to be multi-talented both in engineering and in IT knowledge and skills. The findings also revealed that the future workforce requires advanced skills and knowledge, specifically in the field of IT, communication and automation. The low and moderately skilled workers responded that they feared losing their jobs due to the impact of the 4IR in their respective workplaces. Consequently, the education system is a significant driver towards the preparation of the required workforce.

There are also several implications concerning the government, organisations and workforces. Specifically, the government needs to embark on creating more awareness of the 4IR and stakeholder engagement which is of paramount importance. The government could provide an incentive fund to organisations that are willing to transform and embrace the new forms of work and technologies. Such incentives may then encourage other organisations to embrace the changes. Subsequently, organisations, and particularly human resource professionals, urgently need to minimise the social costs of shifting to the 4IR. Managers should plan and organise retraining programs in order to further develop the existing skills of the workforce to meet the need to support highly skilled, advanced manufacturing requirements over the next five years. There is also a need to address possible job losses due to the implementation of 4IR technologies. As for the workforce, since it is a national aspiration, there are only two options left – that is to embrace the change and position themselves to address the related challenges, or to opt for unemployment.

Therefore, implementing the 4IR has high potential in Malaysia; however, it is crucial that the necessary infrastructure is ready and made available to meet the requirements for the inevitable transition. For example, infrastructure such as internet services requires further development and improved nationwide access in terms of coverage, speed and usefulness in order to fully capitalise the Internet of Things (IoT) and big data. Without these infrastructures, embracing the 4IR will not be fully materialised. As such, the government, organisations and workforces have to work together to realise the national aspiration to completely embrace the 4IR.

Conclusion

This chapter has established that the desire to move forward into the 4IR era is apparent amongst our survey respondents but there is still some uncertainty in relation to 'how' and 'why' it will benefit them. It is evident that effective implementation of 4IR technologies needs government, education and industry support, which involves the participation of managers and workers. However, there are some serious issues that need to be resolved. Firstly, with the implementation of 4IR technologies, the government and industry will need to develop strategies for affected workforces, instead of leaving their future in their own hands. Secondly, HR professionals need to take their services to a different level by embracing supporting technologies and ensuring that employees are being trained/retrained to enable them to be relevant in the digitalisation era. Thirdly, there is an urgency to include courses which address 4IR elements in the existing academic curricula. It is important to have engineers, for example, who are highly skilled in IT. The services sector is also expected to grow at 6.8% per annum and contribute 56.5% to the GDP in 2020, providing 9.3 million jobs. To realise its potential the services sector needs to be transformed to become more knowledge-intensive and innovation-led.

Although Malaysia's GDP was reported as steady in 2017 and 2018, the current government is struggling to strike a balance between growth and the debt left by the previous administration. Hence, the aspiration of becoming a 4IR trendsetter in this region has been somewhat disrupted thus far. However, in line with the government's aspirations, the findings from this study indicate that respondents are ready to prepare for the advent of the 4IR, with the majority of the managerial respondents agreeing that it would be likely to have significant benefits for their organisations in terms of increasing productivity and profitability. In the next five years, future workplaces will need to change rapidly to meet 4IR requirements, particularly in the fields of IT, communication and automation, due to the need to prepare for highly skilled jobs. In particular, a strong manufacturing sector (particularly amongst SMEs) would pave the way to enhancing productivity, job creation and innovation capability.

The majority of respondents were impressed with the government's efforts to date in strengthening policies and frameworks through the participation of various public-private agencies as stakeholders. One key imperative for the vocational and higher education systems is to train the low to moderately skilled workforce, in order to avoid a significant 'job trap' in which an over-supply of low to moderately skilled workers are produced, while there is a simultaneous dearth of highly skilled workers. Managers should plan for skill upgrading and retraining programs in order to further develop the existing skills of the workforce to meet the demands of advanced manufacturing technologies. However, in the pursuit of these desired outcomes, there is also a need to address potential unemployment issues that may result from the implementation of 4IR technologies. Therefore, it is proposed that training/re-training programs or alternative forms of employment should be made a top national priority.

References

Abdullah, D. B., Abdullah, M. Y., & Salleh, M. A. M. (2017). A review on the concept of fourth industrial revolution and the government's initiatives to promote it among youths in Malaysia. e-Bangi. *Journal of Social Sciences and Humanities*, 14 (7). Available at: http://ejournal.ukm.my/ebangi/article/download/22743/7215, accessed 17 February 2019.

Adilla, F. (2019). Budget a testament to gov't ambition in accelerating industry 4.0 adoption. *The Star Online*, Friday, 2 November. Available at: www.nst.com.my/business/2018/11/427724/2019-budget-testament-govt-ambition-accelerating-industry-40-adoption, accessed 19 August 2019.

Asma, N. (2019). *Courses Face New Industrial Revolution 4.0*. Pulau Pinang, Malaysia: Institut Teknikal Jepun. Available at: www.jmti.gov.my/v2/index.php/keratan-akhbar/115-kursus-baharu-hadapi-revolusi-industri-4-0, accessed 11 April 2019.

Deloitte, A. G. (2015). *Industry 4.0 Challenges and Solutions for the Digital Transformation and Use of Exponential Technologies*. McKinsey Global Institute, 13, pp. 1–16. Switzerland. Available at: https://www2.deloitte.com/content/dam/Deloitte/ch/Documents/manufacturing/ch-en-manufacturing-industry-4-0-24102014.pdf, accessed 4 April 2019.

Department of Statistics Malaysia Official Portal (2019). *Principal Statistics of Labour Force, Malaysia*. Available at: https://www.dosm.gov.my/v1/, accessed 17 February 2019.

Duhamel, D. (2019). Is Malaysia ready for industry 4.0? – Digital revolution in manufacturing, healthcare, and logistics industries. *Solidiance.com*. Singapore. Available at: https://solidiance.com/insights/healing/infographics/is-malaysia-ready-for-industry-4-0-digital-revolution-in-manufacturing-healthcare-and-logistics-industries-1, accessed 5 September 2019.

ICEF Monitor (2017). Intense job competition spurring demand for graduate degrees in Malaysia. *Market Intelligence for International Student Recruitment*. Available at: http://monitor.icef.com/2017/10/intense-job-competition-spurring-demand-graduate-degrees, accessed 21 February 2018.

Labour Productivity of First Quarter (2019). *Department of Statistics*. Kuala Lumpur, Malaysia. Available at: https://dosm.gov.my/v1/index.php?r=column/pdfPrev&id=WmtTbys3cktEY2trYVlwSEZlc1ZDdz09, accessed 19 August 2019.

Mahalingam, E. (2019). Is Sabah highway next to get the chop? *Star Online*, Wednesday, 30 May 2018. Available at: www.thestar.com.my/business/business-news/2018/05/30/sabah-highway-next-to-get-the-chop/, accessed 11 April 2019.

Mahpar, N. (2019). Kemahiran digital Sangat Diperlukan Dalam industry Pekerjaan. *Berita Harian*, 17 January. Available at: www.bharian.com.my/bisnes/lain-lain/2019/01/520991/kemahiran-digital-sangat-diperlukan-dalam-industri-pekerjaan, accessed 11 April 2019.

Malaysia External Trade Development Corporation (MATRADE) (2019). Available at: https://twitter.com/matrade/media, accessed 7 February 2019.

Malaysian Investment Development Authority (MIDA) (2019a). *Key Economic Indicators.* Available at: www.mida.gov.my/home/key-economic-indicators/posts/, accessed 11 February 2019.

Malaysian Investment Development Authority (MIDA) (2019b). *Private Investments in Services Sector, 2018 & 2017.* Available at: www.mida.gov.my/home/about-mida/posts/, accessed 11 February 2019.

Might.org.my (2018). *Malaysian Technology Strategic Outlook 2017/2018 Embracing Industry 4.0 – MIGHT Portal.* Available at: www.might.org.my/download/malaysian-technology-strategic-outlook-2017-2018-embracing-industry-4-0/, accessed 15 April 2019.

Ministry of International Trade and Industry (MITI) (2019). *Industry 4wrd: National Policy on Industry 4.0.* [ebook] Kuala Lumpur: Available at: www.miti.gov.my/miti/resources/national%20policy%20on%20industry%204.0/industry4wrd_final.pdf, accessed 19 August 2019.

Mohd Yatid, M. (2019). Why is digital adoption by SMEs not taking off? *The Star Online,* 24 January. Available at: www.nst.com.my/opinion/columnists/2019/01/453789/why-digital-adoption-smes-not-taking, accessed 19 August 2019.

Monash Malaysia (2018). *How Universities Should Prepare for Industry 4.0.* Available at: www.monash.edu.my/news-and-events/pages/latest/articles/2018/how-universities-should-prepare-for-industry-4.0, accessed 4 April 2019.

Mydftz.com (2018). *Digital Free Trade Zone: Strategic Initiative to Intensify Malaysia.* Malaysia Digital Economy Corporation Sdn Bhd Selangor. Available at: https://mydftz.com/, accessed 11 April 2019.

National Policy on Industry 4.0. (2019). *Socio Economic Research Centre,* p. 18. Kuala Lumpur. Available at: www.acccimserc.com/images/researchpdf/2018/20181101%20Malaysias%20National%20Policy%20on%20Industry%204.0.pdf, accessed 5 September 2019.

New Straits Times (2018). 2019 Budget: Finance minister's full speech text. *New Straits Times,* 2 November. Available at: www.nst.com.my/news/nation/2018/11/427605/2019-budget-finance-ministers-full-speech-text, accessed 15 April 2019.

Raj, J. (2019). *DPM:* Govt spent RM2.3b on women entrepreneurs in 2018. *Malay Mail,* Tuesday, 29 January. Available at: www.malaymail.com/news/malaysia/2019/01/29/dpm-govt-spent-rm2.3b-on-women-entrepreneurs-in-2018/1717780, accessed 3 September 2019.

Rosli, L. (2019). Malaysia's E&E paves the way for industry 4.0. *News Straits Times,* 16 November. Available at: www.nst.com.my/business/2017/11/303914/malaysias-ee-paves-way-industry-40, accessed 4 April 2019.

The Star Online (2019). *Malaysia Ranks 37th in Global Innovation Index,* Thursday, 15 June 2017. Available at: www.thestar.com.my/business/business-news/2017/06/15/malaysia-ranks-37th-in-global-innovation-index, accessed 19 August 2019.

Toh, K. I. (2019). Industry 4.0 blueprint on readiness assessment finalised, says Miti. *The Star Online,* Thursday, 15 November 2018. Available at: www.thestar.com.my/business/business-news/2018/11/15/industry-40-blueprint-on-readiness-assessment-finalised-says-miti, accessed 19 August 2019.

World Bank (2019). *"Small Is the New Big" – Malaysian SMEs Help Energize, Drive Economy.* Available at: www.worldbank.org/en/news/feature/2016/07/05/small-is-the-new-big---malaysian-smes-help-energize-drive-economy, accessed 7 February 2019.

Worldbank.org (2019). *GDP (Current US$) Data.* Available at: https://data.worldbank.org/indicator/NY.GDP.MKTP.CD?locations=MYE-MY, accessed 19 August 2019.

Zakariah, Z. (2018). Malaysia's 13 strategies to transform manufacturing & services sector. *News Strait Times.com.my,* 31 October. Available at: www.nst.com.my/business/2018/10/426984/malaysias-13-strategies-transform-manufacturing-services-sector, accessed 11 April 2019.

10 Mauritius

Vikash Rowtho, Karlo Jouan, Sarita Hardin-Ramanan, Shafiiq Gopee, Odylle Charoux

Introduction

This chapter explores the likely impact of the Fourth Industrial Revolution (4IR) on Mauritian industry, workplaces, jobs and employees. In particular, it assesses the preparedness of the government, industry managers and higher and vocational education systems to effectively address the inevitable challenges in this small island developing country context. The chapter begins with a brief explanation of its profile and stages of economic development, before presenting the findings from a study of managerial perspectives on the 4IR. Finally, several key issues are highlighted, together with some recommendations for the government, industry and the education sector in their collaborative attempts to effectively address the challenges posed by the 4IR as a smart island with a circular and inclusive economy.

Country profile

The Republic of Mauritius (referred to later as Mauritius) is a small island economy in the Indian Ocean located off the south-eastern coast of Africa and east of Madagascar. It has a total surface area of around 2011 square kilometres, with the island of Mauritius and Rodrigues (1868 and 110 square kilometres respectively), being the main territories in size and economic activity. Due to its many small outer islands, Mauritius has a large exclusive economic zone of 2.3 million square kilometres, and since 2012 it shares with the Seychelles jurisdiction over an area of 396,000 square kilometres of the Continental Shelf, as shown in figure 10.1.

After a minor settlement by the Dutch, from 1638 to 1710, Mauritius became a French colony from 1715 to 1810. From then on, it remained under British rule for more than 150 years, before acceding to independence in 1968. In terms of governance, the country is a western ministerial-based democratic state with free and fair legislative elections every five years. Separation of powers between the executive, the legislative and the judiciary is guaranteed under the constitution. These checks and balances have been effective in allowing the country to enjoy political stability. Mauritius is a multi-cultural society

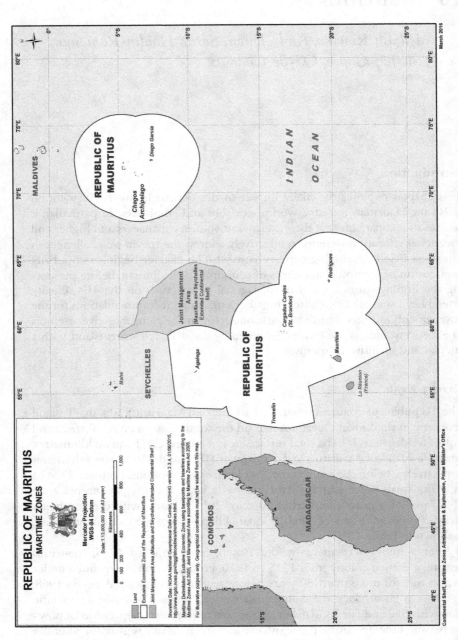

Figure 10.1 The Mauritian Exclusive Economic Zone

Source: Government of Mauritius

consisting of descendants of immigrants from Europe, Africa and Asia – it has no indigenous population. The official language is English although French is also widely used and the population as of 31st December 2018 was estimated at 1.27 million (Statsmauritius.govmu.org, 2019a).

Evolution of the Mauritian economy

During the colonial days, the country was essentially a monocrop, low-income economy based on cane plantations manufacturing sugar. The transport of cane from the fields to factories and the manufacturing of sugar under French rule, as well as during most years of British rule, was undertaken using first industrial revolution technologies. Electricity production, as the key technology of the second industrial revolution, started in Mauritius in 1880. In 1914, the General Electric Supply Company of Mauritius was authorised to go beyond the illumination of some regions and "extend its services to sugar and aloe factories and workshops along the lines of its connections", (Riviere, 2015: 30).

On its way to independence, Mauritius established an import–substitution manufacturing sector during the 1960s. However, the limits of such a strategy intended to tackle the challenges of growth and unemployment, led to a switch towards an export-led growth strategy just after independence. This led to the creation of an Export Processing Zone (EPZ) focused on manufacturing and a tourism industry. After a period of economic difficulties, the country engaged in deep economic reforms in the early 1980s with the adoption of fiscal discipline, as well as rigorous monetary policies to keep inflation in check.

In the early 1990s a labour intensive three-pillar economy (textile/EPZ, tourism and sugar), based on second industrial revolution technologies and extremely reliant on preferential trade agreements, allowed Mauritius to realise robust growth and full employment. After attaining the status of a middle-income economy, the country faced new challenges. These emanated from rising production costs, the elimination of above-market rate prices for sugar and stiffer competition for textiles in export markets. These were due to the erosion of preferential market access that had historically been granted by the European Union to its African, Caribbean, and Pacific (ACP) group of states.

At this point in time, Mauritius needed a new economic strategy based on global competitiveness. Both the EPZ and sugar sectors responded with a move to higher value-added products. The country also prepared itself for introducing information and communications technology to improve productivity gains and explore new development plans. These measures contributed to progressing Mauritius to an upper middle-income economy with a per capita income of $22,570 in purchasing power parity (PPP) as at 2017. At the same time, after peaking to 9.1% in 2006, the unemployment rate has been falling slowly and is now at 7.1% (Statsmauritius.govmu.org, 2019b).

Today, high-speed transfer of data, web development, mobile technology, social media, electronic trading platforms, cloud computing and virtual reality are (inter alia) contributing to service innovation in Mauritius. The more agile economic operators are changing business processes in different areas, such as marketing, training, inventory management and supply chains all of which have contributed to productivity gains. The innovations that have been introduced over the last two decades have also contributed to efforts for further diversification of the economic base, with the emergence of new key sectors such as financial services, information and communication technology (ICT), business process outsourcing (BPO) and real estate. Other new sectors, including a higher education hub, medical tourism and an ocean economy, are still in their early stages. Yet, there is a pressing need for greater attention to technological breadth and depth if they are to be competitive, because of the risk of being driven out by global competitors who make more intensive use of information technology for research and development and product and process innovation, as well as business model innovation.

However, the lack of a strong culture of digital transformation and a skills shortage has restricted the development of e-government, and the possibilities for organisations to innovate and create new business models for significant improvements in quality of life and sustainability. Nonetheless, various policy reforms and the development of IT infrastructure, as well as private and public sector digital initiatives undertaken over the last 25 years in favour of a shift to a digital economy indicate that Mauritius has undeniably embarked on its journey towards the third industrial revolution. Although economic diversification has improved the country's resilience to some external shocks, the declining rate of economic expansion from 2008–2018 (from 5% to 3.5%) constitutes a serious obstacle to achieving the government's Vision 2030 to become a high income and more inclusive economy.

At a time when there are signs that preparation for the Fourth Industrial Revolution (4IR) is already progressing in a number of countries, Mauritius needs to look for opportunities in what is now becoming a world of digital disruption. However, this task is challenging, as it is difficult to assess the country's level of preparedness for the 4IR because Mauritius does not appear in the Automation Readiness Index (see Chapter 1) which assesses how prepared countries are for the challenges and opportunities of intelligent automation. To contribute to an understanding of Mauritius' state of preparedness, this study focused on how well managers and leaders in the country understand the nature and impact of 4IR on their industries and organisations and to what extent they are prepared to address the associated workplace and skills issues.

Research findings: Mauritian managers' perspectives

This study used the conceptual framework and survey questionnaire outlined in Chapter 2. The questions were coded using Qualtrix and the link to the survey was emailed to managers of selected organisations. To ensure sampling was objective, all the key industries of the Mauritian economy (tourism, agriculture, manufacturing, financial services and information and communications technology) and both the private and public sectors, as well as small and medium enterprises were invited to participate in this study.

From the 161 respondents, 60% came from private companies. This was followed by 24% from government business enterprises and public institutions. Multinational corporations represented 16% of the respondents. The private companies included large companies listed on the Mauritian stock exchange as well as small and medium enterprises. The public institutions included ministries and local government as well as government business enterprises.

Data collection took place between December 2018 and April 2019. Respondents had the option of answering online, using their computers or through their mobile phones. Responses were received from 161 of the 450 (36%) organisations which received the survey questionnaire. This response rate is in line with Baruch and Holtom (2008) who recommend that 35% to 40% is an acceptable range for high-level institutional respondents.

Figure 10.2 shows the types of organisations which participated in the study. This constitutes a representative sample of the local context, where the private sector is the largest employer followed by the public sector.

Responses were well distributed between small, medium and large enterprises and respondents were equally divided by organisational size (measured by employee numbers). Specifically, for enterprises employing between 1 and 99 employees there were 34% followed by 33% for enterprises employing between 100 and 499 and the remaining 33% represented those employing over 500 employees, as shown in figure 10.3.

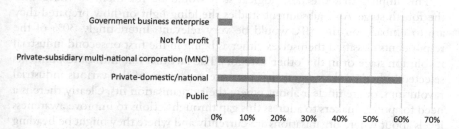

Figure 10.2 Organisation Type

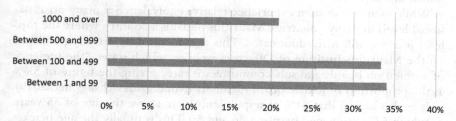

Figure 10.3 Number of Employees in Organisations

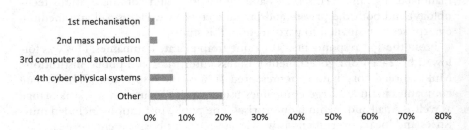

Figure 10.4 Current Technological Stage of Organisations

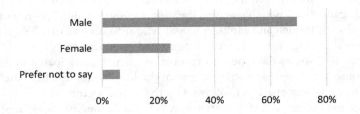

Figure 10.5 Gender of Respondents

Concerning the technological stage in which the respondents situated them-selves, a large majority (70%) considered that their organisations were in the third technological stage, as shown in figure 10.4.

This implies that the next logical step would be for them to move into the fourth stage. Any subsequent studies shedding light on how prepared they are to embark on the 4IR would be very relevant. Interestingly, 30% of the respondents classified themselves either as being in the first or second industrial revolution stage or in the 'other' category. The fact that one fifth of respondents selected 'other' could suggest that they are not aware of the various industrial revolutions, or are unclear about where their organisation fits. Clearly, there is a need for policy makers to address this gap through actions to improve awareness levels about where organisations are currently and where they might be heading

Another interesting aspect of the demographic data relates to respondents' gender. Sixty-nine percent were males with only 24% females represented, as shown in figure 10.5.

While men and women experience relative equivalence at many organisa-tional levels in many countries, Mauritius remains a country where the top-level jobs are still male-dominated. This is evidenced by a study published on the Mauritius Institute of Directors website, which states, "the presence of women on boards and sub-committees is rare" giving the figure of 5.6% as the proportion of female board members (Miod.azurewebsites.net, 2019).

It is also logical that 81% of respondents were above the age of 35 years, of which 51% were aged between 36 and 50. This is usually the age bracket where employees become managers in Mauritius. Respondents were also well qualified, with 55% holding a postgraduate qualification and 33% having a bachelor's degree. Over 70% of respondents held a position of manager or higher which includes directors, CEOs and general managers as well as entrepreneurs. These results show that most managers have at least a bachelor's degree, with a majority having a post-graduate qualification. This is in line with Mauritian recruitment policies from both the public and private sectors.

When asked about information technology (IT) management in their organisations, the majority (70%) reported that it was a centralised IT system, as shown in figure 10.6.

While centralised IT systems allow for lower investment in terms of hardware and provide an easier flow of information between different departments, a drawback of this approach is that it is more difficult to respond quickly to technological change and take advantage of their added capabilities. This is much more relevant in the context of the 4IR, where it is expected that technology will be the disruptor in all industries within a relatively short period of time. Therefore, it is crucial for organisations to be aware of this limitation when devising future strategies, especially in the transition period between the Third and Fourth Industrial Revolutions.

Organisational strategy and 4IR

The current transition period between the third and fourth industrial phase constitutes an excellent opportunity for organisations to review and align their strategic intentions in the context of the usage/implementation of AI software applications. The results of this study show that, in general, respondents adapted and aligned their IT strategies according to strategic business changes, while ensuring that their IT strategies supported and matched their business strategies. While it is good to have appropriate strategic intentions, it is also important to have the support of top management for the implementation of technology change in an organisation. Interestingly, most respondents reported that top management was aware of the benefits and supported the adoption

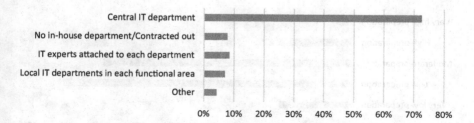

Figure 10.6 Organisation of IT Function

of AI/software/applications, while at the same time, allocating the necessary resources.

Regarding the usefulness of AI/software/applications in their organisations, the majority of respondents reported that they would be useful to employees in performing their tasks and would enhance performance. Most respondents also reported that, because of AI/software/application adoption, organisations will increase revenues, reduce lost sales, enhance profit margins and have a better competitive advantage. However, the findings shown in figure 10.7 indicate that half the organisations have very low, to low, preparedness for the forthcoming changes with regard to AI and other 4IR technologies. With technological changes having already commenced, the fact that 40% of the organisations have only moderate preparation in place should be a cause for concern and draw the attention of policy makers.

Impact on jobs

Concerning the likely impact of the latest technologies on employees' job satisfaction, many respondents tend to believe that it will affect employees positively by enhancing their job satisfaction. However, there were mixed feelings among the respondents regarding job security. Some respondents think that employees are confident that they will continue working for their respective organisations and will keep their jobs, despite the increase in the use of AI/software/applications. On the other hand, some believe that employees worry about the continuation of their careers and fear that they might become redundant in the wake of the 4IR. While it is known that low-level jobs are the most at risk with the forthcoming changes, further investigation is needed to identify the type of employees who might lose their jobs.

In any discussion about changes to jobs, resistance to change is generally a factor to consider. Figure 10.8 shows that only 17% of all respondents anticipate high to very high resistance to the forthcoming changes brought about through technology.

At the same time, 55% of the respondents are of the opinion that there could be moderate resistance. This is a relatively high number, which is probably related to anticipated job security issues.

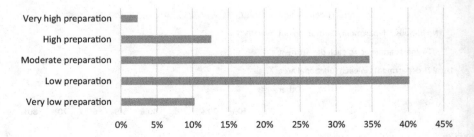

Figure 10.7 Level of Preparation for Forthcoming Changes

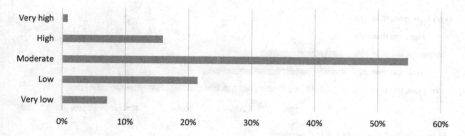

Figure 10.8 Anticipated Resistance to Change

The future of jobs

Respondents also assessed perceived skill needs that are anticipated for the next five years. They reported that skills in data and communications security would be the most sought after in five years' time, followed by data analytics. The findings show that respondents are aware of the importance of security in any technological developments, especially given the fourth technological stage will involve a large number of interconnected devices through networks where there will be an enormous amount of data exchange and processing. What is also interesting is that, while today there is practically no demand in the Mauritian market for data analytics professionals, respondents believe that they will be in high demand in the next five years. This indicates that respondents are well aware that business decisions will increasingly rely on big data analytics in the near future.

When asked about the likely percentage of jobs that will change significantly in different functions in the next decade, due to the impact of artificial intelligence and automation in their organisations, respondents reported that, although there will be changes in all areas, Information Technology, Data and Communications security will be the areas that will undergo the most change. This response is aligned with their opinions about future skill needs where security, communication and analytics featured in the top rankings. Respondents also believe that manufacturing, production and operations would undergo significant changes. The reason might be that the use of technology as a source of competitive advantage is quite common in Mauritius.

Concerning jobs likely to be replaced in different functions over the next decade due to the impact of artificial intelligence and automation, respondents are of the opinion that the nature of jobs will change, rather than these jobs disappearing completely. This is probably why, when asked to estimate the percentage of jobs created overall within their organisation because of new technologies, 80% of the respondents believed that it would be very low to low, as shown in figure 10.9. This is in line with their opinion that very few jobs will disappear completely due to the forthcoming changes.

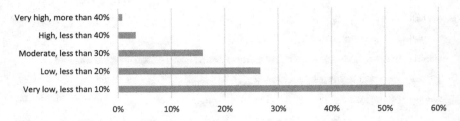

Figure 10.9 Anticipated Job Creation

Some key issues

The first issue identified is preparedness for the forthcoming changes. Although there is growing evidence that the 4IR is happening now, Mauritian employers and their employees in general do not believe that there will be drastic and fast changes. That is probably why most organisations do not have a high level of preparation, including both technological and workforce preparedness where management buy-in and support is critical. Such support ensures appropriate technological acquisitions and facilitates appropriate training and retraining for the continuous upskilling of employees, while contributing to managing resistance to change. Lastly, although government has already taken a number of initiatives to facilitate the transition to the fourth technological stage, most respondents do not seem impressed by government policies.

Technological and workforce preparedness

Schwab (2016) argues that, unlike previous industrial revolutions, the fourth is distinctive in its velocity, scope and systems impact. Hyper-connectivity and digital prowess are multiplying the rate and reach with which new technologies are being developed and deployed. The areas of application, merging the digital, physical and biological realms (Schwab, 2016), are not only far-reaching and breaking new frontiers, but are also questioning and transforming the undisputed foundations of traditional systems of operations. A major concern in the 4IR discourse is, therefore, the importance of preparing (or not preparing) for such unprecedented and profound ramifications and their subsequent impact on business activities. Noticeably, this study revealed that only 14% of the managers surveyed are confident and have a high to very high level of preparedness for the forthcoming changes in AI and robotics technologies.

The first step to preparedness is the awareness of the challenges that such a major shift is going to bring. To this end, Deloitte highlights that "while some people are ready to face the challenge [of the Fourth Industrial Revolution], equipped with the tools to brave the change and take advantage of its effects, others do not even know a storm is brewing" (Deloitte, 2018: 1). As discussed earlier, Mauritian industry leaders appear to be aware of the technological developments stemming from the 4IR. An economy highly dependent on foreign exports and international trade, be it in terms of commodities or services, has always pushed the country in following and adopting international trends to keep up with competition. In fact, there are debates as to whether the drive towards the 4IR is voluntary or a consequence of external forces. On one hand, this study reveals that organisations' top management enthusiastically support the adoption of these disruptive technologies and are generally ready to commit resources towards their adoption. On the other hand, there is also an expectation that, to maintain a competitive edge, companies as a whole will need to embrace these disruptive technologies. For example, one of the survey respondents commented that "AI/Robotics will force itself whether we like it or not". Whether voluntarily or purely as a measure to stay competitive, Mauritian industry leaders have already taken the first step change and also appear to be aware of the potential for forthcoming changes.

The changes or transformations heralded by the 4IR will inevitably have direct consequences not only on business functions but also on the workforce. Schwab (2018) when discussing the way forward comments that businesses will have to approach the 4IR on two fronts. The first, being the capacity to experiment with technology and work out what works best for the organisation and second, with regard to investment in the workforce.

From a technological perspective, although this study did not capture the current investment or actual level of 4IR technology adoption, it can be safely inferred through the various findings and comments that, although companies might not experiment and research new technologies, they are to some degree prepared to implement them when the need might arise. With 70% of the represented organisations being at the third technological stage and having a centralised IT department, it is understood that they have the experience and structure required to deploy company-wide technologies and are also in a position to put in place structures to deploy disruptive technologies.

However, of bigger concern is the impact of the 4IR on the workforce and how best to prepare employees. In the current study, more than 60% of those surveyed disagree, or strongly disagree, that artificial intelligence and associated technologies will not affect the way employees work. There are, however, divergent views on the impact of such a revolution on the workforce.

There is, on one side, a legitimate fear that artificial intelligence and robotics will take over many jobs and will consequently precipitate extensive job losses (Hirschi, 2018). In this study, nearly 55% of respondents agree that employees fear that they might become redundant due to increases in the use of these technologies. Conversely, only 38% feel that employees are very confident that they will be able to keep their jobs despite technology implementation. Fear that the 4IR will engender job losses is very much present and hence makes the issue of preparedness more urgent and important.

That said, without understating the importance and impact of the disruptive technologies on the workforce, there is a growing belief that the 4IR will bring more benefits to employees. The World Economic Forum (2018: 7) in its 'Future of Work' report acknowledged that, just as with previous industrial revolutions, there ought to be the creation of new job roles, but at the same time some more traditional tasks are expected to become obsolete. However, the World Economic Forum reassures us that the "increased demand for new roles will offset the decreasing demand for others" (2018: 7). In the Mauritian case study, the perception that there will be the creation of jobs and enhancement of current job roles is paradoxically very strong, despite (as mentioned earlier) the looming spectre of redundancy.

For example, a little more than half of the respondents believe that their employees think that they will be able to continue working in the organisation despite increased use of artificial intelligence and robotics technologies. Some survey respondents elaborated further in the comments section arguing that the Fourth Industrial Revolution "will change our daily life and make it easier. Access to information and services will improve and the world will be at our fingertips". Another respondent commented that "AI will not replace man but will augment human capabilities". An interesting point raised by one respondent refers to the finer and more detailed difference between jobs and tasks. The respondent argues that "AI may replace tasks, not jobs. Jobs will be shredded but not eliminated. Instead of worrying about job losses, our organisation should be helping to reduce jobs where AI and machine learning take over certain tasks, while humans spend more time with higher-level tasks".

There is a growing body of research supporting the re-training and upskilling of the workforce as a salient facet of the preparation for the 4IR. The World Economic Forum (2018: 11) indicated that "by 2022, no less than 54% of all employees will require significant reskilling and upskilling" to create the "augmented workforce". Along the same line, Shook and Knickrehm (2017) argued that accelerating the reskilling of people is key to the necessary shaping and preparation for the technological advances being deployed. The findings of this study are consistent with these research studies in that Mauritian business leaders are aware of the need to retrain and upskill their staff.

Although not highlighted in the research, the preparation of the workforce for the 4IR will have significant ramifications on human resource activities and policies. For example, Parham and Tamminga (2018: 187) explained that "it is of crucial importance that companies rethink their recruitment and selection strategies, redesign their training and development programs and review all their HR policies to ensure a successful workforce transformation". Hirschi (2018: 199) also argued that HR professionals will have to rethink career development models in light of the fundamental changes to the work structure, with "increasing interconnection between work and non-work". The consequences are boundless. Therefore, in their quest to bring about this transformation and remould existing employees into an augmented workforce, it is advocated that Mauritian companies review their preparation and implementation strategies in order to allow them to have a smooth transition into the 4IR.

Another issue directly linked to the retraining and upskilling of the workforce is resistance to change. There is a plethora of research on the issue in various degrees and forms (Park & Koh, 2017). Resistance to change or resistance towards the adoption of new technologies might be one of the biggest barriers facing organisations in reaping the benefits of the 4IR. Surprisingly, the current study revealed that Mauritian managers are rather confident that there will not be such resistance. A possible explanation could be that, for the past two decades, the country has been involved in a massive endeavour to diversify its economy. The fact that 70% of companies consider themselves to be at the third technological stage is a testament of the transformation that the country has undergone. There have been radical changes at all levels and, although there have been some hiccups, organisations have been faring well in adopting new technologies, methods and processes to ensure that they are abreast of the current developments at the global stage. Notably, a number of countries have already realised that it is crucial to put in place appropriate frameworks and policies to ensure a smooth transition to the new landscape.

Government policies

Government strategies and policies are key to both maximizing the efficiencies brought about by new technologies and to best manage any resulting disruptions. In riding the 4IR wave, governments should not ignore the potential economic and social impacts. Government-driven funds and mechanisms would encourage the development and implementation of innovations from the Fourth Industrial Revolution (World Economic Forum, 2017). These would include investments in required infrastructure and cybersecurity risk management. Governments equally need to contain looming job redundancies and their impact to avoid social unrest. The recent amendment to Mauritian labour laws regarding the portability of severance allowances is to that effect very relevant. Addressing digital inequalities remains another social concern. Facilities for training or upskilling, along with incentives for adaptability to the 4IR would help ease and encourage the adoption of AI. Through collaborations with organisations and society, governments should also develop ethical guidelines for the harmonious co-existence of humans and machines (Reis & Durkin, 2018).

The Mauritian government has worked on a number of strategies and initiatives to endorse artificial intelligence (AI). For example, the last budget speech (2019) announced the following measures:

(1) The setting up of a Mauritius Artificial Intelligence Council (MAIC) to lead, boost and, in some cases, even fund innovative AI initiatives on the island (Budget Speech 2018–2019, 2018; Working Group on Artificial Intelligence, 2018).

(2) The establishment of a Mauritius Innovation and Entrepreneurship Framework to promote idea generation and prototyping of innovative technologies (Budget Speech 2018–2019, 2018).

(3) The provision of Robotics and AI enabled financial advisory services (Budget Speech 2019–2020.

The MAIC is defined in the Mauritius AI Strategy (2018) which, in turn, provides a roadmap for the adoption of innovative technologies in Mauritius. The strategy not only shares AI best practices across several industries, but also dictates the establishment of robust regulations promoting fiscal incentives and training grants to boost AI adoption. In addition to strong measures for cybersecurity, the strategy further recommends the formulation of an ethics committee to ensure an ethical AI ecosystem for a balanced human–machine relationship (Working Group on Artificial Intelligence, 2018).

The Mauritian government is also aware that AI cannot be successful if the island suffers from a dearth of associated talent. To address this issue, the Mauritius AI Strategy (2018) provides several recommendations, including the right framework to attract foreign expertise, a reskilling scheme to train workers with the potential to shift to AI-related positions, revamped university curricula, and advanced AI training. The Government realises that educational institutions have a major role to play, not only in encouraging students to take up mathematical and science subjects, but also in promoting digital literacy and AI knowledge. Already, primary and secondary schools are working with IT companies and the government to offer free training in programming and to encourage students to take an interest in coding through national competitions.

The Mauritius AI Strategy (2018) also stipulates that programming be a mandatory subject across all university courses and that IT courses be reviewed to cover industry-relevant AI skills. The establishment of a "talent watch", responsible for identifying and communicating industry AI needs to educational institutions among other stakeholders, to match related curricula with business needs is recommended. To speed up AI-associated university course offerings, it is suggested that course accreditation by local bodies such as the Mauritius Qualification Authority should be processed more quickly and that universities collaborate in sharing expertise as well as facilities. Inter-university partnerships could also be extended to AI-related research, which currently concerns only a few, isolated projects such as the Government-University of Mauritius Agri-Tech Park initiative for research on digital farming (Tertiary Education Commission, 2018).

The Digital Mauritius 2030 Strategic Plan (2018) also aims to promote AI-adoption on the island. The strategy mentions the allocation of at least 50 scholarships per year for students wishing to study emerging technologies – such as AI. The 2019–2020 budget makes provision for the introduction of a master's degree in AI at one of the local universities, and a six-month AI Skills Development Programme for 100 students organised by the Human Resource Development Council in collaboration with local universities and international experts. Due to the scarcity of local AI talent, the government also undertakes to employ up to 20 international lecturers, and provide a post-study work visa to international AI undergraduates to work in Mauritius for a period of three years (Budget Speech, 2019–2020, 2019).

Creating the right environment and framework for government and industry collaboration is crucial. By hosting the World Artificial Intelligence Show and World Blockchain Summit in Mauritius in November of 2018 (Republic of Mauritius, 2018), the Mauritian government brought together different stakeholders from academia, the public sector and industry to explore the potential of AI for the island. The Mauritius Artificial Intelligence Strategy, including the MAIC as a uniting platform for the public and private sector followed, but has yet to prove its mettle. The same applies to the numerous measures announced in recent budget speeches, which still need to be implemented and their success evaluated. Some of the survey respondents also deplore the lack of clarity around the government AI strategy. As expressed by one of the industry representatives:

> There is not enough information about the AI/Robotics market in Mauritius, the government's stance on AI and its strategy on the promotion of the AI industry. At the educational level, actions to promote AI among students and career prospects for those who have chosen this subject for their studies remain unclear. . . . There are still too many unknown elements on this subject.

This could explain why figure 10.10 shows that 54.4% of respondents were either not impressed or not impressed at all by the government policies put in place to prepare Mauritius for the 4IR.

The Government relies heavily on businesses and educational institutions to implement its AI strategies and, while a number of initiatives have been taken, clearly the expectation from stakeholders is that more needs to be done. On the other hand, business and academia require clear guidelines and a conducive environment for efficient AI training and use (World Economic Forum, 2018).

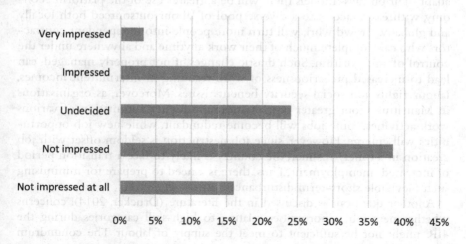

Figure 10.10 Government Policies

Governments are expected to provide incentives for AI training and upskilling, information on associated career paths, and guidance on AI solutions for business optimisation. Although these are mentioned in the Mauritian AI Strategy, Digital Mauritius 2030 Strategic Plan, and both the 2018–2019 and 2018–2020 budget announcements, the country can only succeed if concrete actions come sooner rather than later.

Conclusion

To achieve its vision of becoming a high-income inclusive economy by 2030, Mauritius will undoubtedly need to ride the fourth revolution wave. Pursuing progress with third industrial revolution technologies and hoping to be ready to react to disruptions brought about by the fourth wave, are not substantial enough strategies to support the country to move to the next level. Government will need to put in place appropriate legislative frameworks to facilitate the deployment of new technologies as well as to facilitate the reskilling and upskilling of employees. Some initiatives have been taken recently to develop a strategy for accelerating the implementation of big data analytics, cloud-based business, the internet of things, artificial intelligence, robotics and blockchain in some specific sectors such as smart cities and smart electricity grids. The country is also looking forward to the deployment of 5G wireless networking technology in 2020.

Mauritian policy makers need to bear in mind the need to leapfrog into global leadership. Stepping up research and development, attaining global leadership in one or two targeted areas and unlocking the potential of its vast maritime zone, are all vital for the country to escape the middle-income trap within a reasonable period of time. It is essential to urgently address the current shortage of skills in AI, robotics and blockchain and to promote the emergence of a class of techno entrepreneurs. As Mauritian organisations adapt their business models there will be a greater use of the platform economy, with easier access to a diverse pool of labour outsourced both locally and globally. Crowd work will turn more people into independent contractors who can complete much of their work anytime and anywhere under the control of an algorithm. Such drastic changes, if not properly managed, can lead to increased precariousness of work resulting in intermittent incomes, labour rights and social security benefits issues. Moreover, as organisations in Mauritius adopt greater digitalisation and higher automation of various work activities, some jobs will become redundant, while new job opportunities will emerge. However, since job destruction is seldom offset with job creation in a timely manner, the country is likely to face a transition period of increased unemployment. Thus, there is a need to prepare for minimising such inevitable short-term disturbances.

Another question, as discussed in the literature (Drucker, 2014), concerns whether new job opportunities relating to high-skill categories during the 4IR might not be sufficient to meet the supply of labour. The conundrum for the Mauritian authorities concerns properly addressing the complex balance between adjusting to a more flexible environment with the diversity of labour arrangements in place to facilitate job creation. Unlike previous models of industrial revolution, the 4IR also implies the need to embark on a cultural transformational journey in which the government of Mauritius and businesses cooperate with employees, educational systems and communities to engage in a new model of development, eventually leading to the creation of a smart island with a circular and inclusive economy.

References

Baruch, Y., & Holtom, B. C. (2008). Survey response rate levels and trends in organizational research. *Human Relations*, 61 (8), 1139–1160.

Budget Speech 2018–2019 (2018). *Budget Speech 2018–2019*. Available at: http://budget. mof.govmu.org/budget2018-19/2018_19budgetspeech.pdf, accessed 10 July 2019.

Budget Speech 2019–2020 (2019). *Budget Speech 2019–2020*. Available at: http://budget. mof.govmu.org/budget2019-20/2019_20budgetspeech.pdf, accessed 10 July 2019.

Deloitte (2018). *Preparing Tomorrow's Workforce for the Fourth Industrial Revolution | Deloitte | About*. Available at: https://www2.deloitte.com/global/en/pages/about-deloitte/articles/gx-preparing-tomorrow-workforce-for-the-fourth-industrial-revolution.html, accessed 30 June 2019.

Drucker, P. (2014). *Innovation and Entrepreneurship*. New York: Routledge.

Government of Mauritius (2019). *Ministry of Defence and Rodrigues – Maritime Zone Maps*. Available at: http://mdr.govmu.org/English/defence/Pages/CSMZAE_Maritime_Zone_Maps.aspx, accessed 15 June 2019.

Hirschi, A. (2018). The fourth industrial revolution: Issues and implications for career research and practice. *The Career Development Quarterly*, 66, 192–204.

Ministry of Technology Communication and Innovation (2018). *Digital Mauritius 2030 Strategic Plan 2018*. Available at: http://mtci.govmu.org/English/Documents/2018/Launch ingDigitalTransformationStrategy191218/DM203017December2018at12.30hrs.pdf, accessed 10 July 2019.

Miod.azurewebsites.net (2019). Available at: http://miod.azurewebsites.net/Media/Key%20 Documents/Surveys/20150728-HayGroup-Survey-Directors-Remuneration-Report-Summary.pdf, accessed 1 July 2019.

Parham, S., & Tamminga, H-J. (2018). The adaptation of the logistic industry to the fourth industrial revolution: The role of human resource management. *Journal of Business Management & Social Science Research*, 7 (9), 179–191.

Park, K., & Koh, J. (2017). Exploring the relationship between perceived pace of technology change and adoption resistance to convergence products. *Computers in Human Behavior*, 69, 142–150.

Reis, C., & Durkin, S. (2018). *Workforce of the Future | AusIMM Bulletin*. Available at: www. ausimmbulletin.com/feature/workforce-of-the-future/, accessed 19 July 2019.

Republic of Mauritius (2018). *Republic of Mauritius- Artificial Intelligence Can Ensure a Better Society and Promote Social Inclusion and Safety, Says PM*. Available at: www.govmu.org/English/News/Pages/Artificial-Intelligence-can-ensure-a-better-society-and-promote-social-inclusion-and-safety,-says-PM.aspx, accessed 20 July 2019.

Riviere, M. S. (2015). *Lighting the Way Ahead: History of Electricity in Mauritius (1880–2015)*. Port Louis [Ile Maurice]: The Central Electricity Board.

Schwab, K. (2016). *The Fourth Industrial Revolution: What It Means and How to Respond.* Available at: www.weforum.org/agenda/2016/01/the-fourth-industrial-revolution-what-it-means-and-how-to-respond/, accessed 20 July 2019.

Schwab, K. (2018). The urgency of shaping: The fourth industrial revolution. *Accountancy,* SA (4), 26–27. Available at: https://search-proquest-com.dbgw.lis.curtin.edu.au/docview/20 55024580?accountid=10382, accessed 20 July 2019.

Shook, E., & Knickrehm, M. (2017). *Harnessing Revolution: Creating the Future Workforce, Accenture Strategy, 2017.* Available at: www.accenture.com/_acnmedia/pdf-40/accenture-strategy-harnessing-revolution-pov.pdf, accessed 30 June 2019.

Statsmauritius.govmu.org (2019a). *Statistics Mauritius – Gender Statistics – Year 2018.* Available at: http://statsmauritius.govmu.org/English/Publications/Pages/Gender_Stats_Yr18. aspx, accessed 21 July 2019.

Statsmauritius.govmu.org (2019b). *Digest of Labour Statistics.* Available at: http://statsmauri tius.govmu.org/English/Publications/Documents/Regular%20Reports/labour/Digest_ Labour_Yr18.pdf, accessed 21 July 2019.

Tertiary Education Commission (2018). *Quality Audit Report University of Mauritius.* Available at: www.tec.mu/pdf_downloads/pubrep/UoM_Audit_Report_Final_041218.pdf, accessed 20 July 2019.

Working Group on Artificial Intelligence (2018). *Mauritius Artificial Intelligence Strategy.* Available at: http://mtci.govmu.org/English/Documents/2018/Launching Digital Transformation Strategy 191218/Mauritius AI Strategy (7).pdf, accessed 27 May 2019.

World Economic Forum (2017). *The Global Competitiveness Report 2017–2018.* Available at: http://www3.weforum.org/docs/GCR2017-2018/05FullReport/TheGlobalCompeti tivenessReport2017–2018.pdf, accessed 30 June 2019.

World Economic Forum (2018). *The Future of Jobs Report 2018.* Available at: www.weforum. org/reports/the-future-of-jobs-report-2018, accessed 30 June 2019.

11 Nepal

Subas P. Dhakal, Devi P. Dahal and Simon Dahal

Introduction

The nexus between innovation and economic progress features prominently within the United Nation's (UN) sustainable development goals (SDGs). While the techno-centric view of the economic opportunities associated with digital transformations has received significant attention in the context of the Fourth Industrial Revolution (4IR), the gap between developed and developing nations remains significant. For example, more than two and a half billion people in developing countries do not have access to constant electricity. Similarly, over four billion people lack access to the Internet, an overwhelming majority of whom live in developing countries (UN, 2019).

If the 4IR is an opportunity to harness converging technologies in order to create an inclusive, human-centred future (WEF, 2018), this chapter contends that the premise of the 4IR must complement the aspirations contained within the UN's SDGs – widely accepted as a blueprint for an inclusive world. Under the assumption that there are fertile prospects to judiciously foster transformative technologies and advance the SDGs, this chapter focuses on an inclusive 4IR scenario using a case study of Nepal, one of the developing countries in South Asia. While Dhakal (2018a) observed that the state of socio-technological development in the region – Afghanistan, Bangladesh, Bhutan, India, Maldives, Nepal, Pakistan and Sri Lanka — varies significantly, recent UIS (2018) data indicates that some of these countries lag behind the rest of the world in terms of the research and development (R&D) share of their gross domestic product (GDP) expenditure. On the one hand, R&D expenditure in India and China, two neighbouring countries, are 0.8% and 2% of GDP respectively (UIS, 2018), indicating a significant difference between two rapidly growing economies. On the other, since Nepal only spends about 0.3% of its GDP on R&D (UIS, 2018), the country's preparedness for the 4IR (or lack thereof) can offer useful insights into the potential of transformative technological innovations as vehicles to advance the SDGs in developing countries. It is in this context that this chapter explores the central research question of: "How ready are countries like Nepal to harness the 4IR to meet their sustainable development priorities?" contending that the quest for an inclusive 4IR in the developing world needs significant attention in the era of the SDGs.

The chapter is structured in four parts, with the next section providing a general country profile. The inclusive 4IR is then reviewed in the context of the Diffusion of Innovations Theory (DIT) and the Digital Divide Theory (DDT). The next sections of the chapter subsequently describe data collection and findings from the study, as well as discussing the implications, before presenting concluding remarks.

Country profile

The Federal Democratic Republic of Nepal is a landlocked nation in South Asia, located between China and India. It is currently recovering from two recent major crises: a decade-long armed conflict that ended in 2006, in addition to the devastating 2015 earthquake. The conflict claimed the lives of over 13,000 people and approximately 200,000 were internally displaced (Singh et al., 2007). The 2015 earthquake killed 9,000 people, injured 22,000, and destroyed or damaged almost one million homes (Dhakal, 2018b). The latest census data indicates that Nepal has a population of over 29 million people (CBS, 2018). There are approximately 21 million people in the workforce, with a labour force participation rate of 83% and an aggregate unemployment rate of 11.4% (CBS, 2018). Over one-fifth of the workforce in Nepal depends on agriculture/forestry (21.5%) to make a living, and the manufacturing (15.1%) and construction (13.8%) sectors are the second and third most significant sectors for employment generation (CBS, 2018).

Nepal is one of the world's 47 Least Developed Countries (UNCDP, 2018) and is ranked 149th out of 189 countries in the Human Development Index, which is based on three key variables: life expectancy, educational achievement and income (UNDP, 2018). Other global indicators suggest that Nepal is ranked at the lower end of competitiveness (ranked 109th out of 140 countries), innovation (ranked 108th out of 126 countries), information and communications technology (ICT) development (ranked 140th out of 170 countries) and human capital (ranked 102nd out of 157 countries) indices (see ITU, 2017; Transparency International, 2018; UNDP, 2018; WEF, 2017). For example, its lacklustre standing in terms of the Human Capital Index (HCI) – which incorporates four variables, a) *capacity* – the existing stock of education across generations, b) *deployment* – the active participation in the workforce across generations, c) *development* – current efforts to educate, skill and upskill the students and the working age population, and d) *know-how* – growth or depreciation of working-age people's skillsets through opportunities for value-adding employment (WEF, 2017: 5) – does not bode well in terms of the country's 4IR-readiness. It has also been argued that the country's poor performance in terms of controlling corruption (Transparency International, 2018), as well as fostering innovation, have stifled its economic growth (World Bank, 2014). The recent Global Innovation Index (GII) (Cornell University et al., 2018), alongside the HCI, suggests that concerted efforts towards good governance and digital infrastructure are urgently needed to promote long-term economic growth, improved productivity and employment creation in developing countries like Nepal.

The Fourth Industrial Revolution in Nepal: enabling divide or inclusion?

As discussed earlier in this book, the World Economic Forum (2018) has argued that the world has entered the era of the 4IR. One of the ways to comprehend this phenomenon is by making transitional linkages between the Third and Fourth Industrial Revolutions. The Third Industrial Revolution was about the rapid uptake of information and communication technologies (ICT) with the increasing convergence of communication and energy (Rifkin, 2011) based on the use of ICT and the networking of computers to expand human activities from offline to online (Lee et al., 2018). The 4IR, on the other hand, concerns the creative connection between ICT and society that potentially leads to the development and application of transformative technological advancements towards improving industrial efficiency and human productivity, as well as enhancing individual and community well-being in line with the UN's SDGs. Nonetheless, what is important to consider here is the extent of the divide between developed and developing countries in terms of their access to and adoption of ICTs in the context of the 4IR.

Warschauer (2003) stated that the "digital divide" as a notion is not simply about a binary divide of "haves" versus "have nots", where a single overriding factor can be seen to determine or bridge such a divide. Moreover, Dhakal (2011) suggested that ICTs do not exist as an external variable needing to be injected from the outside in order to bring about certain changes; instead, such technologies are intertwined in a complex network of social systems and processes. For instance, the World Bank (2018a) data indicates the significant differences in binary division of Internet use between high-income and low-income countries (such as, over 85% of Australians are Internet users compared to less than 20% of Nepalese).

Although such division at least partially explains Nepal's relatively low ranking in terms of innovation and competitiveness, a variety of socio-economic challenges, including but not limited to poverty and gender inequality, means that the divide is also much wider between men and women in developing nations. For example, a recent report (GSMA, 2019) indicates that: a) more than a billion women in low- and middle-income countries are not mobile internet users, and b) female mobile users are 18% less likely than their male counterparts to use the mobile internet (p. 3). These socio-economic realties of developing nations as well as evidence from developed economies (Dhakal, 2014) confirm that measures that increase access to ICTs alone are not sufficient to overcome the digital divide without actually addressing the root causes of existing social challenges such as corruption or poverty.

Although an optimistic school of thought has argued that the 4IR can potentially close the digital divide (Vercruysse & Reid, 2018), a less sanguine school of thought suggests that it might actually exacerbate the existing socio-technical inequalities (Park, 2016). Consequently, the digital divide is a matter of concern for countries like Nepal because the diffusion and appropriate utilisation of technologies can provide immense innovation opportunities for accomplishing SDGs, whereas their absence is likely to accentuate any pre-existing inequalities. The innovation process is fundamentally driven by the knowledge, technology, infrastructure and cultures that these societies have created or learned (DIISR, 2011). In this context, the Diffusion of Innovations Theory (DIT) also makes an attempt to explain the social nuances pertaining to the digital divide.

The DIT describes the process of 'homophily', in which actors (individuals, businesses or countries) with better social, financial and human resources will generally be the first ones to adopt new technologies (Rogers, 1995). From this point of view, at any given time there will always be actors (individuals, communities or countries like Nepal) that do not have adequate resources to access and benefit from technological advancements. However, as indicated earlier, the divide concerns not only the material access to technologies but also the skills and literacies that enable various actors to harness the potential of existing and emerging technologies. Consequently, unlike the DIT's proposition that the divide is simply a technological phenomenon, the Digital Divide Theory (DDT) espoused by van Dijk (2005) can assist in ensuring that the 4IR is inclusive. Drawing on the DDT, this chapter postulates the following:

- Existing inequalities (education, innovation, employment) produce an unequal distribution of resources;
- An unequal distribution of resources leads to unequal access to transformative technologies;
- Access depends on the capacity of actors to invest in education, innovation and employment opportunities by harnessing transformative technologies; and
- The lack of capacity reinforces inequalities and the unequal distribution of resources.

It is clear from the propositions outlined previously that, if the 4IR is to be an inclusive vehicle that bridges the existing socio-technical divide, the potential of associated transformative technologies in developing countries such as Nepal, needs to be examined and understood within a range of social complexities. This chapter therefore considers the prospect of transformative technologies to be a driver of equity – relative to the developed economies – for the developing nations. As Dhakal et al. (2013) noted, the utility of this proposition applies not so much to innovation in the sense of digital technologies, but in the contextual understanding of its applications, including responsible innovation (Stilgoe et al., 2013). For the purposes of this chapter therefore it is important to explore the factors that contribute to the quest for an inclusive 4IR in Nepal and suggest a potential way forward by which the divide may be bridged.

Research study design

As low-income countries transition to middle-and high-income economies, the potential of the 4IR to foster such aspirations is increasingly significant from the perspective of the SDGs. Drawing on the perspective of the inclusive 4IR, this chapter utilises an interpretivist case study approach to examine the research question: "How ready are developing countries such as Nepal to harness the 4IR to meet their sustainable development priorities?" According to Yin (2017), case studies describe, "a contemporary phenomenon within its real-life context, especially when the boundaries between a phenomenon and context are not clear and the researcher has little control over the phenomenon and context" (p. 13). More importantly, an interpretivist perspective accepts that multiple realities and meanings coexist, and assumes that the social reality is context-dependent (Oates, 2006) and is co-created by the researchers (Lincoln et al., 2011). The overarching purpose of this chapter is to gain an in-depth understanding of the 4IR-readiness status of Nepal. Since case study research generally uses a wide range of evidence from multiple sources such as documents, artefacts, interviews and observations (Rowley, 2002), a two-pronged approach was adopted to examine the research question.

First, based on the three pillars of the Automation Readiness Index (EIU, 2018), discussed in Chapter 1, a document analysis of sectoral policies in Nepalese innovation, education and employment sectors was undertaken. Second, this study utilised a purposive sampling technique to conduct semi-structured interviews (n=11) of stakeholders representing various sectors. Interviews were conducted between March 2018 and April 2019 in accordance with the RMIT University ethics approvals. Each interviewee was provided with a research information sheet and signed a consent form to indicate they understood the research process. The main purpose of the interviews was to gather the perspectives of diverse stakeholders about national preparedness for the unfolding 4IR in Nepal. In order to protect the privacy of the respondents, findings have been presented using a code (table 11.1) assigned to each respondent without specifically naming the interviewees.

There are two key limitations associated with this research design. First is the small sample of interviewees (n=11) selected via purposeful sampling. Second, unlike most of the other countries featured in this book, a survey questionnaire was not used in Nepal – due to the lack of willingness of adequate number of organisational participants to undertake the survey. Despite attempting to resolve the identified issues through triangulation methods, implications of the findings cannot be generalised. Future studies might use a multi-method approach to improve the rigour of findings with quantitative techniques.

The education, employment and innovation policies landscape

Given that the three pillars of the Automation Readiness Index constitute education, employment and innovation aspects (EIU, 2018), whether sectoral policies reflect on the changes being brought forward by the 4IR needs to be assessed in the Nepalese context. Although the potential of the education-employment-innovation nexus is obvious in the context of the 4IR, so too are the perils related to the disruption of existing educational and employment related opportunities. Policies related to investment in ICT infrastructure and increases in ICT uptake need to be adaptive and evolve with the changing times, primarily because disruptive technologies associated with the 4IR have outpaced the ability of policymakers even in developed nations (OECD, 2018).

First, ADB (2015a) highlighted the fact that Nepal does not have a clear policy framework or regulations related to the higher education (HE) sector assisting with the country's sustainable development aspirations (p. xii). In addition, ADB (2015b) identified that the Technical Vocational Education and Training (TVET) sector is not necessarily market-responsive, and the linkages between industry and TVET service providers are either missing or weak, where they do exist (p. x). A review of the 2012 TVET Policy of Nepal conducted by UNDP (2018) highlights the need for implementing a National Vocational Qualification System (NVQS) (p. 2), but TVET-specific 4IR or ICT-oriented interventions remain completely overlooked. These policy shortcomings, coupled with very limited employment opportunities and political instability (Upadhyay, 2018), mean that thousands of Nepalese students leave the country each year to pursue university qualifications overseas. According to the ICEF Monitor (2015), Nepal is one of the fastest-growing markets for universities in developed nations to recruit international students. For example, over 67,000 students went abroad to pursue tertiary qualifications in 2017 (GoN-MoE, 2018: 47). Meanwhile, the latest data indicates that nearly 400,000 students are currently enrolled in HE institutions in Nepal, of whom less than one-tenth are studying science and technology programmes (GoN-MoE, 2018: 52). As mentioned earlier, Nepal ranks 102nd out of 157 countries in the global HCI, at least partially due to the overall weak educational policy landscape and low number of students in the science and technology fields.

The utilisation of ICT in education has become a priority for the government in recent years. For example, the School Sector Development Plan (2016–2023) aims to implement and expand bottom-up ICT initiatives to enhance teaching/learning outcomes in every school in the country (GoN-MoE, 2016). The plan also aims to produce technology-savvy graduates by utilising ICT as a vehicle to improve classroom delivery, increase access to learning materials and enhance the efficiency and effectiveness of educational governance (p. 61). The government has also formulated the 2015 ICT policy with a vision to transform Nepal into an informed and knowledge-based society by 2020 through massively expanding its capacity to utilise ICT across the country. For instance, the policy aims to increase digital literacy rates to over 75% of the population and provide access to broadband internet to 90% of the population (GoN-MoE, 2016: v). However, the specifics of how these ambitious aims will be achieved in a timely manner are not clear.

Second, international aid organisations active in Nepal point out that inadequate infrastructure, insufficient energy supply, and inept, inefficient and ineffective public administrations have critically constrained the prospect of sustainable growth and employment opportunities (ADB, 2015c; Basnett et al., 2014; World Bank, 2015). For example, 85% of the total jobs in the country are in the informal sector (CBS, 2018). The CBS (2018) data also indicates that the so-called "growing" IT sector only provides approximately 60,000 formal jobs, thus employing less than one percent of the country's workforce. The lack of employment and conducive policy environment to foster entrepreneurship means that, on average, over 450,000 people seek overseas employment each year (MoLE, 2018). It has been estimated that three and a half million Nepalese work in the Middle East and Malaysia, with remittances contributing to a quarter of the country's total GDP (MoLE, 2018).

Third, the newly promulgated Constitution of Nepal 2015 focuses on science and technology, including ICT, playing a central role in advancing the SDGs. For example, the 2015 ICT policy is intended to lay the foundations for an overarching vision of "Digital Nepal" and views ICT as a driving force in transforming Nepali society into a knowledge and information-based society and strengthening Nepal's pursuit of inclusive economic growth (GoN, 2015). There are three specific goals of the policy that are relevant in the context of this chapter. First, the country aims to enhance its overall national ICT readiness, with a target of being ranked in the top second quartile of the international ICT development index. This is quite ambitious, given that its current ranking is 140th out of 174 countries (ITU, 2017). The second goal is to ensure digital literacy for at least three-quarters of the population by 2020. Although the third goal is to provide broadband access to 90% of the population by 2020, the World Bank (2018b) estimates that 0.77% of the population has fixed broadband subscriptions, significantly lower than the regional average of 1.61% for South Asia.

In a significant recent development, the government has developed the 2019 Digital Nepal Framework (GoN-MCIT & Frost & Sullivan, 2019) as a blueprint for the ICT and sustainable development nexus. The framework provides a roadmap for digital initiatives to foster: a) economic growth, b) innovative solutions to socioeconomic problems, and c) harness opportunities for the country to participate in the global economy. The framework has identified eight sectors – digital foundation, agriculture, health, education, energy, tourism, finance and urban infrastructure – and proposed a total of 80 digital initiatives across the sectors ranging from smart classrooms to intelligent waste management in order to envisage Digital Nepal of the future. Nonetheless, while the framework admits that Nepal is yet to fully exploit digital opportunities, the main shortcoming of the new framework is that it acknowledges the unfolding 4IR only once in a 352 pages long comprehensive document: "emerging business models and disruptive technologies such as artificial intelligence (AI), robotics, and the Internet of things (IoT) are transforming the way work is done" (p. 17).

Thematic findings from interviews

As table 11.1 demonstrates, nine out of the eleven interviewees were male, representing government agencies, private, not-for-profit and HE sectors. The analysis of the interview findings revealed four main themes: a) the extent of government readiness, b) business opportunities, c) not-for-profit agencies as innovation leaders and d) ethical concerns in the context of the potential and pitfalls associated with the 4IR in Nepal. The thematic findings will subsequently be presented and discussed.

Government readiness

The actual role of the Nepalese government, as well as 4IR policy design and directions, were a matter of concern for most of the interviewees, as reflected in the following comment:

> If you want to discuss 4IR in the context of [a] poor country like Nepal, we have to ask what the role of our government is. It should ideally play a leading role to stimulate sectoral collaboration so that [the] main socioeconomic challenges that we face today can be resolved. However, there is no governmental accountability, corruption is at an all-time high level, and there is no genuine desire to empower people with or without technology. You can look at any industry or innovation policies, the targets are so unrealistic that it is almost comedic. As if the lack of infrastructure and years of inadequate investment is not even a variable when designing ICT policies . . . it's a joke.
>
> [3HEI]

Poor government policy and infrastructure seem to be a common issue throughout Asia and the Pacific region as well. For instance, Jones and Pimdee

Table 11.1 Code, Position, Sector and Gender of Interviewees

Code	Current position	Sector	Gender
1NFP	AI developer and researcher	Education and research	M
2NFP	AI researcher	Education and research	M
3HEI	Academic (private university)	Education and training	F
4HEI	Academic (public university)	Education and training	M
5ADM	Education policy expert	Professional/Scientific services	M
6BUS	Business system analyst	Banking and finance	M
7BUS	HR manager	Travel and tourism	F
8BUS	Medical practitioner	Health care	M
9BUS	Business facilitator	Manufacturing	M
10BUS	Chief executive officer	Housing/Real estate	M
11BUS	Director	Information and technology	M

(2017) examined the disconnect between a country's policy and its people's understanding of the 4IR in the context of socio-economic development in Thailand. Their analysis concluded that: "no matter how much money is thrown at Thailand 4.0 (Industry 4.0/Fourth Industrial Revolution), without skilled workers, researchers, engineers, technicians, and teachers to implement the unicorns [start-ups worth billions of dollars], educate the smart farmers, or SME digital entrepreneurs, the whole plan falls apart" (p. 23).

Business opportunities and societal concerns

The digital opportunities associated with some of the disruptive technologies (pre-4IR) came up frequently during some of the interviews. One of the interviewees said:

> What the Tootle [a motorbike ride sharing app similar to Uber] has done in Nepal, you know, it is almost like [a] gig job for those without adequate education or skills to enter the labour market. And our so-called policymakers are not even aware of these technology-driven changes, so government support or regulation in disruptive technologies is out of the question in the foreseeable future. . . . Also, have you heard of Foodmandu? It delivers food in the Kathmandu Valley. It has changed the way people consume food – some are happy to pay almost half of the cost of an entire meal on delivery charges. [Businesses] are certainly riding a profit wave in the absence of legislative framework . . . but we also sense societal concerns around empowering people to benefit from the 4IR and protecting them from exploitation, e.g. minimum wage.
>
> [7BUS]

The sentiment expressed by the interviewee indicates that proactive government initiatives to harness the opportunities associated with disruptive technologies are necessary if the country does not want to fall further behind in terms of the digital divide. For example, Prabhat et al. (2019), whilst reporting on an ethnographic study of Uber drivers in India, observed that "recognizing the potential, in October 2016, Uber along with the Telangana Government started the scheme where the government subsidises about 60% of the on-road price of the vehicle and Uber impart necessary driving and communication skills and training. The scheme was implemented in association with the Backward Classes Welfare Corporation and Tribal Welfare Corporation of Telangana" (p. 4).

However, not all of the participants were convinced that 4IR-associated opportunities will be helpful for the socio-economic aspirations of countries like Nepal. For example, one of the interviewees suggested that:

> From the perspective of [the tourism] sector, there are certainly 4IR-related opportunities to improve the market share, efficiency and productivity.

However, as a country, we are not only falling behind but likely to be left out, as much of the advancements within the sector focus on customer service and engagement on digital platforms. The reality is that our partner organisations and agencies in remote/rural areas don't have access to decent internet speed – unless there is an emphasis on digital infrastructure and high-speed connectivity – the 4IR will be another layer of competitive disadvantage for us.

[8BUS]

Not-for-profits leading the way

In the absence of government led initiatives, not-for-profit (NFP) organisations seem to be the leaders in exploiting the potential of the 4IR for Nepal. For example, one of the interviewees [9BUS) indicated that rural populations in Nepal have no access to proper healthcare facilities, the problem being compounded by the lack of road infrastructure and low doctor/patient ratios. An emerging not-for-profit (NFP) organisation – the National Innovation Centre (NIC) – is developing an AI-enabled "medical drone" designed by young local graduates in order to improve the delivery of healthcare services in remote parts of the country (Sharma, 2018). Another NFP – Artificial Intelligence for Development (AID) – is also at the forefront of harnessing the transformative potential of the 4IR towards the broader sustainable development aspirations of the country. The AID is a research and development institution that specialises in applied artificial intelligence solutions to existing community problems by linking domain experts with AI developers to address contemporary problems in Nepalese society (AID, 2018). The innovative opportunities associated with the 4IR for countries like Nepal were highlighted during some of the interviews. One of the interviewees provided an interesting example:

> After the 2015 earthquake, we wanted to play a constructive role in the post-disaster recovery. A team led by us came up with the Post-Disaster Rapid Response Retrofit (PD3R). The Deep Learning Model analyses multiple images of a property provided by the owner via a mobile phone app. The app classifies the image and provides an assessment of whether or not the damaged property can be retrofitted, saving time and money [so a] structural engineer [does not have to] visit the house and analyse [it] by hand. This process will speed up the retrofitting process. The PD3R earned 2nd place in the 2018 Call for Code Global Challenge, an award of USD $25,000.
>
> [1NFP]

This contribution in terms of NFPs' innovation and leadership in harnessing the 4IR to solve real-world problems is not unique to Nepal or the region. For example, the Sri Lanka Association for Artificial Intelligence (SLAAI) is a not-for-profit scientific association formally established in 2000. It has been working towards understanding the mechanisms underlying thoughts and intelligent behaviour and their emulation in machines (SLAAI, 2019). In the neighbouring country of Bangladesh, an NFP called the Bangladesh Robotics Foundation (BRF) was established in 2017, primarily for enhancing skills and education in the field of robotics to create a better research community through ensuring innovation for humanity (BRF, 2019).

Ethical concerns

Some of the interviewees were particularly concerned about the 4IR's ethical aspects in the context of winners and losers. For example, one of the interviewees pointed out that:

> I am not sure [whether] you know this or not, but some of the fast food restaurants here in the valley have started using robots to serve their customers. Although we are not at the stage of jobs being replaced by robots, but it's worth contemplating that they are already here. What does this mean for countries like Nepal and its sustainable development aspirations? I am not sure, but it will eventually be a tool for corporate profits here as well, the more robots, the less unionized workers and so forth. I am [a] little concerned that the ethical aspects of 4IR have not received as much attention as [they] should have, even your research brief that you emailed to me doesn't really take ethics into account.
>
> [4HEI]

Robotics-driven automation has been the focus of a local technology start-up called Paaila Technology (2019), which is helping a variety of companies in Nepal to integrate AI technologies as an innovative way to improve customer services and experiences. Consequently, various restaurants have showcased waiter robots as part of the dine-in experience. However, corporate ethics and responsibility around automation is a burgeoning issue (Walsh, 2017). For instance, Cathy O'Neil (2016), in her highly acclaimed book, equates some of the 4IR-associated developments to "Weapons of Mass Destruction". She uses Google as a case and states that "whether it's bed and breakfast or an auto repair shop, [business] success hinges on showing up on the first page of search results" (p. 115). The author argues that humans' key to success will be to learn what machines are looking for and that the digital universe touted as being fair, scientific and democratic is not necessarily true.

One cannot help but notice that there are two different schools of thought on the ethical aspects of transformative technologies. On the one hand, Elon Musk (a billionaire and the founder of Tesla) has argued that AI is far more dangerous than nuclear weapons for humanity (Clifford, 2018). On the other, Mark Zuckerberg (a billionaire and the founder of Facebook) has expressed a firm belief that AI is going to make human lives better in the future (Harwell,

2018). Ongoing research on AI and its impact on the future of work in developed countries like Australia do suggest that societal concerns over the adverse impacts of emerging technologies and the potential, as well as the limitations, of what government regulations can and cannot achieve should not be overlooked (Begley et al., 2019), especially if an inclusive 4IR is to be a priority in developing countries like Nepal. For example, in neighbouring India, the National Strategy for Artificial Intelligence (Ayog, 2018) has specifically highlighted the fact that there is an urgent need to spread awareness among individuals about the importance of consent, ethics and privacy while dealing with technology (p. 88).

Discussion and conclusion

This chapter has explored the central research question of: "How ready are developing countries like Nepal to harness the 4IR to meet their sustainable development priorities?", and argued that the quest for an inclusive 4IR in developing countries needs significant attention in the era of the SDGs. While acknowledging that the trends in 4IR-related opportunities and challenges have not been well-documented in Nepal, the chapter has reviewed the existing policy landscape in the education, employment and innovation sectors, alongside exploring the perspectives of various stakeholders.

There were two key findings that are worth revisiting here. First, it is clear from the assessment of various policies that Nepal lacks 4IR policy preparedness. Second, a thematic analysis of interviews indicated that policymakers are largely unaware of 4IR-related impacts and businesses are uncertain, while NFPs are innovation leaders and ethical concerns remain overlooked. The aspiration for an inclusive 4IR is highly unlikely without an associated responsible code of conduct. For example, the IBM Corporation (2018) states that AI systems should be developed with a moral compass if the full potential of the 4IR is to be realised while reducing the risks. However, it has been acknowledged, that no matter the country or its economic stage, a lack of rigorous, relevant evidence typically complicates attempts to draft impactful sectoral policies in terms of education, employment and innovation opportunities (OECD, 2018). Given the size of the informal economy and the state of socio-economic progress in Nepal, an inclusive 4IR can only materialise when policy directions in all three sectors strategically complement each other (figure 11.1).

It is clear from the Nepalese case, that if transformative technologies associated with the 4IR are to potentially contribute to SDG aspirations, the current policy landscape is ill-equipped. What this means is that the desired economic transition towards middle income status necessitates substantial investment in education, employment and innovation so that the country is strategically prepared to exploit the potential of the 4IR. The fact that Nepal ranks so poorly in many of the global indicators means that there exists an urgent need to integrate employment and education strategies driven by an emphasis on investment in

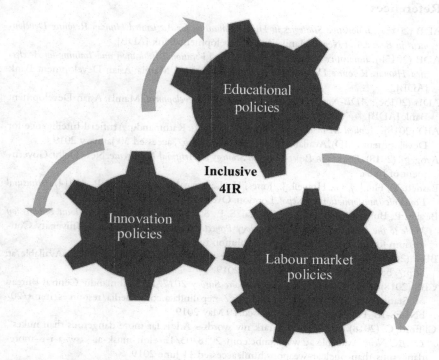

Figure 11.1 The Alignment of Sectoral Policies for an Inclusive 4IR in Nepal

Source: Conceptualised by the authors

ICT-related hard and soft infrastructure. This strategic intervention is particularly pivotal in the case of Nepal if it is to benefit from its proximities to the rising economies of China and India.

Inevitably the role of HE and TVET sectors in producing a highly skilled and competent workforce in Nepal (Dhakal, 2018a) to cope with the 4IR-driven changing employment landscape is paramount. For instance, as the entire landscape of TVET in the country is on the verge of systemic change through the adoption of the NVQS, it is crucial that sectoral priorities must be geared towards developing skills and competencies associated with digitisation and automation. However, this study focused solely on the Nepalese context, which possesses distinctive characteristics such as its lower standing in various global indices, thereby restricting the generalisability of its findings to other countries in the region. Future studies can build on the analysis of education, employment and innovation policies presented in this paper and utilise a comparative perspective between countries in the South Asia to examine the 4IR and SDGs nexus at the regional level.

References

ADB (2015a). *Innovative Strategies in Higher Education for Accelerated Human Resource Development in South Asia Nepal.* Manila: Asian Development Bank [ADB].

ADB (2015b). *Innovative Strategies in Technical and Vocational Education and Training for Accelerated Human Resource Development in South Asia Nepal.* Manila: Asian Development Bank [ADB].

ADB (2015c). *ADB-Nepal Partnership for Inclusive Development.* Manila: Asian Development Bank [ADB].

AID (2018). *Applied AI to Bring Community Solutions.* Kathmandu: Artificial Intelligence for Development (AID). Available at: http://ainepal.org/, accessed 30 January 2019.

Ayog, N. (2018). *Discussion Paper National Strategy for Artificial Intelligence.* New Delhi: Government of India.

Basnett, Y., Henley, G., Howell, J., Jones, H., Lemma, A., & Pandey, P. R. (2014). *Structural Economic Transformation in Nepal.* London: Overseas Development Institute.

Begley, P., Burgess, J., Connell, J., Dhakal, S. P., & Nankervis, A. (2019). *A Joint Submission Made to the Human Rights and Technology Project.* Melbourne: AHRI and University Consortium for the Fourth Industrial Revolution research.

BRF (2019). *Our Objectives.* Dhaka, Bangladesh: Robotics foundation (BRF). Available at: http://bdrf.org.bd/, accessed February 2019.

CBS (2018). *Report on the Nepal Labour Force Survey 2017/18.* Kathmandu: Central Bureau of Statistics [CBS]. Available at: https://nepalindata.com/media/resources/items/20/bNLFS-III_Final-Report.pdf, accessed 10 May 2019.

Clifford, C. (2018). Elon Musk: "Mark my words – A.I. is far more dangerous than nukes". *CNBC News.* Available at: www.cnbc.com/2018/03/13/elon-musk-at-sxsw-a-i-is-more-dangerous-than-nuclear-weapons.html, accessed 11 June 2019.

Cornell University, INSEAD, & WIPO (2018). *The Global Innovation Index 2018: Energizing the World with Innovation.* Fountainbleau: Ithaca, Fontainebleau, and Geneva.

Dhakal, S. P. (2011). Can environmental governance benefit from ICT-social capital nexus in civil society? *TripleC: Cognition Communication Cooperation,* 9 (2), 551–565.

Dhakal, S. P. (2014). ICT-mediated adaptive capacity of environmental third sector in Australia. *Journal of Community Informatics* (Special Issue on Urban Planning and Community Informatics), 10. Available at: http://ci-journal.net/index.php/ciej/article/view/1088, accessed 12 July 2019.

Dhakal, S. P. (2018a). The state of higher education and vocational education and training sectors in Nepal: Implications for graduate work-readiness and sustainable development. Chapter 10. In Cameron, R., et al. (eds.), *Transitions from Education to Work: Workforce Ready Challenges in the Asia Pacific.* London: Routledge, pp. 189–204.

Dhakal, S. P. (2018b). Analysing news media coverage of the 2015 Nepal earthquake with the lens of community capitals: Implications for disaster resilience. *Disasters: The Journal of Disaster Studies, Policy and Management,* 42 (2), 294–313.

Dhakal, S. P., Mahmood, M. N., Wiewiora, A., Brown, K., & Keast, R. (2013). The innovation potential of living-labs to strengthen small and medium enterprises in regional Australia. *Australasian Journal of Regional Studies,* 19 (3), 101–119.

DIISR (2011). *Key Statistics – Australian Small Business.* Canberra: Department of Innovation, Industry, Science and Research (DIISR).

EIU (2018). *The Automation Readiness Index: Who Is Ready for the Coming Wave of Automation?* London, Economist Intelligence Unit (EIU) Limited. Available at: www.automationreadiness.eiu.com/static/download/PDF.pdf, accessed 7 May 2019.

GoN (2015). *National Information and Communication Technology Policy, 2015.* Kathmandu: Government of Nepal (GoN). Available at: www.youthmetro.org/uploads/4/7/6/5/47654969/ict_policy_nepal.pdf

GoN-MCIT & Frost & Sullivan (2019). *2019 Digital Nepal Framework Unlocking Nepal's Growth Potential.* Kathmandu: Government of Nepal-Ministry of Communication and Information Technologies (GoN-MCIT). Available at: http://mocit.gov.np/application/resources/admin/uploads/source/EConsultation/EN%20Digital%20Nepal%20Framework%20V8.4%2015%20July%20%202019.pdf, accessed 5 September 2019.

GoN-MoE (2016). *Nepal School Sector Development Plan 2016–2023.* Kathmandu: Government of Nepal-Ministry of Education (GoN-MoE). Available at: www.globalpartnership.org/content/nepal-school-sector-development-plan-2016-2023, accessed 12 May 2019.

GoN-MoE (2018). *Education in Figures 2017 (At A Glance).* Kathmandu: Government of Nepal-Ministry of Education (GoN-MoE). Available at: https://moe.gov.np/assets/uploads/files/Education_in_Figures_2017.pdf, accessed 12 May 2019.

GSMA (2019). *Connected Women the Mobile Gender Gap Report 2019.* London: GSM Association. Available at: www.gsma.com/mobilefordevelopment/wp-content/uploads/2019/02/GSMA-The-Mobile-Gender-Gap-Report-2019.pdf, accessed 23 July 2019.

Harwell, D. (2018). *AI Will Solve Facebook's Most Vexing Problems, Mark Zuckerberg Says: Just Don't Ask When or How.* Available at: www.washingtonpost.com/news/the-switch/wp/2018/04/11/ai-will-solve-facebooks-most-vexing-problems-mark-zuckerberg-says-just-dont-ask-when-or-ow/?noredirect=on&utm_term=.d607c88babd5, accessed 9 July 2019.

IBM Corporation (2018). *The Business Case for AI in HR.* New York: IBM Corporation.

ICEF Monitor (2015). *Nepal Emerging as an Important Growth Market for International Education.* Bonn: International Consultants for Education and Fairs [ICEF]. Available at: http://monitor.icef.com/2015/12/nepal-emerging-as-an-important-growth-market-for-international-education/, accessed 2 January 2019.

ITU (2017). *Measuring the Information Society Report,* Vol. 1. Geneva: International Telecommunication Union (ITU). Available at: www.itu.int/en/ITU-D/Statistics/Documents/publications/misr2017/MISR2017_Volume1.pdf, accessed 9 July 2019.

Jones, C., & Pimdee, P. (2017). Innovative ideas: Thailand 4.0 and the fourth industrial revolution. *Tạp chí Nghiên cứu dân tộc,* 22, 39–45.

Lee, M., Yun, J., Pyka, A., Won, D., Kodama, F., Schiuma, G., & Yan, M. R. (2018). How to respond to the fourth industrial revolution, or the second information technology revolution? Dynamic new combinations between technology, market, and society through open innovation. *Journal of Open Innovation: Technology, Market, and Complexity,* 4 (3), 21.

Lincoln, Y. S., Lynham, S. A., & Guba, E. G. (2011). Paradigmatic controversies, contradictions, and emerging confluences, revisited. *The Sage Handbook of Qualitative Research,* 4, 97–128.

MoLE (2018). *Report on the Nepal Labour Force Survey 2017/18.* Kathmandu, Ministry of Labour and Employment [MoLE]. Available at: https://asiafoundation.org/wp-content/uploads/2018/05/Nepal-Labor-Migration-status-report-2015-16-to-2016-17.pdf, accessed 29 March 2019.

Oates, B. J. (2006). *Researching Information Systems and Computing.* Los Angeles: Sage Publishing.

OECD (2018). *Science, Technology and Innovation Outlook 2018: Adapting to Technological and Societal Disruption.* Paris: OECD.

O'Neil, C. (2016). *Weapons of Math Destruction: How Big Data Increases Inequality and Threatens Democracy.* New York: Broadway Books.

Paaila Technology (2019). *The Power of Robotics to Benefit Humanity.* Kathmandu: Paaila Technology. Available at: https://paailatechnology.com/, accessed 29 March 2019.

Park, H. A. (2016). Are we ready for the fourth industrial revolution? *Yearbook of Medical Informatics*, 25 (1), 1–3.

Prabhat, S., Nanavati, S., & Rangaswamy, N. (2019). *India's Uberwallah: Profiling Uber Drivers in the Gig Economy*. Proceedings of the Tenth International Conference on Information and Communication Technologies and Development, ACM, p. 43.

Rifkin, J. (2011). *The Third Industrial Revolution: How Lateral Power Is Transforming Energy, the Economy, and the World*. New York: Palgrave Macmillan.

Rogers, E. M. (1995). *Diffusion of Innovations*. New York: The Free Press.

Rowley, J. (2002). Using case studies in research. *Management Research News*, 25 (1), 16–27.

Sharma, G. (2018). *Nepal's Medical Drones Bring Healthcare to the Himalayas, Thomson Reuters Foundation*. Available at: http://news.trust.org/item/20180430000050-xvs99/, accessed 18 April 2019.

Singh, S., Sharma, S. P., Mills, E., Poudel, K. C., & Jimba, M. (2007). Conflict induced internal displacement in Nepal: Medicine. *Conflict and Survival*, 23 (2), 103–110.

SLAAI (2019). *Sri Lanka Association for Artificial Intelligence*. Colombo, Sri Lanka. Available at: https://slaai.lk/, accessed 18 April 2019.

Stilgoe, J., Owen, R., & Macnaughten, P. (2013). Developing a framework for responsible innovation. *Research Policy*, 42 (9), 1568–1580.

Transparency International (2018). *Corruption Perceptions Index 2018*. Available at: www.transparency.org/files/content/pages/2018_CPI_Executive_Summary.pdf, accessed 18 April 2019.

UIS (2018). *How Much Does Your Country Spend on R&D?* Paris: UNESCO Institute for Statistics (UIS). Available at: http://uis.unesco.org/apps/visualisations/research-and-development-spending/, accessed 18 April 2019.

UN (2019). *Goal 9: Industry, Innovation and Infrastructure*. New York: United Nations (UN). Available at: www.undp.org/content/undp/en/home/sustainable-development-goals/goal-9-industry-innovation-and-infrastructure.html, accessed 15 July 2019.

UNCDP (2018). *List of Least Developed Countries (as of December 2018)*. New York: United Nations Committee for Development Policy (UNCDP). Available at: www.un.org/development/desa/dpad/wp-content/uploads/sites/45/publication/ldc_list.pdf, accessed 18 April 2019.

UNDP (2018). *Human Development Indices and Indicators: 2018 Statistical Update*. Kathmandu: United Nations Development Programme (UNDP). Available at: http://hdr.undp.org/sites/all/themes/hdr_theme/country-notes/NPL.pdf, accessed 18 April 2019.

Upadhyay, J. P. (2018). Higher education in Nepal. *Pravaha*, 24 (1), 96–108.

van Dijk, J. (2005). *The Deepening Divide: Inequality in the Information Society*. Thousand Oaks: Sage Publications.

Vercruysse, J., & Reid, F. (2018). *The Fourth Industrial Revolution Can Close the Digital Divide, This Is How*. Geneva: World Economic Forum (WEF). Available at: www.weforum.org/agenda/2018/09/how-do-we-close-the-digital-divide-in-the-fourth-industrial-revolution/, accessed 18 April 2019.

Walsh, T. (2017). *It's Alive: Artificial Intelligence from the Logic Piano to Killer Robots*. Melbourne: La Trobe University.

Warschauer, M. (2003). Demystifying the digital divide. *Scientific American*, 289 (2), 42–47.

WEF (2017). *The Global Human Capital Report 2017*. Geneva: The World Economic Forum (WEF). Available at: http://www3.weforum.org/docs/WEF_Global_Human_Capital_Report_2017.pdf, accessed 18 April 2019.

WEF (2018). *Fourth Industrial Revolution*. Geneva: The World Economic Forum (WEF). Available at: www.weforum.org/focus/fourth-industrial-revolution, accessed 18 April 2019.

World Bank (2014). *A Vision for Nepal Policy Notes for the Government: Three "I"s for Growth – Investment, Infrastructure, Inclusion.* Washington, DC: The World Bank.

World Bank (2015). *Nepal Country Snapshot.* Washington, DC: The World Bank.

World Bank (2018a). *Individuals Using the Internet (% of Population).* Washington, DC: The World Bank. Available at: https://data.worldbank.org/indicator/IT.NET.USER.ZS, accessed 18 April 2019.

World Bank (2018b). *Fixed Broadband Subscriptions (per 100 People).* Washington, DC: The World Bank. Available at: https://data.worldbank.org/indicator/IT.NET.BBND.P2, accessed 18 April 2019.

Yin, R. K. (2017). *Case Study Research and Applications: Design and Methods.* London: Sage Publications.

12 Thailand

Monthon Sorakraikitikul

Introduction

This chapter explores the challenges of the Fourth Industrial Revolution (4IR) for the government, industry and the education sector in Thailand in effectively addressing its impacts on labour markets, productivity, competitiveness and the future of work. It begins with a brief country profile, including labour market characteristics and current government strategies and policies, followed by an exploration of the proactive 'Thailand 4.0' project and a discussion of key current and future technologies. The research findings are then presented, prior to an analysis of their implications for the Thai government, industry, and both higher and vocational education systems.

Country profile

Unlike some of the other regional countries explored in this book, Thailand has experienced a relatively stable and consistently growing economy over the last few decades, despite occasional lapses into social and political disruption. Wailerdsak (2015), for example, observed that Thailand experienced 'rapid and sustainable economic growth after the mid-1980s and is regarded as one of the high performing Asian economies' (p. 26). As a key indicator of this strong economic performance, Cooke (2018) reported that Thai gross domestic product (GDP) had 'five-year highs in 2017, with business-friendly fiscal policies and planned spending on infrastructure expected to support further expansion in 2018' (webpage). Its strengths lie in its sound infrastructure, persistently low unemployment levels, and the dominance of the private sector supported by pro-investment government policies, and strong export performance. With respect to recent infrastructure developments, three new rapid transport lines are planned for Bangkok to address major traffic congestion, supplemented by more than a hundred new transport projects in Thailand's Eastern Economic Corridor, some of which are supported by artificial intelligence technologies (Cooke, 2018), as discussed later in this chapter.

Government policies

Government policies have been particularly important in supporting private sector innovation by encouraging foreign direct investment and offering social provisions such as family planning and protecting the rights of retirees. For example, recent amendments to the Labour Protection Act (2017) have given employees, rather than employers, the right to decide when to retire – 'Where the retirement age is not specified or the retirement age is over 60 years of age, the employee can retire by notifying the employer that he/she wishes to retire' (Thonguthaisri, 2017: 2). This amendment is important in view of the aging of the Thai population and its workforce, and perhaps even more significant in the shadow of the Fourth Industrial Revolution (4IR). Particularly where pragmatic employers may be keen to use workforce aging as an opportunity to reduce the number of older workers who may be presumed to be less adaptable than their younger colleagues. Some employers have already demonstrated their willingness to do this. For example, in the automobile industry, where some observers suggest up to 44% of workers may be lost due to the 4IR. Moreover, Toyota and the Thai Suzuki Motor Company have been accused in the Thai press of using 'voluntary layoff' provisions to reduce their workforces in the face of new technologies without providing legally-required compensation (Maneechai, 2018).

Labour market issues

Some observers have highlighted the potential threats to future economic growth and development from structural weaknesses in the country's labour market (ILO, 2013). It has been proposed that they might compound the adverse workplace effects of the implementation of the new technologies posing 'a high risk of significant negative side-effects on macro-economic performance' (EIU, 2018a). With respect to these structural weaknesses, some researchers point to the difficulties the Thai government has experienced in controlling population growth, the significant (and regionally-shared) aging of the workforce, and the reducing supply of skilled workers which is exacerbated by 'little progress . . . in science and technology education' (Wailerdsak, 2015: 27). As in many other developed and developing nations, it has been estimated that up to a fifth of the Thai population will be aged over 60 by 2022 (Anonymous, 2015) or even 25% by 2030 (ILO, 2013: 3).

Other compounding demographic, social and labour market factors include the narrow composition of the industry landscape, limited literacy and higher education participation levels, gender workforce imbalances and the significance of precarious work in the overall economy. Whilst there are conflicting data on the proportion of employees in the key industry sectors in Thailand, it is generally agreed that agriculture employs between 39–41%, services (41–48%) and manufacturing (15–20%) of the total workforce. Whilst agriculture is declining, services (retailing, hospitality and professional) are, and will become, the prime industry sector especially with the impact of the 4IR. Associated with these sectoral proportions, the majority of semi-skilled jobs are currently in agriculture and manufacturing (38%), with approximately 23% in sales and services and serious shortages are reported in senior official and managerial positions (ILO, 2013: 6).

Whilst labour force participation rates are healthy (around 75%), they are gender imbalanced with more than 80% males and only 65% females actively involved. According to ILO data, many of Thailand's workers are engaged in vulnerable or precarious jobs, especially in the agricultural and manufacturing sectors. In common with their counterparts in other regional countries, over 60% are employed largely without employment protection in the ubiquitous 'informal' economy (ILO, 2013: 13). In addition, approximately 65% of the total population in 2010 had only basic elementary education level qualifications – vocational and higher education completions are growing but at a relatively slow rate (ILO, 2013: 4). As a consequence of these economic and labour market weaknesses, together with Thailand's relatively rapid uptake of 4IR technologies, some observers have suggested that more than 56% of current jobs are likely to be displaced in Thailand (Panyaarvudh, 2018). Others have adopted a more positive perspective maintaining that Thailand has an 'enabling environment to create growth for people' (Chansrichawla, 2017). In response to these challenges, the Thai government has formulated a development plan entitled 'Thailand 4.0' which is discussed in the following section of the chapter.

Thailand 4.0

According to the Ministry of Information and Communication Technology (2016), 'Thailand 4.0 is an economic model that aims to unlock the country from several economic challenges resulting from past economic development models which place emphasis on agriculture (Thailand 1.0), light industry (Thailand 2.0), and advanced industry (Thailand 3.0)'. These challenges include 'a middle-income trap', 'an inequality trap', and 'an imbalance trap'. It aims to 'shift the economic focus away from production and towards service' (Cooke, 2018), targeting four specific industry sectors (bio-economy, electronic and robotic parts, aviation-related and medical industries – Deloitte, 2018: 14; Jones & Pimdee, 2017: 6) as well as revitalising some of the more traditional sectors.

Its key objectives are:

1   *Economic Prosperity*: to create a value-based economy that is driven by innovation, technology and creativity. The model aims to increase Research and Development (R&D) expenditure to 4% of GDP, increase economic growth rate to a full capacity rate of 5–6% within five years, and increase national income per capita from 5,470 USD in 2014 to 15,000 USD by 2032.

2   *Social Well-being*: to create a society that moves forward without leaving anyone behind (inclusive society) through realization of the full potential

of all members of society. The goals are to reduce social disparity from 0.465 in 2013 to 0.36 in 2032, completely transform to social welfare system within 20 years and develop at least 20,000 households into "Smart Farmers" within 5 years.

3 *Raising Human Values*: to transform Thais into "Competent human beings in the 21st Century" and "Thais 4.0 in the first world. Measures under Thailand 4.0 will raise Thailand's Human Development Index (HDI) from 0.722 to 0.8 of the top 50 countries within 10 years, ensuring that at least five Thai universities are ranked amongst the world's top 100 higher education institution within 20 years.

4 *Environmental Protection*: to become a liveable society that possesses an economic system capable of adjusting to climate change and a low carbon society. The targets are to develop at least 10 cities into the world's most liveable cities and reduce terrorism risks.
(https://thaiembdc.org/thailand-4-0-2/)

In pursuit of these objectives, the government has designed the following five broad and integrated 'agendas', together with a road map for their implementation:

Agenda 1: Prepare Thais 4.0 for Thailand becoming a first world nation
Agenda 2: Development of Technology Cluster and Future Industries
Agenda 3: Incubate Entrepreneurs and Develop Networks of Innovation-Driven Enterprise
Agenda 4: Strengthening the Internal Economy through the Mechanisms of 18 Provincial Clusters and 76 Provinces
Agenda 5: Integrating with ASEAN and Connecting Thailand to the Global Community

Through their strategy to achieve these bold objectives, the Thai Ministry of Labour has established a Manufacturing Automation & Robotics Academy (MARA) as a joint venture between the Department of Skill Development and the Federation of Thai Industries. The intention is to analyse the current and future capabilities of the labour market, an initiative that may help to address some of the earlier challenges. There has also been discussion of the promulgation of a 'robot tax' to pay for compensation to displaced employees, in accordance with the government's new legal requirements for voluntary retirement (Maneechai, 2018). Despite these achievements, Thailand is not included in the Economist Intelligence Unit's (EIU's) Automation Readiness Index discussed in Chapter 1 (EIU, 2018b).

In addition, the Thai Ministry of Digital Economy and Society has a plan to help and facilitate Thai society to enable a smooth transition towards Thailand 4.0. Six Thailand Digital Strategies are included, namely:

1 developing internet connection to cover all parts of Thailand
2 enabling the usage of new technology in industry and service sectors

3   ensuring a healthy society in which people have technology literacy to improve health and life
4   transforming towards a digital paperless government system
5   developing people and the workforce to be ready for digital society, and
6   building confidence in using ICT technology.

The outputs from this plan are intended to transform the Thai economy in many sectors including food and agriculture, health and wellness, industry and automation, society and culture. Farmers would have access to advanced technology; there will be more new technological startups; and technology will help the service sector to have more capability in order to respond to various and different customer needs. Finally, Thailand would have the ability to create its own technology and thus buy less from overseas (Ministry of Information & Communication Technology, 2016). This Thailand Digital Economy and Society Development Plan was introduced as one of the main strategies for improving Thailand's competitive advantage in its 20-year plan (2017–2037).

In summary, Thailand's economy is currently in good shape, but potential political instability, its outdated industry structure, the relatively low education and skills levels of many members of its workforce, gender inequalities, and the continuing dominance of informal (and largely unprotected) work in the economy may render it increasingly vulnerable to the adverse impacts of the 4IR. However, like some of its regional counterparts (notably Singapore, Malaysia, Indonesia, China and India), the Thai government has promulgated a bold initiative – Thailand 4.0 – as outlined earlier, to better address these future challenges.

The next section of this chapter explores the particular technologies which will be most important for key Thai industry sectors, and how they might be implemented without excessive disruption to future workplaces, jobs and employees.

Key current and future technologies

Artificial intelligence technology has been taught and researched at Thai universities for over three decades, notably at Kasetsart and King Monghut institutions. Currently, Chulalongkorn and King Mongkut's universities offer double degrees in artificial intelligence and robotics engineering programs in an attempt to meet the annual demand for more than 10,000 jobs. This is supported by government funding of US$6 billion (Lung, 2018). An AI Research Roadmap was established between 2000–2005, resulting in an ICT Master Plan (2001–2010) to 'make Thailand a knowledge society with five areas of strength – e-government, e-education, e-society, e-industry and e-commerce' (Kawtrakul & Praneetpolgray, 2014: 83–85). Between 2006–2010, the government refined these admirable priorities in a national development plan to 'Smart Health, Smart Farm and Digitized Thailand', reflecting its focus on the medical, agricultural and information technology sectors (Kawtrakul & Praneetpolgray, 2014: 86).

The Thailand 4.0 program has both broadened and focused these priorities, including the intention to create one hundred Smart Cities in the next two decades (Martinidis, 2018). Thus, the Thai government strategy is to integrate the adoption of 4IR technologies not only in key industry sectors but also within urban and rural environments. As examples, enhanced traffic management systems incorporating facial recognition, ATM security, and traffic light synchronisation systems are planned to ease traffic congestion in the major Thai cities and to provide increased security for the population (Martinidis, 2018). Alibaba's Chinese 'City Brain' technology project in Hangzhou is being used as a template for this program.

The industries targeted in the contemporary version of Thailand 4.0 have expanded to ten key sectors – namely, automotive, medical, petrochemical, digital, electrical and electronic, automation and robotics, agro-processing, aerospace, tourism and textiles (Jones & Pimdee, 2017: 8–9) – with a special interest in 'unicorn enterprises', or 'promising businesses that truly represent the evolving global digital economy' (Jones & Pimdee, 2017: 14). Some examples of particular applications include the:

(a) *Retail sector* – 7-Eleven Thailand uses facial recognition software across its 11,000 Thai stores to analyse customer behaviour and reward customer loyalty, monitor stock levels, measure real time performance and conduct competitor analyses (Anonymous, 2018); and the Thai Beverage Group uses more than a thousand robots in Thailand, Cambodia, Myanmar and Laos in its tea factories (Prakash, 2017)

(b) *Media sector* – has 'the second highest number of organisations adopting AI among all Southeast Asian nations', using applications to improve the 'management and delivery of content', automate operations and to report on live events (Eade, 2018)

(c) *Medical sector* – organisations employ robotic radiology scans to enhance its popular medical tourism industry (Shafer, 2017); provide physicians with evidence to support treatment decisions; assist oncologists to monitor and analyse new cancer research publications; and chatbots for more accurate and efficient customer services (Leesa-Nguansuk, 2017)

(d) *Legal and accounting* – organisations use AI for repetitive tasks such as document reviews, invoice data extraction, processing and payments processing; as well as more complex activities such as providing legal advice and legal analytics (Chinsanyaram, 2018; Rukkiatwong & Khurancharea, 2018).

Accordingly, Thailand has been described as 'one of the countries in the Asia Pacific where the 4IR has been incorporated into the national policy agenda' (APAIE, 2018) due to the active role of both the government and the private sector; the 'demand-driven' policy in the public sector; the ongoing pursuit of both global and regional networks; and especially the bold government infrastructure projects discussed earlier in this chapter. Thus, Thailand appears in good shape to withstand the impact of the 4IR, especially with respect to its understanding of the benefits and its preparatory planning at the governmental and high-tech industry levels. However, as a counter-balance to this optimistic view and as discussed earlier in this chapter, it might be suggested that structural issues in Thailand's industry composition, labour market characteristics, the formal versus the informal economy and the legal framework, provide significant challenges for the successful adoption of 4IR technologies in many (if not most) Thai public and private organisations.

Research method and findings

This section of the chapter investigates the preparedness of a sample of Thai managers to address these challenges through a quantitative research study where data was gathered by a survey questionnaire. An on-line platform survey was applied in this case, in order to reach a target population of managers in a variety of organisations. The questionnaire was translated from English to Thai in order to facilitate the collection of data from Thai managers. With on-line survey technology, both English and Thai questionnaires were provided. This was to ensure that respondents would read and understand the questions. A purposive sampling technique was employed in order to obtain the data from the right sources. The survey was conducted from January 2019 until the end of April 2019. In total, 130 respondents participated in the survey. The IP addresses were checked in order to ensure that no double cases were used for data analysis. After checking and deleting incomplete data sets, there were 101 responses ready for analysis.

Sample demographics

Table 12.1 illustrates the genders, educational levels and positions of the respondents.

As table 12.1 indicates, the majority of respondents (60%) were female, with most aged between 18 to 35 (68%) or between 36 to 50 years (28%). Only a small proportion were over 50 years of age. The majority possessed undergraduate qualifications (67%) with many (32%) also having a postgraduate degree. Whilst 56% categorised themselves simply as 'staff', the remainder were in line, middle or senior management roles.

Table 12.2 shows the industry sectors represented, organisational types and sizes, the perceived stage of automation and the organisation of their information technology functions.

As table 12.3 illustrates, most respondents worked in the manufacturing (18%), education and training (13%), health care and social assistance (12%) and utilities (11%) sectors respectively. They mainly represented private organisations, either local (35%) or MNC subsidiaries (55%). Their organisational sizes were primarily large (1,000 workers or more – 45%) and to a lesser extent, small and medium enterprises (100 and 999 people – 37%).

Table 12.1 Description of Respondents

		n (101)	Percentage of sample (%)
Gender	Female	60	60
	Male	37	37
	Prefer not to say	4	3
Age categories	Between 18 and 35	68	67
	Between 36 and 50	28	28
	Between 51 and 65	5	5
Education Levels	High school or lower	1	1
	Undergraduate qualification	68	67
	Postgraduate qualification	32	32
Positions represented	Staff	57	56
	Team leader/Supervisor	24	24
	Manager	11	11
	Senior manager	6	6
	Director/CEO/General manager	2	2
	Business owner/Entrepreneur	1	1

Unexpectedly, the majority of the sample also perceived that their organisation was in the 4IR or Cyber Physical Systems stage (62%). Most reported that their organisations had centralised their IT system (70%), although a significant minority (18%) aligned IT with functional areas.

Strategic alignment of 4IR technologies, management support and organisational benefits

Table 12.3 demonstrates respondents' opinions about the strategic alignment of 4IR technologies; and the perceived extent of management support, value and impact, and the capacity of these technologies to improve organisational performance.

Although respondents rated the usefulness of 4IR technologies highest at a mean of 4.15, they were unsure whether they would help improve their performance (3.88) or enable them to accomplish their work faster. Overall, the respondents perceived that these new technologies could help to improve organisational performance (3.88). Respondents agreed that the IT strategy supported and matched the business strategy, and generally agreed that it would contribute to changes in business strategy (3.91). Some were concerned about levels of management support, as the mean score was the lowest at 3.46. Most, however, agreed that top management showed enthusiasm in supporting the adoption of new technologies, and were aware of the benefits of implementing them. However, they were concerned about the allocation of sufficient resources during the implementation process.

Table 12.2 Industry Representation, Types, Number of Employees, Automation Stage and IT Structure

		n (101)	Percentage of sample (%)
Industry sector	Manufacturing	18	18
	Education and training	13	13
	Health care and social assistance	12	12
	Electricity, gas, water and waste services	11	11
	Financial and insurance services	9	9
	Professional, scientific and technical services	9	9
	Administrative and support services	8	9
	Retail trade	6	6
	Others	14	13
Organisation type	Private – domestic/national	36	35
	Private- subsidiary Multi-National Corporation (MNC)	30	30
	Public	20	20
	Government business enterprise	8	8
	Not for profit	7	7
Number of employees	Between 1 and 99	18	18
	Between 100 and 499	34	34
	Between 500 and 999	3	3
	1,000 and over	46	45
Organisation automation stage	1st mechanisation	3	3
	2nd mass production	11	11
	3rd computer and automation	20	20
	4th cyber physical systems	63	62
	Other	4	4
Organisation of IT system	Central IT department	70	70
	No in-house department/ Contracted out	8	8
	IT experts in each department	4	4
	Local IT departments in each functional area	19	18

Table 12.3 Strategic Alignment, Management Support and Organisational Impacts

	Mean	SD
Strategic alignment of implementation	3.91	.815
Top management support	3.46	.951
Usefulness of 4IR applications	4.15	.526
Impacts of 4IR applications on organisational performance	3.88	.649

Respondents rated their leaders' roles in relation to innovation–oriented behaviours, creating and nurturing an innovative environment, and directing the investment in innovation. Of these, the first received the highest rating at 3.76. Leaders were perceived to strongly encourage staff to apply and use new technologies by empowering them to handle clients' problems. Respondents also reported that their leaders actively created and nurtured an innovative environment (3.72), encouraged them to create new ideas and induced creative thinking. However, respondents rated the role of their leader in directing innovative investment as relatively low at 3.66. However, in general, it was reported that leaders understood the importance of technological investment and the value added from such innovations, as well as determining how to use personal and resources to make innovations more successful. Then, the leader may consider to invest in creating a socialisation space for people in an organisation (Panyaarvudh, 2018). This would enable them to have an opportunity to socialise in order to think and to get hands–on experience, which is the first step for innovative behaviours (see Table 12.4).

4IR and job satisfaction, job security and future skills needs

The mean response for the effect of the implementation of 4IR technologies on job satisfaction in the workplace was relatively low (3.46), and most respondents agreed that the new technologies would affect the way they currently work. Regarding their job security, the sample reported a mean score of 3.34. However, most felt that they would keep their job, and continue to work in the organisation; although they also indicated that they were worried about the continuation of their careers and were unable to predict whether jobs might be made redundant with the impact of these new technologies.

Table 12.5 shows respondents' opinions of the new technological skills requirements predicted for the next five years. As the table indicates, specific technological skill requirements were generally rated more highly than non-technical skills. The highest mean score was for data/communication security skills (4.27), which it was anticipated would be in very high demand in the future. Data analytics (3.94), collaboration software (3.91) and IT infrastructure (3.84) were also seen as critical.

Regarding attitudes toward change management, respondents generally felt that their organisations were only moderately prepared for the likely changes

Table 12.4 Organisational Leadership and 4IR

	Mean	SD
Leader – Directing innovation investment	3.66	.764
Leader – Creating and nurturing an innovative environment	3.72	.774
Leader – Innovation-oriented behaviour	3.76	.853

Table 12.5 Skill Needs for the Next five Years

	Mean	SD
Data security/Communications security	4.27	0.991
Data analytics	3.94	1.129
Collaboration software	3.91	1.030
IT infrastructure	3.84	1.007
Automation technology	3.76	1.059
Development of application assistance systems	3.76	1.096
Non-technical skills: systems thinking and process understanding	3.76	0.928

Table 12.6 Attitudes Toward Job Changes in Particular Job Clusters

	Likely to change		Likely to be replaced	
	Mean	SD	Mean	SD
Manufacturing production and operations (Product design or engineering)	3.60	1.11	3.65	1.16
Research and development	3.86	0.94	3.16	1.17
Purchasing	3.39	1.02	3.34	1.10
Information technology/data security/ Communications security	4.21	0.90	3.74	1.20
Marketing, sales, distribution and customer support	3.87	0.93	3.45	1.07
Human resource management	3.50	1.02	3.22	1.18
Accounting and finance	3.75	0.96	3.64	1.10
Transport and logistics	3.65	1.20	3.77	1.17
General administration	3.49	1.02	3.39	1.06

effected by the 4IR (3.00). Resistance to change was considered to be moderate (3.12), but higher than the preparedness for change. Further analysis of the likely changes in particular organisational sections and related jobs is outlined in table 12.6.

According to respondents, the job clusters likely to change (in order of significance) included information technology/data security/communications security (4.21); marketing, sales, distribution and customer support (3.87); and research and development (3.86). The function considered least likely to change was purchasing (3.39). The functions and their jobs considered most likely to replaced included transport and logistics (3.77), information technology/data security/communications security (3.74), manufacturing production and operations – product design or engineering (3.65) and accounting and finance (3.64). Research and development (3.16) was considered the function least likely to be replaced by 4IR technologies.

Government policy and 4IR

As in other regional countries discussed in this book, most respondents were unimpressed with current government policies and strategies introduced to address the challenges of the 4IR (2.61). This was a somewhat surprising finding, given the range and scope of the Thai government's progressive 'Thailand 4.0' strategy.

Summary

Findings were reported from 101 respondents, holding undergraduate degrees or higher qualifications. Most were between 18 and 35 years of age and they mainly worked as 'staff' in a broad range of industries. They perceived that their workplaces were already at the 4th industrial revolution stage, they primarily used central IT departments and believed that 4IR technologies will add value to their workplaces. However, these benefits will require their leaders to build conducive and nurturing work environments together with supportive, innovative behaviours.

There were significant concerns about the effect of the implementation of 4IR technologies on jobs and workplaces. Whilst most expected that they would continue in their current jobs they were fearful about how long those jobs would last which may help to explain the low scores on both job satisfaction and job security. The key skills required over the next five years were expected to be in data and communication security, and the least important were reportedly non-technical skills, although some respondents felt that they would still be important skills to develop. Most anticipated that resistance to these changes brought about by the 4IR would occur.

Implications for the Thai government, industry and the education sector

Thai government

The findings from our study indicate that most respondents are aware of the 4IR, and of the associated government strategies, plans and policies discussed earlier in this chapter. This suggests that the government has communicated effectively with many industry sectors in Thailand and has promulgated supportive legislation. However, the government could further support the development of the 4IR by considering the following issues. In order to further support successful implementation of these new technologies it is important to ensure top management support, which was ranked the lowest in this study. In this regard, the Thai government could assist in changing public attitudes by providing information and support to top management. Such support might include enhancing leaders' innovative behaviours by supporting an innovation investment mentality and the ability to create and nurture an innovation environment in all organisations.

These initiatives might also include support in developing skills that will be necessary for the future such as technical skills related with data security/communication, data analytics, collaboration software, IT infrastructure and automation technology, and non-technical skills. Such actions would equip Thai workers to be ready to accept and effectively adopt 4IR technologies in their organisations. In addition, the non-technical skills would enable Thai workers to better cope and become able to adapt themselves to the inevitable changes in their jobs and workplaces. In creating these skills, the government could enhance both the IT infrastructure and people skills for the coming 4IR (Panyaarvudh, 2018).

Thai industry

As suggested by this research study, it is likely that, in the future, industry may require a smaller number of workers with more specialised skills and competencies. Accordingly, the findings indicated relatively high levels of concern about future job satisfaction and job security. During this transition to the 4IR era, employees will need to be encouraged and assisted to develop themselves to have the necessary skills to keep them upgraded to cope with new job requirements. These skills include both technical skills and non-technical skills. Hence, organisations will need to provide additional (and more sophisticated) learning and development opportunities either separately or in collaboration with government and educational systems.

With regard to change management, both employee and managerial preparedness and resistance to change require attention by all organisations. In order to assure positive and proactive approaches towards these changes, new organisational cultures and more innovative leadership styles will be required in most (if not all) industry sectors. When employees and managers are equipped with these skills, resistance to change is likely to be reduced.

Education systems

The key role of education systems is to prepare students with the knowledge, skills and capabilities to successfully transition from graduation to the workplace. However, in order to prepare or enhance future workforce skills, both technical and non-technical skills are equally important. Technical skills enable workforces to be capable for work in the near future. Non-technical skills equip workforces to sustain their capabilities in dealing with further changes. Thus, it will be the responsibility of education systems (whether secondary school, vocational or higher education) to collaborate with both the government and industry in order to identify the new skills and competencies required in the 4IR era; to design both innovative curricula and pedagogies to ensure that these skills and competencies are embedded; and finally, to communicate the outcomes of these initiatives to the government, industry and the broader community, thus ensuring their continuing relevance within the 4IR era.

Above all, effective responses to the 4IR in Thailand will inevitably require collaboration between all relevant stakeholders; and innovative strategies, plans, policies and programs, implemented in a proactive and ongoing manner. Some of these approaches have already begun in Thailand but will need to be continuously developed in order to reap real benefits.

Conclusion

The existing reports and scholarly literature on the preparedness of the Thai government, and (especially) larger organisations in Thai industry for the 4IR, suggest that stakeholders are relatively aware of the associated challenges and have implemented proactive strategies and policies to address them. Many of the respondents in the study agreed with these views and were positive about the potential benefits for productivity and competitiveness. However, many also had concerns about possible adverse impacts on job satisfaction, job security and future career opportunities. The key implications from the study are that the government needs to invest more in funding research and development programs associated with the implementation of 4IR technologies; to develop plans for the reskilling and/or upskilling of both current and future employees; and to encourage collaboration between all stakeholders. Industry managers are recommended to design future-oriented human resource plans, including analyses of new skills needs and the implementation of ongoing learning and development programs. Higher and vocational education systems need to review their courses and pedagogies in order to include more industry-relevant content and work-based skills, in conjunction with industry managers.

References

Anonymous (2015). Thai labour market faces dual challenges. *The Nation*, 28 February.

Anonymous (2018). 7-Eleven to introduce AI in 11,000 stores. *Inside Retail Asia*, 16 March.

APAIE (2018). *Impact of the Fourth Industrial Revolution on Thailand's Higher Education*. Bangkok: APAIE.

Chansrichawla, S. (2017). With the FIR comes "HR 4.0". *The Nation*, 25 February.

Chinsanyaram, C. (2018). Legal AI comes to Thailand as Weeranoy C & P picks Luminance. *Artificial Lawyer*, 21 May.

Cooke, P. (2018). That was 2017. This is 2018. Thai economy. *The Thaiger*. Available at: https://thethaiger.com/news/2017-year-thai-economy, accessed 18 January.

Deloitte (2018). *Economic Outlook Report 2018*. Bangkok: Deloitte.

Eade, P. (2018). How AI will accelerate growth in Thailand's media industry. *The Nation Weekend*, 7 October.

EIU (2018a). *Thai Economy*. Economic Intelligence Unit. Available at: www.country.eiu.com/Thailand

EIU (2018b). Who is ready for the coming wave of automation? *The Automation Readiness Index*, EIU Ltd. Available at: www.automationreadinessindex.com, accessed 25 July 2019.

ILO (2013). *Thailand: A Labour Market Profile*. Geneva: ILO.

Jones, C., & Pimdee, P. (2017). Innovative ideas: Thailand 4.0 and the fourth industrial revolution. *Asian Journal of Social Sciences*, 17 (1), 4–32.

Kawtrakul, A., & Praneetpolgray, P. (2014). A history of AI research and development in Thailand: Three periods, three directions. *Worldwide AI*, 83–92, Summer.

Leesa-Nguansuk, S. (2017). AI and 4.0 forefront. *IBC Asia Pacific*, 5 June.

Lung, N. (2018). Unis in Thailand join hands to offer degree in AI and robotics engineering. *Bangkok Post*, 2 February.

Maneechai, T. (2018). Robots versus labour: The state of the car industry in Thailand: The politics of the robot wave. *Prachatai English*, 11 November.

Martinidis, G. (2018). AI technology to help in the development of Thailand's smart cities. *Intelligent Cities, Smart Cities*, 8 November.

Ministry of Information and Communication Technology (2016). *Thailand Digital Economy and Society Development Plan*. Available at: www.mdes.go.th

Panyaarvudh, J. (2018). Reskilling urged to shore up jobs as AI sweeps in. *Bangkok Post*, 8 August.

Prakash, A. (2017). Global AI: Robotics race stretches from Norway to Thailand. *Robotics Business Review*, 19 May.

Rukkiatwong, N., & Khurancharean, K. (2018). How to succeed in the age of AI. *Insight Labour*, 8 August.

Shafer, M. (2017). Is Thailand preparing for the AI assault? *The Nation*, 12 September.

Thonguthaisri, N. (2017). *Drklae Talk no.161: Thailand's New Labor Law Amendment no.6 B.E.2560(2017)*. Dherakupt International Law Office Ltd. Available at: www.drkilaw. com/Lawtalk/Commercial/2Labour/drklaw161.pdf, accessed 15 August 2019.

Wailerdsak, N. (2015). Labour market and economic performance in Thailand and the Philippines: Demand imbalance and the ASEAN economic community. *International Journal of East Asian Studies*, 25–34, March.

Part 3

Fourth Industrial Revolution – The Asia Pacific and beyond

13 Comparisons and conclusions

Alan R. Nankervis, Julia Connell and John Burgess

Introduction

This book explores a range of challenges and the associated implications of the Fourth Industrial Revolution (4IR) on organisations situated in the Asia Pacific region and beyond. The chapter authors investigated, using a standardised survey questionnaire, the perceptions of managers in Australia, China, India, Indonesia, Malaysia, Mauritius, Singapore and Thailand – about their organisations' preparedness to address the potential impact of the 4IR. The key research question was 'How prepared are you and your organisation to face the impact of the 4IR?', with a particular focus on implications for present and future labour markets, workforces, skills development, leadership styles and change management strategies. The key objectives of the study, as expressed in Chapter 1, were to assess:

a. What changes are occurring within organisations that are linked to technological developments associated with the 4IR?
b. What are the drivers and impediments to such developments and applications?
c. What is the impact on work, workplaces and employment?
d. What preparations are organisations making for the 4IR?
e. To what extent is there a national policy program that is guiding and leading organisational developments with respect to 4IR?

The following sections of this chapter and Appendix 1 summarise the key, comparative findings of the study and discuss their implications for industry managers, their organisations and associations, government policy, education strategies, and nations more generally. In the process some insights are offered towards addressing the earlier questions.

The chapter authors focusing on Nepal and Taiwan took a different approach, for reasons explained in their chapters, using case studies and interviews, rather than surveys. The Automation Readiness Index, the Human Development Index, and the UN Sustainable Development Goals frameworks are used throughout the book to provide a broader perspective on the national contexts of the countries studied. These are discussed in the next section of the chapter before a comparative analysis of the study findings is presented.

The Automation Readiness Index

The Automation Readiness Index (ARI), compiled by the Economist Intelligence Unit (EIU, 2018) and discussed in more detail in Chapter 1, is also referred to throughout this book to enable comparisons of the research data with assessments of the relative 'readiness' status of the various countries included. This assisted analysis of 'which countries are better positioned to take up the policy challenges that automation poses' (EIU, 2018: 8). The ARI focuses on three policy areas: innovation policy (government and industry), education policy (secondary, vocational and higher education systems) and labour market policy (government, industry and educational systems). Only six of the countries discussed in this book (Australia – 10; China – 12; India – 18; Indonesia – 25; Malaysia – 14; and Singapore – 3) are ranked in the 25 countries included in the ARI which limits the comparability of findings to that index. We can see from the ARI that the countries featured in the index are favourably positioned (Singapore), mid-ranking (Malaysia) and low ranking (Indonesia) in terms of preparation for the challenges of the 4IR. This final chapter of the book examines the findings from the country chapters to determine whether the findings resonate with the ARI assessment.

Human development index and US sustainable development goals

Although this study was intended to examine the preparedness of industry managers (or otherwise) for the micro (organisational) impact of the 4IR, it also considered the broader macro (national/country) implications, using the frameworks of the Human Development Index (http://hdr.undp.org/en/countries) and the associated US Sustainable Development Goals (www.un.org/sustaina bledevelopment/sustainable-development-goals/). In this way 4IR readiness can be analysed according to the more inclusive – developed versus developing nation contexts – 'a blueprint for an inclusive world'. In particular, factors related to the predominance of the unprotected informal labour sectors in the latter, and the significance for all economies of technology-led innovation. Differences are also highlighted between technology adoption and its economic, social and cultural impacts across the range of diverse countries included in the book. Reference to the HDI suggests the scope of the challenges linked to the 4IR. In several of the country studies, large rural populations, a large agricultural and self-employment sector and poor infrastructure (Indonesia, Nepal) suggest that, for large sections of the community and industry the 4IR will have limited relevance. However, there is still some relevance for trade, capital and labour movements, and for the potential to improve access and services across communities.

Key research findings

Across the countries studied, 1669 survey responses were received in total – Australia (250), China (164), India (118), Indonesia (226), Malaysia (317), Mauritius (161), Singapore (332) and Thailand (101). In Nepal and Taiwan case studies and interviews were utilised, rather than a survey.

Research samples

The samples from the different countries were generally representative of the nature and spread of industries in their context, with respondents from large local (and/or multinational) private companies predominant in India, Thailand, Singapore and Australia. Conversely, the Malaysian, Mauritian and Indonesian samples represented mainly small to medium size local organisations, and the Chinese respondents came primarily from large government and private organisations.

The respondents themselves also varied with respect to gender, age and position. Thus, the Indian and Mauritian respondents largely comprised middle-aged males with undergraduate and/or postgraduate qualifications holding middle to senior management positions, and in China, Singapore and Malaysia respondents reflected equal proportions of well-educated younger males and females, holding middle management positions. The Thai and Australian respondents were mainly young females with undergraduate and/or postgraduate qualifications and held line or middle management positions. The industries they represented differed according to national industrial structures. For example, the Indian and Singaporean samples focused on banking and finance, IT and the media and education sectors; China on government agencies; Thailand, Mauritius and Indonesia on tourism, health, manufacturing, education, transport and logistics; Australia on professional services and health; and Malaysia on agriculture, forestry and fishing, together with the public sector.

The samples are neither nationally representative nor are they matching samples. The analysis was determined based on responses from those in managerial positions who have experiencing changes associated with the 4IR. Respondents were requested to reflect on their organisational and national experiences with and responses to the challenges that have been identified as being associated with the 4IR.

Comparative research findings

Industrial revolution stage

It is generally accepted that there have been three previous 'Industrial Revolutions', with the present stage characterised as the 'Fourth Industrial Revolution' (4IR). For the purposes of the study, all country collaborators (and respondents) were provided with the following descriptors of these revolutionary (or evolutionary) stages of industrial and technological development:

First Industrial Revolution: Mechanisation, Water & Steam Power
Second Industrial Revolution: Mass Production, Assembly Line & Electricity
Third Industrial Revolution: Computers & Automation
Fourth Industrial Revolution: Cyber-Physical Systems.

All but four countries considered that their organisations were still in stage three (computer and automation), with only China, India, Thailand and Singapore reporting 'significant progress' or 'evidence of momentum' towards the 4IR (cyber-physical systems) 4th stage. This is interesting given the ARI rankings as only Singapore appears in the top 10 countries in the index that are recognised for their level of preparation for the 4IR. Thailand is not ranked, and both India and China are given mid ranking.

These national assessments are supported by the existence of clear government strategies in the four countries. Specifically, China's 'National Medium and Long-Term Science and Technology Program' together with its subsequent 'Innovation-Driven Development Strategy', and the more recent 'Made in China 2025' initiative; India's comprehensive 'Digital India' program; the Thai government's 'Thailand 4.0' strategy; and Singapore's 'Smart Nation' and 'Digital Economy Framework', together with its related 'Workforce Qualifications Scheme'. This scheme has led it to being recognised as the digital leader in Southeast Asia. Indonesian respondents reported that their country was on the cusp of moving towards the 4th stage, supported by the government's '1000 New Start-Ups' and 'Smart City' initiatives. China's land mass, geography and complex diversity complicate government attempts to develop comprehensive approaches, although it promulgated a 'Next Generation Artificial Intelligence Development Plan' in 2017.

Both the Malaysian and Mauritian samples reported that, whilst most organisations were in the third stage of technological development, some were still in the second stage (Appendix 13.1), undoubtedly reflecting their industrial structures. In Australia, despite some encouraging developments, including the establishment of several university-based 4IR institutes (for example, the 3A Institute at the Australian National University, the Machine Learning Institute at the University of Adelaide), and dedicated artificial intelligence professorial positions created at some universities, few coordinating strategies or policy initiatives with respect to the future of work have been developed to date by either state governments or the Australian federal government. This is surprising given that Australia ranks 10th in the terms of the ARI ratings.

Organisational strategy, top management support and value of 4IR technologies

The majority of respondents in almost all the countries reported that their organisations could be considered to be strategic and agile. Most suggested that the adoption and implementation of 4IR technologies was likely to be aligned with their broad organisational strategies, although as the detailed country data suggest, few such technologies have been employed to date in many of their organisations. The exceptions to these optimistic predictions were evident in relation to the Malaysian and Australian data in particular. In these cases, respondents were more sanguine, with many feeling (respectively) that their top managers were indecisive about the technologies; that their organisations were not strategic in decision-making; and/or that the small size or family culture of many organisations precluded either the adoption of 4IR technologies or necessitated the development of formal strategies and policies.

With respect to top management support to prepare for and support employees in the adoption and implementation of these technologies, again the majority of country respondents felt that their senior managers were aware of the potential benefits to their operations and encouraged their use but felt that insufficient resources were (or would be) allocated to enable the most effective utilisation. The exceptions to this were evident from the Indonesian, Malaysian and Mauritian data which suggested that adequate resources would be provided; and the Australian respondents who reported lower levels of top management support for the adoption and implementation of 4IR technologies than some of the other countries. The Chinese study found strong links between management support, usefulness, ease of use of the technologies and employee satisfaction, but weaker links to perceived improvements in task accomplishment or customer satisfaction due to technology adoption.

Impacts on organisational performance, productivity and innovation

Almost all the respondents from the countries studied agreed that artificial intelligence, robotics and machine learning technologies are likely to have a positive effect on organisational productivity and both individual and collective work performance, as well as in supporting employees in their jobs. The outliers were Australia, China, India and Singapore which were sceptical of the ability of employees to fully exploit technology for increased work performance and productivity. The Australian research sample was mixed in its assessment of the usefulness of 4IR technologies in enhancing performance, productivity and innovation; whilst the Chinese respondents suggested that the value and effectiveness of the technologies in achieving these outputs would be dependent on the levels of top management support and innovative leadership strategies. In the latter case, the national innovation strategies, policies and plans discussed previously are likely to provide strong encouragement to organisational managers to adopt such proactive leadership roles.

Employee job satisfaction, job changes, job security and the future of work

The majority of respondents from all the countries except Australia, China and India were positively inclined to agree that 4IR technologies would most likely increase employee satisfaction. The three outlier countries modified the prediction respectively to add cautions regarding the unknown nature of the impact of these technologies, the importance of employee perceptions in relation to their usability and their ease of use or innovation potential. These views most likely reflect respondents' concerns about implementation strategies, including communication between management and employees; the need to develop staged organisational plans; and ongoing information about the effects of the new technologies on the existence of current jobs and the nature of skills required in the human–technology interface at their workplaces.

These concerns reflect significant underlying themes prevalent in discussions of the impact of the 4IR – namely, the likelihood of significant job changes, new competency expectations and the possibility of job losses in the foreseeable future. In some cases (for example, in Australia and India) they may also be associated with potential resistance from unions or employee associations in industry sectors where they have strong membership.

Given the plethora of recent reports (for example, UNCTAD, 2018; World Economic Forum (WEF), 2018) which have predicted widespread job losses in a range of industry sectors, it is not surprising that most country respondents reported concerns about the lack of confidence in the ability of organisations to retain the number and types of current jobs in the wake of the 4IR. Chinese, Indian, Indonesian, Malaysian, Mauritian and Thai managers were marginally more positive about future job security than their Singaporean counterparts. The Australia sample was the most concerned, with the expectation that there would be labour displacement, especially in routine service jobs.

Overall, most respondents agreed, however, that there will be substantial changes in the nature of many (if not most) jobs due to the implementation of new technologies. These changes are highly likely to involve de-skilling and the acquisition of new skills, requiring organisations to enhance their learning and development programs, potentially on an ongoing basis. The job clusters reported to be the most vulnerable to change or replacement included manufacturing, purchasing, accounting and finance. The types of new skills suggested by respondents varied between technical (for example, data and communications security, data analytics, collaboration software and IT infrastructure development) and non-technical or soft skills (innovation, systems thinking, process understanding, general communication and interpersonal). The majority suggested that there will be a 'high to very high' need for skill development across all roles and functions in future workplaces but none were supportive of the notion that the 4IR might result in widespread job creation.

Organisational preparedness and resistance

All country respondents suggested that their organisations possessed a low to moderate level of preparedness to face the challenges posed by the 4IR, regardless of whether their respective governments (as discussed earlier in this chapter) had developed dedicated strategies and policies to promote and address them. Similarly, all reported low to moderate levels of potential managerial and/or employee resistance with regard to the implementation of new technologies.

Government strategies and policies

Despite the evidence of 4IR government strategies and policies in many of the countries studied (as discussed earlier), all country respondents were dissatisfied with their effectiveness. The large majority of respondents from all countries reported that they were either 'very unimpressed' or 'unimpressed' with their governments' current approaches to encourage research and development in 4IR technologies; to assist them in implementing them; or in preparing for the inevitable workplace, labour market and human resource development consequences. There was, however, a small proportion of respondents who remained 'undecided'. Clearly, more work on these issues is required to support smooth transitions from the 3IR to the 4IR stages. For this to occur governments, industry and education sectors will need to collaborate further to achieve this crucial outcome.

Global perspectives on the 4IR and stakeholder implications

Whilst the research findings focus on managers' views from a broad range of industry sectors in the countries studied, it is necessary to locate their assessments within broader global frameworks such as the Human Development Index and the UN's Sustainable Development Goals (see earlier), given that five of the ten countries (Indonesia, Mauritius, Nepal, Taiwan and Thailand) are usually categorised as developing countries. We have chosen in this book to group China and India as 'intermediary' rather than 'developing' countries, due to their impressive economic growth trajectories and rapid stages of recent development. The UNCTAD (2018) maintains that the 4IR could be considered to be a 'blueprint for an inclusive world'. Accordingly, if the potential of the 4IR is embraced then it could assist a move towards a trajectory where developing countries achieve developed nation status. The creation of sustainable and innovative global economies results from 'harnessing the benefits of technology, transformation and globalisation, taking into consideration national needs, priorities and circumstances' (G20, 2019: 1). Thus, the research findings presented here can provide some insights into some of the challenges the ten featured countries may face as they move further towards the 4th stage of the 4IR and opportunities that could be grasped to assist along the way.

These imperatives are included in both the UN's Sustainable Development Goals and the OECD's Recommendations on Artificial Intelligence (inclusive growth, sustainable development and well-being, human-centred values and fairness, and accountability – G20, 2019: 4) referred to as 'human-centred artificial intelligence'. It is argued they should be the foundation for the implementation of 4IR technologies at national, societal and institutional levels. Evidence of these links are provided in almost all of the national strategies and policies promulgated so far in the countries included in this book and discussed earlier in this chapter. The associated challenges posed by the 4IR in achieving these goals have been characterised as 'transitions in the labour market, privacy, security, ethical issues, new digital divides, and the need for artificial intelligence capability-building' (G20, 2019: 3), and are the joint responsibilities of all stake-holders including international organisations, governments, civil society, industries and their managers as well as vocational and higher education suppliers.

The chapter on Nepal highlighted the challenges of an inclusive and accessible 4IR process. Many developing economies lack the infrastructure and expertise to take advantage of the digital economy. Challenges include limited and unreliable energy supplies; limited and unreliable internet access; low levels of education, skills and ICT literacy. The challenge set out in the Nepal chapter is whether 4IR will serve to intensify economic divisions across regions, industries and the community through concentrating the benefits to those who have access to the infrastructure, know-how and resources.

In pursuit of these goals the International Bank for Reconstruction and Development suggests that there are six priorities for the development of a strong digital economy in Southeast Asia and beyond, namely:

1   Improve affordable, high speed internet
2   Strengthen the population's digital skills through education and industry training
3   Governments need to become 'more digital' themselves
4   Need to move from high level masterplans to 'detailed, time-based plans with clear performance indicators and monitoring frameworks'
5   More effective links between governments, the private sector and educational systems and work towards more effective
6   (Asia Pacific) regional cooperation and integration.

(DDP, 2019: 11–12)

In a similar vein, UNCTAD cautions against both 'digital utopianism that attributes boundless opportunities for developing countries to leap-frog into high value-added and job-creating activities' and 'the potential adverse employment and income effects of digital technologies', arguing for a balanced approach that involves stakeholders at global, national, industry and education system levels (UNCTAD, 2018: 94). The G20 Statement (G20, 2019) suggests that national government, societal and industry responsibilities in this regard should include long and medium-term public and private investment in 4IR research and development. This includes developing a 'digital eco-system', providing an 'enabling policy environment' for these new technologies while building human capacity and preparing for associated labour market transformations (G20, 2019: 12–13). To effectively meet these imperatives, governments, employers and education systems will need to engage collaboratively in ongoing social dialogue, lifelong learning and development, support for retrenched workers and create new job opportunities for future workforces (G20, 2019: 13). In addition, as Lovelock (2018) proposes these challenges are also going to require policies that will be necessary 'to reinforce the development of digital awareness, skills, knowledge and training . . . to manage the growth of the digital economy' (p. 15). Table 13.1 outlines a range of

Table 13.1 Strategies Required to Address the 4IR

Sector	Strategies required
Government	Develop more detailed technology adoption and implementation policies and programs; strengthen information technology infrastructure; encourage and fund 4IR research and development projects; analyse and address impacts on broad and narrow labour markets; renegotiate new employment standards and conditions with industry; design intensive communication and engagement programs to prepare for inevitable challenges; collaborate with education systems and industry sectors to identify, design and monitor more innovative learning and development opportunities to ensure effective knowledge transfer and skills development; and monitor the outcomes of these activities.
Industry	As above need to engage with governments and education systems to achieve successful joint outcomes; to communicate and work with employees regarding changes; plan labour market strategies and new skills requirements; work to mitigate any job losses due to the implementation of new technologies.
Education	Engage with governments and industry; evaluate the currency of their courses and graduate outcomes; contribute to research on the impacts and effects of the 4IR on broad labour markets and particular industry sectors; enhance their practical industry links through the employment of dedicated artificial intelligence and/ or machine learning via research and teaching.

strategies it is proposed are necessary to address the challenges arising and changes required from the impacts of the 4IR in relation to governments, industry and education.

The research presented here did not specifically address the macro-perspectives concerning the impact of the 4IR. However, as discussed earlier in this chapter, the individual and collective country findings support some of the UNCTAD, UNDP and World Bank recommendations. In general, the majority of respondents across all countries reported that their organisations were both relatively unaware and unprepared for the projected challenges to their workforces, workplaces and skills posed by the 4IR. Many believed that their organisations did not have clear alignments between business and new technology strategies; were uncertain about the benefits of these technologies to their operations; and they did not indicate that sufficient resources were likely to be allocated to effectively implement the requisite changes. Moreover, the potentially negative impacts on employee satisfaction, job security and job changes were a matter of concern. On the positive side, many respondents suggested that their top managers were generally supportive of the potential value of the technology changes to organisational systems, productivity levels and employee performance. That said, very few respondents were satisfied with current government strategies and policies regarding the 4IR, even in countries which appear to have developed clear and comprehensive programs and accompanying institutional processes to support them.

Limitations of the research

The book provides a scoping of the issues, challenges and perspectives of the 4IR within a largely regional context. Whilst this provides some limitations, however, it does capture the challenges facing developed, intermediary and developing economies, so it does have a global application. The study did not include all countries in the region, with notable absences being Japan, Korea and Vietnam. The primary focus of data collection was managers, and they represent only one stakeholder in the 4IR evaluation process. The research sampling was convenient and opportunistic and is not representative of the different nations. As the 4IR is an ongoing and dynamic process, the book captures developments at one point in time.

Further research

This book represents an attempt to understand the issues and challenges linked to the 4IR largely within one region. Technological and structural change is not new, skill augmentation and de-skilling is not new, job destruction and job creation are not new; what is new is the technology, the reach and the potential of the technology to create and destroy jobs, skills and workplaces. This book opens up the research agenda on a topic that has relevance to all the countries included. There is an opportunity to develop the research further in terms of systematically examining government policies across the region; carefully investigating the responses of key institutions such as the education sector to the 4IR; and analysing the impact of new and emerging technologies on employment and skill development; and finally, examining the impact of the 4IR technologies on sectors that cross the technology spectrum from agriculture and mining, through to manufacturing, health, retail and education.

Conclusion

Finally, in response to the conundrum posed in the book's title – does the Fourth Industrial Revolution constitute a 'revolution', or merely a natural stage in the 'evolution' of the technology-human interface? We would argue that it is probably both. There is no doubt that the issue is complex; in terms of scope, breadth and rapidity of its influence and impact with huge potential for both positive and adverse effects on all economies and their labour markets. From a short-term perspective, it is likely to be as the World Economic Forum suggested 'different from previous industrial revolutions' (WEF, 2018). However, from a broader and longer-term perspective, it has similar characteristics to those of the earlier industrial revolutions. In hindsight, the 4IR may in fact be considered as just a further evolutionary stage of the relationship between humans and technology – only time and history will tell.

References

DDP (2019). *The Digital Economy in Southeast Asia: Strengthening the Foundations for Future Growth*. Washington, DC: International Bank for Reconstruction and Development, World Bank.

EIU (2018). *The Automation Readiness Index: Who Is Ready for the Coming Wave of Automation?* Geneva: ABB.

G20 (2019). *Ministerial Statement on Trade and the Digital Economy*. Tokyo, Japan, 8–9 June.

Lovelock, P. (2018). *Framing Policies for the Digital Economy: Towards Policy Frameworks in the Asia-Pacific*. UNDP Global Centre for Public Service Excellence, NUS. Available at: http://hdr.undp.org/en/countries

UNCTAD (2018). *Trade and Development Report 2018: Power, Platforms and Free Trade*. New York: UN.

World Economic Forum (2018). *The Global Competitiveness Report 2018*. Available at: www.weforum.org/reports/the-global-competitveness-report-2018, accessed 20 August 2019.

Appendix 13.1 Brief summary of comparative country findings

	India	Thailand	Singapore	Malaysia	Mauritius	Indonesia	Australia	China
Organisation type	High proportion of large companies and MNCs in IT, media, banking and finance	High proportion of private sector organisations in health, manufacturing, education and training	Equal numbers of small/very large private organisations in IT and media, banking, education and training	High proportion of small organisations in administration, services and agriculture, forestry/fishing	High proportion of SMEs, private sector organisations in IT and media, manufacturing, transport and warehousing	High proportion of SMEs, private sector organisations in accommodation and food services, transport and warehousing	High proportion of large, private sector organisations in professional, scientific and technical, health care and social assistance	More than three quarters government businesses
Progress towards the 4IR	Some progress towards the use of cyber physical systems	Significant progress toward cyber-physical systems	Progress towards use of cyber physical systems	A third at 2IR and limited evidence of progress toward 4IR	70% in 3IR	Equal proportions in 3IR and 4IR	Majority in 3IR and 4IR	Mostly 3IR, but a minority in 4IR
Management support and provision of resources	Aware of benefits encourage use but insufficient resources allocated.	Aware of benefits encourage use but insufficient resources allocated.	Aware of benefits encourage use but insufficient resources allocated.	Aware of benefits, encourages use and allocates resources	Aware of benefits, encourages use and allocates resources	Aware of benefits, encourages use and allocates resources	Moderate level of management support evident	Management understanding and support unreliable
Evidence of leadership and innovation	Strong evidence in some sectors, but patchy in others	Strong innovation/ leadership in creative thinking and encouraging autonomy	Weak innovation/ leadership in coaching for creativity but strong in openness	Innovation leadership is excellent	Some evidence but needs to be strengthened by government, industry and educational institutions	Not yet clear – differs between sectors	Moderate	Moderate

AI software benefits perceived for productivity, performance and employee usefulness	Yes	Yes	Yes	Yes	Yes	AI/software will not necessarily be useful to employees	Perceptions of usefulness associated with management support/ innovative leadership
AI software will help improve profitability and sales and, particularly, competitive advantage	Yes	Yes	Yes	Yes	Yes	AI will improve organisational performance when perceived to be useful/easy to use	Possibly – depends on competencies of managers in communicating benefits and implementation effectiveness
AI/software improves productivity, innovation, customer satisfaction and management control	Yes	Yes	Yes	More than half respondents agreed	Yes	May not	Strategic intention and innovation leadership are associated with these factors
AI/software likely to increase employee satisfaction and change work patterns	Evidence of indecision despite acknowledgement that AI/software will change work patterns	Yes	Not provided	Yes	Yes	Yes when it is perceived to be useful and easy to use	Yes when it is perceived to be useful and easy to use

(Continued)

(Continued)

	India	Thailand	Singapore	Malaysia	Mauritius	Indonesia	Australia	China
Perceptions that AI might lead to job loss	Equally balanced perceptions of employee confidence and concern about potential job loss	Perceptions of employee confidence slightly outweighed concern about potential job loss	Perception of employee concern slightly outweighed confidence about potential job loss	Equally balanced perceptions of employee confidence/concern about potential job loss	Equally balanced perceptions of employee confidence/concern about potential job loss	Perception of employee confidence slightly outweigh observation of concern	Those who did not agree AI/software was useful/easy to use more likely to have greater concern than confidence	Yes, especially in traditional jobs and skills
Level of satisfaction with government policy and strategy	High level of indecision	Mainly undecided or unimpressed	Mainly undecided or unimpressed	Mainly impressed or very impressed	Mainly unimpressed or undecided	Mainly impressed or very impressed	Very unimpressed	Some useful policies (e.g., 'Made in China') but more needs to be done
Skill needs to prepare for the 4IR	Low to moderate need, with highest need for non-technical skills	High need especially in data and comms security	High to very high need especially in data and comms security	High to very high need across all specified functions	High need across all specified functions	Moderate to high need in data and comms security	Technical and non-technical skills	Level of innovativeness impacts upon need for different skills
Organisational level of preparedness for AI/robotics	Low	Moderate	Low	Moderate	Low	Moderate	Low to moderate	Moderate
Perceived organisational resistance to change	Low	Moderate	Moderate	Moderate	Low	Moderate to high	Moderate	Low, partly because workers are not aware of the impacts

Degree of change in different functions	Low to moderate; highest for IT-related and lowest for HRM	Moderate to high, especially in IT-related jobs	Moderate to high degree of change, especially IT-related jobs	Moderate to high degree of change	Moderate to high degree of change, especially IT-related jobs	Low to moderate degree of change	Moderate to high	Moderate to high, especially in IT-related jobs
Potential job losses and functions	Highest job losses in manufacturing and purchasing	Moderate to high job loss across all functions	Highest job losses in manufacturing and accounting and finance	Moderate to high job loss across all functions	Low to moderate job loss across all functions	Yes, jobs will be lost, mainly in manufacturing, hospitality and tourism	Mixed – there will be significant job losses in some but not all industries	Yes, especially in traditional jobs and skills
Potential job creation and function	Low to moderate levels of job creation, but high for IT-related jobs	Moderate level of job creation	Moderate to high job creation, especially IT-related	Moderate to high levels of job creation across functions	Low to very low levels of job creation	Moderate to high level of job creation in the organisation	Low to moderate, but in particular industry sectors	Low support

Index

Note: page numbers in *italic* indicate a figure and page numbers in **bold** indicate a table on the corresponding page.

2IR *see* Second Industrial Revolution
4IR *see* Fourth Industrial Revolution
7-Eleven 77–78, 80, 81, 189

AI *see* artificial intelligence
Allen, E.R. 117
Amazon Web Services 63
ARI *see* Automation Readiness Index
artificial intelligence **213–215**; *see also* individual countries
Artificial Intelligence for Development 176
ASEAN Economic Community 5, 10
Asian Digital Transformation Index (ADTI) 56
Australia 13, 33–48, 205, 206, **212–215**; Automation Readiness Index (ARI), **9**, 43; demographics, 34; education, 204; government strategy, 45, **45**, 46, **214**; health care sector, 35–37, **42**, 45; ICT sector, 37–39, **42**, 45; labour market trends, 33–34, 44, **45**; stages of automation, 42–43, **43**; survey, 41–45, **42**, **43**, **44**, **45**; technologies, 43, **43**; tourism sector, 39–41, **42**, 45–46
Australia Bureau of Statistics (ABS) 37, 39
Australia Human Resources Institute (AHRI) 13, 33
Automation Readiness Index (ARI) 8, 47, 171–172, 187, 202; categories, 8, **9**; country ranks, 9, **9**, 12

Bali 119
Bandung Institute of Technology 128
Bangladesh Robotics Foundation 177
Baruch, Y. 153
Bhaskaran, M. 53–54
BINUS University 128

Braun, V. 118–119
Brynjolfsson, E. 4
Bukalapak 128, 129

Cedefop, K. 11
CekMata 128
Chalmers, P. 3, 4
Changi Airport 67
Cheng, T-Z. 71–72, 81
China 7, 14, 84–96, 205, 206, 207, **212–215**; artificial intelligence, **91**, **93**, 93–94, 204; Automation Readiness Index (ARI), **9**; developmental stages, 84–88; education, 86, 95–96; government policy, 94–95, **214**; Innovation-Driven Development Strategy, 204; IT strategies, 89–90, **90**; job security, **92**; labour, 86–87; Made in China 2025, 95, 204; National Medium and Long-Term Science and Technology Program, 204; Next Generation Artificial Intelligence Development Plan, 204; One Belt, One Road, 87–88, 95; opening-up policy, 84–85; patent law, 85; skills, 91–93, **92**, **93**; socialist market economy, 85–87; supply side reforms, 87–88; survey, 88–94, **90**, **91**, **92**, **93**; World Trade Organisation and, 87
Clarke, V. 118–119
Cooke, P. 184
Coursera 64
crowdfunding 128, 129
Crowdo Indonesia 129

DBS Bank 128
Deloitte 71, 158–159
Dhakal, S. 11, 169, 170

Diffusion of Innovations Theory (DIT) 168, 170
Digital Divide Theory (DDT) 168, 170
Doll, W.J. 102

East Nusa Tenggara 119
economic categories 7
Economist Intelligence Unit 8
Economist, The 12
education 5, 46–47

facial recognition 77–78
Foodmandu 175
Fourth Industrial Revolution (4IR) 26–28, 27; components of, 4–5; definition, 3, 71; infrastructure and, 9–10; man and machine relations, 4; survey and, 20–21
FoW *see* Future of Work
Foxconn 71
Frey, C.B. 12
Future of Work (FoW) 26–28, 27

General Electric Supply Company 151
Gleason, N. 64
Global Innovation Index (GII) 56, 132
Go-Jek 125, 128
government policy 6; *see also* individual countries

Habibi Garden 128
HCI *see* Human Capital Index
HDI *see* Human Development Index
Helien 128
Henderson, J.C. 90
Hirschi, A. 160
Holtom, B.C. 153
homophily 170
Hota 76–77, 80
Human Capital Index (HCI) 11
Human Development Index (HDI) 11, 201, 202, 207

IBM Corporation 178
India 7, 14–15, 100–112, 205, 206, 207, **212–215**; artificial intelligence, **106**, **107, 108, 109**, 110, 178; Automation Readiness Index (ARI), **9**; Digital India program, 204; government policy, 101, 111, 175, **214**; information technology, 101–102, **104**; JAM trinity, 101; job satisfaction, 108, **108, 110**; National Strategy for Artificial Intelligence, 178;

service sector, 100–101; skills, 109–110; strategic intentions, 105; survey, 102–110, **103, 104, 105, 106, 107**
Indonesia 15, 114–129, 202, 205, 206, **212–215**; 1000 Start-Ups Movement, 127, 204; artificial intelligence, *120*, 120–124, *121, 122, 123, 124*, 124–127, *125, 126, 127*, 128; Automation Readiness Index (ARI), **9**, 118; education, 116, 127; government policy, 116–118, 124, 127, **214**; Hub ID, 127; information technology, 117–118, 119, *119*; interviews, 118–119; labour market, 115–116; Smart City initiative, 114–115, 116, 125–126, 204
industrial revolution stages 204
inequality 5, 12
infrastructure 6, 46
internet of things (IoT), 78, 79

Jakarta 114, 119
Job Characteristics Model (JCM) 7, 8
Jones, C. 174–175

Kaskus 125
Kata.ai 128
Keretapi Tanah Melayu Berhad (KTMB) 133
Kibar 127
King Monghut University 188
KitaBisa.com 128
Knickrehm, M. 160
Kumparan 128

leadership 21–22
Lee Kuan Yew 55
Lovelock, P. 208–209

Mahathir Mohamad 131–132
Maier, C. 23
Malaysia 15–16, 131–147, 204, 205, 206, **212–215**; Aerospace Malaysia Innovation Center (AMIC), 133–134; artificial intelligence, 140, *141, 142*, 143–144; Automation Readiness Index (ARI), **9**; debt, 132; Digital Free-Trade Zone (DFTZ), 134; government policy, 131–132, 134–135, *141*, 145, 146, **214**; Industry Digitalisation Transformation Fund, 136; Malaysia 11th Plan 2016–2020 (MP11), 131; Malaysian Industry-Government Group for High Technology (MIGHT), 133; Malaysian Performance Management and Delivery

Unit (PEMANDU), 135; Malaysian
Productivity Corporation, 134–135,
136; Ministry of Higher Education, 135;
Ministry of International Trade and
Industry (MITI), 133, 134, 135–136;
Readiness Assessment Guidelines,
134, 135; Readiness for the Future of
Production Report, 132; skills, 135, *139*,
140, **143**, 145; survey, **136**, 136–143, *137*,
138, *141*, *144*; technology stage, *138*,
139; unemployment, 133; Vision 2020,
132–133
Mauritius 16, 149–165, *150*, 204, 205,
206, **212–215**; artificial intelligence,
156, 157, 158–159, 160, 161–164;
Digital Mauritius 2030 Strategic Plan,
162, 164; economic history, 151–152;
Export Processing Zone (EPZ), 151;
government policy, 161–164, *163*,
214; history, 149–151; information
technology, 155, *155*; Mauritius AI
Strategy, 162–164; Mauritius Artificial
Intelligence Council (MAIC),
161; Mauritius Innovation and
Entrepreneurship Framework (MIEF),
161; skills, 157, 160, 161–163; sugar, 151;
survey, 152–158, *156*, *157*, *158*;
tourism, 151
McAfee, A. 4
Melville, N. 90
Mesko, B. 37
Microsoft 64, 72, 128
Mobticket 133
Morris, M.G. 23
mosquito venues 75
Musk, E. 177

National Innovation Centre 176
National University of Singapore 64
Nepal 16, 20, 167–179, 202; 2019 Digital
Nepal Framework, 173; artificial
intelligence, 176–177, 178; corruption,
168–169, 174; economic profile, 167,
168–169; education, 172–173; ethics,
177–178; government policy, 171–175,
179; infrastructure, 174, 179; interviews,
171, **174**; not-for-profit (NFP)
organisations, 176–177, 178; tourism
sector, 175–176
NVIDIA 128

O'Neil, C. 177
organisational change-readiness 24
organisational performance 24
Osborne, M.A. 12

Paaila Technology 177
Parham, S. 160
perceived ease-of-use 22
perceived usefulness 22
Peters, M.A. 12
Pimdee, P. 174–175
policy *see* government policy; *see also*
individual countries
Prabhat, S. 175
Price Waterhouse Coopers Workforce of
the Future Report 5
Productivity Commission (PC) 46, 47

Rajah, R. 115
Republic of Mauritius *see* Mauritius
Romero, D. 4

Schumpeter, J. 67
Schwab, K. 158
SDG *see* UN Sustainable Development
Goals
Second Industrial Revolution 72
Shook, E. 160
Singapore 13–14, 52–69, 205, **212–215**;
artificial intelligence (AI), 56–57,
60, **63**, 64–65, 66–67; Automation
Readiness Index (ARI), **9**; big data,
57–58; Committee of Singapore's
Competitiveness, 65; demographics,
52–53, **53**; Digital Economy Framework,
57, 204; Digital Government Framework,
57–58; education, 64; government
policy, **61**, 61–62, 68, **214**; IT strategies,
59, 66; labour market trends, 54–55;
Model Artificial Intelligence Governance
(MAIG), 56–57; SkillsFuture program,
64, 67–68; Smart Nation policy, 55–56,
57; stages of automation, 58–59, *59*;
survey, **58**, 58–62, **62**; Workforce
Qualifications Scheme, 204
Singapore Polytechnic 65
skills training 5, 62–64, 206
socio-technical theory (STS) 7–8
South Korea: Automation Readiness Index
(ARI) 9, **9**
Sri Lanka Association for Artificial
Intelligence (SLAAI) 176–177
strategic orientation 21
STS *see* socio-technical theory
survey: components, 20–24; data processing,
26; instrument, 24–25; objectives, 201;
pre-test, 25; results, 26, 201–211, **209**,
212–215; samples, 203; translation, 25; *see
also* individual countries
Suzuki Motor Company 185

Taiwan 14, 20, 71–81; 7-Eleven, 77–78, 80, 81; artificial intelligence, 75; case studies, 76–81; demographics, 72–73; Digi 2025: Upgrade 5+2 Industries Through Tech Revolution, 75; economy, 73–74; government policy, 74–76; green energy, 75–76; healthcare industry, 78–79; Hota, 76–77, 80; Industry Innovation Upgrade Fund, 75; Productivity 4.0, 75; robotics, 80, 81; societal factors, 72–74
TAM *see* Technology Acceptance Model
Tamminga, H-J. 160
Tan, K.S. 53–54
task innovation 22
task productivity 22–23
Technology Acceptance Model (TAM) 22
Thai Beverage Group 189
Thailand 16–17, 184–197, 206, **212–215**; AI Research Roadmap, 188; artificial intelligence, 188, 189; Automation Readiness Index (ARI), 187; Eastern Economic Corridor, 184; education, 186, 195–197; government policy, 185, **214**; ICT Master Plan, 188; information technology, 188; labour market, 185–186; Labour Protection Act, 185; Manufacturing Automation & Robotics Academy, 187; Ministry of Digital Economy and Society Development Plan, 187–188; Ministry of Information and Communication Technology, 186–188; Ministry of Labour, 187; skills, **194**, 196; survey, 190–195, **191**, **192**, **193**, **194**; Thailand 4.0, 16–17, 186–188
Tokopedia 128
Tootle 175
Torkzadeh, G. 102
Toyota 185
trade war 74
Traveloka 128

Uber 160, 175
Udacity 64
Udemy 64
UN Sustainable Development Goals (SDG) 16, 167, 169, 202, 207
UNCTAD 208–209

van Dijk, J. 170
Venkatesh, V. 23
Venkatraman, H. 90

Wailerdsak, N. 184
Warschauer, M. 169
WEF *see* World Economic Forum
World Bank 115
World Bank Report (2019) 4, 5, 6, 7
World Economic Forum (WEF) 10–11, 38, 160; Future of Work Report, 160

X-Mart 128

Yin, R.K. 171

Zuckerberg, M. 177–178

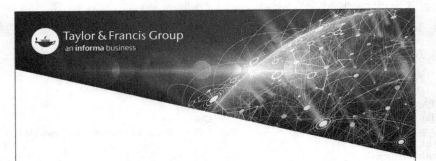

Printed in the United States
by Baker & Taylor Publisher Services